LATIN AMERICA WESTERN EUROPE AND THE U.S.

POLITICS IN LATIN AMERICA
A HOOVER INSTITUTION SERIES

General Editor, **Robert Wesson**

Copublished with Hoover Institution Press,
Stanford University, Stanford, California

LATIN AMERICA
WESTERN EUROPE
AND THE U.S.

Reevaluating the Atlantic Triangle

Edited by
Wolf Grabendorff and Riordan Roett

PRAEGER

PRAEGER SPECIAL STUDIES • PRAEGER SCIENTIFIC

New York • Philadelphia • Eastbourne, UK
Toronto • Hong Kong • Tokyo • Sydney

Library of Congress Cataloging in Publication Data

Latin America, Western Europe and the U.S.

(Politics in Latin America)
Bibliography: p.
Includes index.
1. Latin America—Foreign relations—Europe.
2. Europe—Foreign relations—Latin America. 3. Latin America—Foreign relations—United States. 4. United States—Foreign relations—Latin America. 5. Latin America—Foreign economic relations. I. Grabendorff, Wolf, 1940–   II. Roett, Riordan, 1938–
III. Series.
F1416.E85L37 1984   327.804   84-15891
ISBN 0-03-000533-7 (alk. paper)

The Hoover Institution on War, Revolution and Peace, founded at Stanford University in 1919 by the late President Herbert Hoover is an interdisciplinary research center for advanced study on domestic and international affairs in the twentieth century. The views expressed in its publications are entirely those of the authors and do not necessarily reflect the views of the staff, officers, or Board of Overseers of the Hoover Institution.

**Published and Distributed by the
Praeger Publishers Division
(ISBN Prefix 0-275)
of Greenwood Press, Inc.,
Westport, Connecticut**

Published in 1985 by Praeger Publishers
CBS Educational and Professional Publishing
a Division of CBS Inc.
521 Fifth Avenue, New York, New York 10175 U.S.A.

© 1985 by Praeger Publishers

56789 052 987654321

Printed in the United States of America

EDITOR'S FOREWORD

The English edition of Wolf Grabendorff's and Riordan Roett's book (Spanish and German editions are to appear simultaneously) is a valuable addition to the Politics in Latin America series. Its subject, the expanding relations of Latin America with Western Europe and the triangle consequently formed with the United States, is of growing importance as the dominance of the United States in the hemisphere tends to recede and the economic and political influence of Western Europe grows. It is imperative that we understand how Latin Americans and Europeans interact. Political evolution in Latin America, especially in South America, is not to be understood without taking into account the European role.

It is particularly fortunate that the distinguished editors have been able to focus on this subject by presenting the views of outstanding European and especially, Latin American scholars. The world seen through their eyes is by no means the same as that to which North Americans are accustomed.

It is hoped that this book will contribute to the understanding that is essential for the harmony of the great triangle.

Robert Wesson

ACKNOWLEDGMENTS

The three meetings of the New Atlantic Triangle Conference held in 1981 and 1982, under the auspices of the Center of Brazilian Studies at the Johns Hopkins School of Advanced International Studies in Washington, D.C., would not have been possible without the generous financial and logistical support of a number of individuals. We received major financial support from the University of Brasília, the Ford Foundation, the Friedrich Ebert Foundation, the Fritz Thyssen Foundation, the Johnson Foundation, the Rockefeller Foundation, and the Tinker Foundation. Additional financial support came from the Foundation Center for the Study of Foreign Trade (Rio de Janeiro, Brazil), the International Studies Program of Latin America (RIAL) (Santiago, Chile), the Konrad Adenauer Foundation, the Johns Hopkins University Center of Brazilian Studies, and the Stiftung Wissenschaft und Politik (Ebenhausen, West Germany).

Many people provided the organizational support that made the whole undertaking possible. We are most grateful to all of them, even though we cannot thank each individually here. Mention must be made of the following, however, to whom we are particularly deeply indebted: Rita Johnson and Kay Mauer of the Johnson Foundation; the Rector, Dr. José Carlos de Almeida Azevedo, and the Dean of Extension Services, Dr. Carlos Henrique Cardim, of the University of Brasília; Professor Klaus Ritter, the Director of the Stiftung Wissenschaft und Politik; Don Gabriel Valdes, President, and Dr. Luciano Tomassini, Academic Coordinator, RIAL. Diane C. Monash and Kathleen L. White of the staff of the Johns Hopkins University Center of Brazilian Studies and Latin American Studies Program, and Helga Strasser of the Latin American Program of the Stiftung Wissenschaft und Politik, were important to the success of the meetings. Our thanks for a job extremely well-done.

Felicity Skidmore, the conference editorial and manuscript consultant, patiently and artfully brought order and style to a collection of manuscripts originally written in a variety of languages. Genevieve Mittnacht did a superb typing job.

The Triangle Conference meetings drew a wide spectrum of participants from the academic world, government, business, foundations, and the press. It was our hope to generate increased discussion among all these groups about the recent and important phenomenon of a changing relationship involving Latin America, Western Europe, and the United States. The degree of involvement from paper writers, discussants, and those attending each of the three meetings confirms the existence of a high degree of interest in this topic. It is our hope that this volume will encourage other research and policy publications about this important theme in today's international relations.

CONTENTS

REEVALUATING THE ATLANTIC TRIANGLE: AN OVERVIEW

Wolf Grabendorff

> The Atlantic Triangle rests on a broad foundation. A sense of Western consciousness links Europe, North America, and many areas of Latin America, and is expressed by multiple ties: historic, religious, political, economic, military, and cultural.[1]

These words were written 20 years ago to epitomize one of the principal ideas of Western international politics, the Atlantic Triangle. In the last 20 years, the nature of the relationships among the three points of the Atlantic Triangle has undergone such profound changes that the entire concept needs to be reevaluated.

The goal of this book is to contribute to such a reevaluation by focusing on the relationship between two of the three components of the triangle, Western Europe and Latin America. The Atlantic Alliance and the relationship between the United States and the southern members of the American hemisphere have been well studied. However, the growing silent partnership[2] between Europe and Latin America has received neither the political nor the intellectual attention it deserves—particularly in the context of the separate relationships between each of them and the United States. The essays in this volume begin to fill this gap.

To understand the effect of the European–Latin American relationship on the Atlantic Triangle, it must be examined in the context of the general changes that have taken place in the international system since World War II. Before that time, and for a while thereafter, the political power and economic might of the United States made it the unquestioned and unquestioning hegemonic center of the triangle.

In the decades since then, its position has been eroding at the same time as Western Europe's impact has grown to some degree and Latin America's voice in the international context has reached an entirely new prominence.

Two decades ago, the United States could be seen as the link between Western Europe and Latin America; today both regions challenge the idea of the United States as the principal spokesman for and interpreter of their overall role in the international system. It has become evident to all that the United States alone can no longer be relied on to manage the economic or political crises evolving in the context of the triangle. Both Western Europe and Latin America are increasingly willing to assume more responsibility; but by the same token they expect a larger role in the overall management of triangle affairs. The structure of the so-called triangle has therefore become unstable. Since the original hierarchy of power has now been questioned, agreement on identification of the common interest versus individual interests has become much more difficult, and patterns of cooperation and conflict shift constantly. Whether new burden-sharing or power-sharing arrangements can restore the stability of the triangle and therefore, its relevance as a concept in the international arena, is the principal question for the years to come.

The authors of these essays, and the numerous participants in three conferences—one in Brazil, one in the United States, one in West Germany—bring to the subject a wide variety of regional, national, and transnational interests and expertise.[3] To channel these into some common ground for reevaluating the Atlantic Triangle, all were asked five basic questions.

1. Is there a community of interest between leading Latin American countries, Western Europe, and the United States? If so, of what does such a community of interest consist, and to what extent has it changed over time?

There is clearly no consensus among the partners of the Atlantic Triangle on the answer to this question. The relatively strong cultural consensus among the three is insufficient to forge any enduring agreement on economic or security issues. The declared shared values of human rights, social justice, economic development, and democratic government have all too often been subjected to the requirements of *realpolitik*. This is especially true with regard to United States and Western European willingness to tolerate the denial of all or most of these values to the majority of Latin Americans. Such values have been understood as guidelines for internal use at best, hardly enforceable within the context of the Atlantic Triangle, given the traditional stress on national sovereignty. Western concepts of development—within the general framework of the market mechanism—are no longer seen by many Latin Americans as the most promising ways to reach either economic progress or social justice. This may be the most profound change of all within the Atlantic Triangle.

2. Is there a community of interest between Western Europe and the United States versus leading Latin American countries, along the lines of status seekers versus status defenders in the international system?

With respect to what is important in regard to Latin America, such a community of interest does exist. Western Europe and the United States share the following consensus:

- To work against the transferring of additional Latin American states to the socialist camp;
- To work against regional and internal instability coming from interstate or intrastate violence;
- To work toward close economic cooperation with Latin American states through the support of free market economies.

There is also agreement in general to work toward binding the new power centers in Latin America to the West. However, the reduced capacity and willingness to aid the development process in Latin America through large resource transfers and privileged access to the markets of the United States and Western Europe endanger such policies. In addition, no political strategy as yet has been developed to meet the demands of those seeking status within the triangle.

3. Is there a community of interest between Western Europe and Latin America versus the United States, as the hegemonic power of the West?

The process of emancipation from United States dominance has very different origins for these two regions and offers a different set of possibilities and limitations for each. The asymmetry of power between one great nation and the two regional systems has made it difficult for the two regional systems to express their interests in a concerted form.

Nevertheless, parallels between the Atlantic Alliance and the Inter-American System, the two most successful subsystems in the international system, are striking. Each dominated the international ties of their respective regions for many decades. In each case, the United States has been able to secure cooperation on a wide range of issues, in exchange for security guarantees. Development of new interregional subsystems tends to threaten the dominance of each in the international system, and will continue to do so in the near future.[4] These similarities in the two regions make it clear that their community of interest is mainly to gain a larger independent role in international affairs, while at the same time demonstrating their willingness to support the global position of the United States, for security reasons.

4. Are there discrepancies between Western Europe and the United States with regard to their respective approaches and strategies toward Latin America?

A variety of such discrepancies exists because of the asymmetry of power and influence between the hegemonic superpower of the United States (weaker though it is than formerly) and the secondary powers of Western Europe. These can best be explained by their different historical experiences and geopolitical situations. The United States tends to view social change in Latin America in general, and in the Caribbean Basin in particular, in a national security context. Western Europe seems resigned to accepting greater ideological pluralism in the different developmental models in Latin America, as in the Third World in general. This difference in tolerance results partly from the greater need of Western Europe to cooperate with the Third World economically. However, it also reflects the wide variety of ideological perceptions about Third World developments in Western European society, as exemplified by the approaches toward Latin America of the European Christian and Social Democratic parties. The United States tends to cooperate with business and military elites in Latin America to ensure stability;[5] Western Europe emphasizes cooperation with political parties and trade unions, and stresses the need for social change as a prerequisite to future stability and development within a democratic context. From a Latin American viewpoint, the greater willingness of Western Europe to accommodate Latin American demands, results at least partly from the lack of power to pursue their interests in the same form as the United States. This leads to such intrawestern discrepancies being seen in Latin America as a chance to enhance the bargaining power of Latin America within the context of the Atlantic Triangle.

5. Are there any interest and/or policy differences among the three points of the Atlantic Triangle and if so, are there any chances they could be resolved, or at least lessened, in the near future?

Differing and changing international status and bargaining power make the stakes of the three partners in the Atlantic Triangle differ widely and diverge increasingly over time. The specific super-power interests and preoccupations tend to make the "lesser" issues in the Atlantic Triangle context (El Salvador, Grenada) especially controversial; the "central" issues (trade, debt, energy, technology transfer) are often resolved transnationally. Any lessening of the structural conflicts among the three regions can be expected only in the event of three developments:

- a massive change in the distribution of resource allocations (oil crisis);
- an increase in the power of Latin America to cause chaos in and between other countries (debt crisis);
- an external threat by an outside power to one of the members (security crisis).

Any complete resolution of the problems seems possible only in the highly unlikely event of the simultaneous settlement of the North–South and East–West conflicts, since both conflict systems outweigh any forces (internal and external) advancing the Atlantic Triangle concept.

HISTORICAL BACKGROUND OF THE ATLANTIC TRIANGLE

The first section of the book (chapters 1 through 4) deals with the political and economic dimensions of the relations between Latin America and Western Europe. The basic reason for looking at the period before and through World War II is to demonstrate that the relationship has been much stronger than it is today, and that the overwhelming importance of the United States for Latin America in the postwar years has been a result mainly of the decline of Western Europe during and immediately after World War II.

Stanley E. Hilton demonstrates that the political interaction between Europe and Latin America has always been intense, even though concentrated on different issues and countries in different periods. Werner Baer shows that the dominant economic presence of Western Europe in the nineteenth and early twentieth centuries was by no means to the long-term benefit of Latin America, whereas the new European presence may contribute to increased stability and bargaining power for Latin America in the international arena. Gerhard Drekonja uses his examination of Western European interests in the last two decades in order to describe the interplay of clichés, (mis-)understandings, and half-hearted attempts at dialogue, as well as the transfer of ideologies that has led to sharp dissent between the United States and Western Europe over political developments in Latin America. Roberto Russell puts recent developments in the interregional relationship into the wider context of the North-South conflict, especially criticizing the negative impact of the policies of the European Economic Community on Latin America. He emphasizes that Western European interests continue to be principally economic, and are therefore concentrated on the more important countries because of their (potential) markets and natural resources.

DYNAMICS WITHIN THE ATLANTIC TRIANGLE: THE CASE OF BRAZIL

Given the special role Brazil plays as one of the leading countries of the Third World, not only in U.S.–Latin American but also in Western European–Latin American relations, this section of the book (chapters 5 through 7) evaluates the foreign policy orientation of that nation and its impact on the Atlantic Triangle.

Roberto Fendt Jr. traces the changes and principal orientations of the bilateral and multilateral relations of Brazil and demonstrates how the developmental imperatives of the country have shaped its pragmatic foreign policy. Walder de Góes points out that the diversification of Brazil's economic relations took place at the expense of the economic interaction between the United States and Brazil, and that Brazil's aim to become a global power has also colored its relations with Western Europe. Carlos Perez Llana sets out to correct Western

European (and implicit U.S.) perceptions of Brazil as the decisive Latin American country in the Atlantic Triangle context. He argues for the inclusion of Argentina, Mexico, and Venezuela in a new Western European policy toward middle-level countries (and regional powers) in Latin America.

CRITICAL ISSUES: INTERDEPENDENCE WITHIN THE ATLANTIC TRIANGLE

The third section of the book (chapters 8 through 11) identifies the most critical issues in the triangular relationships: debt, energy, and security.

Rosario Green puts the interdependent factors of the Latin American debt crisis into the larger context of the role of international banks and Third World demands for a "new financial order." She describes the origins and effects of the growth of Third World foreign debt and the "concentration," "privatization," and "bilateralization" process. She proposes the creation of a negotiating group of the most important debtor countries from not only Latin America but the entire Third World.

Looking at the energy problems of the partners in the Atlantic Triangle, Carlos J. Moneta discusses the strengths and weaknesses of Latin American oil producers and exporters. He also criticizes the lack of an overall regional policy on that important issue which, in his judgment, could contribute to the strengthening of Latin America's bargaining power.

Alexandre de Souza Costa Barros looks skeptically at defense and security issues in the Atlantic Triangle context, noting that threat perceptions in Latin America are radically different from those in Western Europe or the United States. In his view, the defense of the South Atlantic, which seems to be the most important strategic issue for all parties concerned, does not seem to be enough justification for an enduring triangular relationship in the security area.

Ulrich Albrecht puts the security issue into the wider perspective of Third World interests, and assesses West Germany's role in supplying military aid and weapons transfers to the South. He concludes that informal participation in Latin American security issues is more promising and more likely than any formal triangular relationship.

A NEW ATLANTIC TRIANGLE?

The last section of the book (chapters 12 through 14) sums up the international implications of the Atlantic Triangle concept in the early 1980s and points to possible future developments, seen from the perspective of all three regions.

Riordan Roett asks pointedly about the future of the United States in Latin America, and analyzes the principal reasons for the decline of U.S. influence and the rise of Western Europe's role. He argues that employing the East–West prism to look at Latin American developments hinders understanding of the realities and acceptance of the ideological pluralism of the Western Hemisphere, which might prove essential to long-term U.S. interests.

Juan Carlos Puig looks from a Latin American viewpoint at the role of both the United States and Western Europe in the international relations of the region. He discusses the various forms of dependence and autonomy that are available for Latin America in its relations to the dominant power. Comparing the historical European hegemony with the current American–Soviet dominance, he looks for Latin American maneuverability and concludes that any strengthening of European–Latin American political relations will inevitably transform some of the foundations of the current international system.

Wolf Grabendorff contrasts the forms of influences of the United States and Western Europe in Latin America, and finds a certain mutual attractiveness between the ideological currents in Latin America and Western Europe. He characterizes the relationship between the United States and Western Europe in Latin America as an uneasy partnership, since competition and cooperation tend to exist side-by-side. As Latin American states become increasingly assertive, he argues, neither historical and cultural ties nor traditional hegemonic presumptions will be reason enough for Latin America to give Western Europe or the United States special preference. Rather, it will continue to form new alliances wherever it finds its national or regional interests best served.

Whether or not that place will be the Atlantic Triangle will remain, at best, an open question for a long time to come.

NOTES

1. Reidy (1964). The concept also had been discussed earlier by Whitaker (1951).
2. See Roett in the conclusions of this book and Grabendorff (1983).

3. The papers in this volume resulted from three New Atlantic Triangle conferences held in 1981 and 1982. The format of the conferences—which included policymakers, academics, businessmen, and journalists from each of the three regions—allowed for careful consideration of the papers. The written comments supplied by participants of the conferences have been of great help to the authors in revising the papers for publication.

4. See Grabendorff (1982).

5. For an outstanding treatment of the U.S. policies toward the Third World, see Feinberg (1983).

REFERENCES

Feinberg, Richard E. *The Intemperate Zone: The Third World Challenge to U.S. Foreign Policy.* New York: Norton, 1983.

Grabendorff, Wolf. "El papel de Europa Occidental en la Cuenca del Caribe." *Foro Internacional*, 33:4 (April-June 1983):400–422.

———. "Latin America and Western Europe: Towards a New International Subsystem?" In Jenny Pearce (ed.), *The European Challenge: Europe's New Role in Latin America.* London: Latin American Bureau, 1982, 41–58.

Reidy, Joseph W. "Latin America and the Atlantic Triangle." *Orbis*, 8:1 (Spring 1964):52–65.

Whitaker, Arthur P. "The Americas in the Atlantic Triangle." In *Ensayos sobre la Historia del Nuevo Mundo.* Mexico, 1951, 69–96. Reprinted in Lewis Hanke (ed.), *Do the Americas Have a Common History?* New York: Knopf, 1964, 141–164.

LATIN AMERICA WESTERN EUROPE AND THE U.S.

LATIN AMERICA AND WESTERN EUROPE, 1880–1945: THE POLITICAL DIMENSION

Stanley E. Hilton

The subject of political relations between Latin America and Western Europe from the late nineteenth century to the end of World War II is vast, with diverse ramifications. Political interaction between states occurs typically at many levels and through the media of often numerous actors (Rosenau 1969). The task of defining such interaction in this case is all the more complex because it involves two large geographic areas, each of which embraces several individual countries. The dividing line between politics and economics, moreover, is frequently a fine one. The subject becomes manageable within the confines of a single essay only if analytical limits are imposed. This essay, therefore, concentrates on Brazil, Argentina, and Mexico on the Latin American side, and Germany and the United Kingdom on the European side. Relations are evaluated, furthermore, at the state–state or intergovernmental level, with emphasis on policy rather than on the policy-making process. Two major themes are addressed: Latin America as a factor in great power rivalries, and the political response of Latin America to Europe. In other words, how did European governments approach Latin America politically? How did that region enter into their strategic calculations? What role did it play in the competition between and among major European nations and the United States? How, for their part, did representative Latin American governments react to European developments? What benefits did Latin America derive from relations with Europe? How and for what political or strategic purposes did Latin American states utilize such relations?

FROM THE EUROPEAN SIDE

Before the Great War

The historical importance of the European-Latin American connection is profound. It was, after all, European colonization that broke down Latin American isolation from the rest of the world and began the process of its integration into the international economy. From Europe's standpoint during the colonial era, Latin America's foodstuffs, raw materials, and precious metals facilitated state building and national expansion. The end of formal European political control over most of the region in the early 1800s did not affect substantially the quickening pace of Latin America's integration into what would become a global ecumene at the end of the century. Indeed, the abandonment of Iberian mercantilist controls, coupled with the rapid spread of the Industrial Revolution across Western Europe and North America, with its accompanying free trade and free migration of peoples and capital, pulled Latin America tightly into the expanding capitalist system of the late nineteenth and early twentieth centuries (Mosk 1948; Platt 1973).

Brazil, for example, in good measure because of European (especially British) capital, technology, and demand for primary products, solidified its position in the international system after 1850 as an importer of manufactured goods and an exporter of such commodities as coffee, sugar, tobacco, rubber, and hides. European immigrants—primarily Italians, Portuguese, Spaniards, and Germans—flooded the country, bringing new economic attitudes and skills, and contributing significantly to commercial and manufacturing development (Baklanoff 1969; Graham 1972; Dean 1969).[1] Argentina is a classic example of an underdeveloped economy transformed by European capital, technology, and consumption demand into a major supplier of primary products to Europe's industries and burgeoning populations. Late in the nineteenth century, as a result of a veritable "revolution on the pampas" (Scobie 1964), Buenos Aires became, as Thomas F. McGann (1957, p. 17) put it, "a spigot from which poured a torrent of wheat and meat for Europe."[2] The European demographic impact on Argentina during this time was likewise dramatic, as millions of Italians, Spaniards, and Germans sought new opportunities in that country, where they constituted a valuable pool of human capital and entrepreneurial talent, taking the lead in developing local manufacturing (Cortes Conde 1974; Beyhaut et al. 1965; Cornblit 1967; Fleming 1979; Solberg 1969). Mexico, too, entered a phase of modernization and intensified economic specialization under the aegis of U.S. and European investors, technicians, and markets, although it failed to attract the immigrants that its leaders ardently desired (Tischendorf 1961; Pletcher 1958; Katz 1964; Schiff 1967).

European countries were not only critical markets and sources of loans, investments, technology, and immigrants; they were also the major suppliers of military hardware to Latin America. As a U.S. official (see Bastert 1959, p. 395) ruefully commented, with regard to the War of the Pacific between Chile, Peru, and Bolivia (1879–1883), "Chile got ironclad ships from England [and] Chilean soldiers marched to Peru clad in uniforms of English cloth, with English muskets on their shoulders." The United Kingdom did dominate sales of warships to Latin American countries in the pre-World War I era; but transactions were actually few, the largest single order coming in 1907, when Brazil gave major contracts for fleet renewal to British yards (Platt 1973). Hotly disputed Argentine naval contracts, however, went in 1910 to U.S. builders, in preference to British, German, or Italian competitors (Etchepareborda 1978). Imperial Germany was the principal source of artillery and infantry weapons, with Krupp and the Deutsche Waffen und Munitionsfabrik (DWMF) enjoying a near monopoly of sales to Brazil, Chile, and Argentina until World War I (Brunn 1969; Rodríguez 1966; Schaefer 1974). French competition was severe nonetheless; Krupp lost to Schneider an important contract with the Mexican army in 1889 and again in 1902, although Mexican troops were equipped with DWMF-supplied Mauser rifles and carbines (Schiff 1959; Katz 1964).

German arms exporters benefited greatly from the presence of German military missions in several South American countries after the 1880s and from the training of Latin American officers in Germany. Chile took the lead in contracting Prussian instructors, with the result that by 1910 it had the "best equipped land fighting forces and the best educated officer corps in Latin America" (Nunn 1970, p. 300).[3] Venezuela and several other Spanish American countries subsequently drew indirectly on German expertise by sending cadets to study in Chilean academies (Nunn 1975). German military influence was likewise extensive in Argentina by World War I, a consequence of German assistance in organizing and staffing her Escuela Superior de

Guerra. From 1904 to 1914, furthermore, over 150 Argentine officers studied or served in Germany (Epstein 1954; Potash 1969; Atkins and Thompson 1972; Schaefer 1974). Efforts by Berlin to place instructional missions in Brazil and Mexico at this time were unsuccessful for various reasons, but both those countries sent officers to Germany in the early 1900s. In Brazil's case, several of them later formed a "young Turk" movement and became an influential force for army reform and a channel for German influence within the officer corps (Schiff 1959; Katz 1964, 1981; Brunn 1971). France, for its part, sent a military training mission to Peru in the late 1890s; and the powerful Brazilian state of São Paulo contracted a group of French army officers in 1906—Foreign Minister Rio Branco had urged the governor to import German methods—to train the 5,000-man state militia (Nunn 1975; de Abreu Dallari 1976).

Also worthy of emphasis is the fact that the European experience provided Latin America with political, ideological, and cultural models after the area gained independence. French literary, philosophical, and general cultural influence dominated Latin American elite circles notoriously until well into the twentieth century. McGann (1957, pp. 18–19) referred to it graphically as the "hypnotic spell" that French (and British) culture exercised over the governing class in turn-of-the-century Argentina, "an economic colony of Great Britain and a cultural vassal of France." Indeed, said a British observer during World War I, "an Argentine takes off his hat to an Englishman, but tucks his arm in that of a Frenchman" (Kirkpatrick 1981, p. 50).[4] The pervasive impact of Comtean positivism in the major Latin American countries late in the nineteenth century, especially in Brazil and Mexico, was one well-known reflection of elite receptivity to French thought. The British parliamentary system was a model for the post-independence Brazilian constitutional framework, and British liberalism had a tremendous influence on key Brazilian political leaders of the late empire and early republic. Joaquim Nabuco, Brazil's first ambassador to the United States (1902–1908), alluding to his previous career as an imperial congressman, wrote that he had been so dedicated to the tenets of English liberalism that it was "as if I were working under the orders of Gladstone." A prominent fellow traveler was Ruy Barbosa, early republican finance minister and later head of Brazil's delegation to the Second Hague Conference (1907), who once remarked that "in the press, in parliament, on the speaker's platform, England has always been the great teacher for my liberal principles" (Graham 1972, pp. 252–276).[5] German analysts bemoaned the ideological success of Anglo-French adversaries. "One cannot trust those people," Kaiser Wilhelm II himself commented late in 1906 with regard to the Brazilians, "because they have French or English sympathies" (Brunn 1969, p. 314). More radical European doctrines such as socialism, Marxism, and anarchism also filtered into Latin America, frequently carried by immigrants, and made some impact on working class groups, especially in Brazil, Mexico, and Argentina (Dulles 1973; Walter 1977). The Brazilian elite, furthermore, was profoundly influenced by European racial thought up to World War I (Skidmore 1974).

Viewed from the European angle, the importance of Latin America in the prewar era is perhaps best gauged by the intensity of the rivalry between and among the great powers for influence in the region. Great Britain had a competitive edge over other major countries in most Latin American markets until 1914, among other reasons because of an industrial head start and the strength of her merchant marine. In Brazil's case, there was the additional advantage of England's previous long-standing special trade relationship with Portugal, which facilitated commercial penetration of the former Portuguese colony. In the field of investments in Latin America as a whole, British capital substantially outdistanced European and American rivals; on the eve of World War I, one-fifth of Britain's overseas investments were in Latin America. By the early 1900s, nonetheless, the British lead was facing a stiff, and in some fields and in certain countries successful, challenge from the United States, Germany, and even (to a much lesser degree) France, which had three shipping lines to Latin America by the turn of the century (Ferns 1960; Manchester 1964; Graham 1972; Rippy 1948, 1977; Ford 1975; Stone 1977; Platt 1973; Brunn 1971; Tischendorf 1961; Schiff 1967). There were instances of cooperation between foreign firms in some countries— Mexico, for example—but it usually proved short-lived and was followed by the sharp, aggressive competition, accompanied by official pressures or appeals for official intervention that was characteristic of the worldwide scramble for markets in the "age of imperialism." One well-documented and apparently typical case was the struggle between U.S. and British oil interests in Mexico in the early twentieth century (Vagts 1928; Katz 1961).

Economic rivalries were intense; but what about the political interests of the European powers in Latin America? Early in the nineteenth century political quarrels in Europe had found ample reverberations in the region, but political interest gave way rapidly until late in the century to overwhelmingly commercial concerns. European countries had territorial possessions—British Honduras, the Guianas, and various Caribbean islands—which implied a political stake in Western Hemisphere affairs, but with the exception of the ill-fated Mexican venture of Napoleon III, only Spain among the European powers showed any keen political interest in the region until the 1890s. The most influential foreign power in Latin America—Great Britain— restricted itself to commercial undertakings. "Strategic interests were slight or nonexistent," D. C. M. Platt observed in 1967, "and Latin America, after the 1820s, took no part in the problems of a European balance of power which preoccupied Victorian statesmen." For Platt, Britain's "static, largely negative" diplomacy in Latin America during the nineteenth century was characterized "by its minor diplomatists yearning for comfortable postings in Europe; by its third-rate legations, staffed simply by a Minister, his clerk, and a local archivist, sometimes besieged by claimants, more often idle" (Platt 1978, pp. 21–39). A more recent study confirms the judgment that British policy in that period was "a combination of indifference, ignorance, and neglect, based on the reality that Latin America possessed no political or strategic importance for Britain" (Smith 1979, p. 21). Furthermore, Platt and others have argued cogently that the Foreign Office did not even actively or unduly seek to encourage or protect British commercial interests in Latin America (Platt 1978; Jones 1980).

Following the collapse of Napoleon's dream of erecting a European monarchy on the southern flank of the United States in the 1860s, Paris likewise displayed no serious political preoccupation with Latin America. Typically, the new minister assigned to Brazil in 1869 thought that country "a professional dead-end" (Skidmore 1974, pp. 29–30). French publicists did seek to disseminate ideas of an ill-defined Pan-Latinism in the region, in opposition to the growing American influence there, and after 1880, when Washington launched the Pan-American movement, such propaganda sharpened in tone; but there was no apparent underlying political concern except a certain anxiety about possible Yankee designs on European colonies. Certainly France was in no position to pursue grand strategy in Latin America. "All that could be done by criticism, denunciation, and propaganda, Frenchmen did; and they proved themselves the more able in these lines of effort because there was little else they could do," J. Fred Rippy (1928, p. 134) aptly observed. The Auswärtiges Amt, like the Foreign Office and Quai d'Orsay, largely ignored Latin America. Diplomatic posts there were "very unpopular" with nineteenth century German envoys, one of whom announced that he would rather resign from the service than become minister to Brazil (Cecil 1976, pp. 170–171), and national strategists found little reason to include Latin America in their speculations—until the 1890s.

The twin catalysts for a shift in Germany's attitude were changes in the political configuration of Europe itself and the growing industro-military strength and expansionism of the United States. Indeed, throughout the post-1890 period, the Latin American policies of not only Germany, but of England as well, were vitally influenced by intra-European politics (i.e., the deepening Anglo–German schism), and by the relations of each with the United States. As Platt (1967, p. 37) stated it, regarding much of the story of British relations with Latin America, they were "merely an eddy off the main current of British relations with Washington." The attitude of the latter toward Latin America, in turn, was largely a function of suspicions and anxiety about European activities in the hemisphere.

The Pan-American movement generated by Secretary of State James G. Blaine in the 1880s was conceived of precisely as a means of impeding European interference in the hemisphere. On the one hand, Blaine, who was imbued with "marked suspicion and ill will" toward England, feared that armed conflict in Latin America provided a dangerous opportunity for European intrigue, hence his desire to establish a system of inter-American arbitration (Bastert 1959, pp. 377–378, 383–384, 411–412). On the other hand, Washington's interest in an inter-American customs union was, in part, a function of a desire to weaken European competitors. British and German observers understandably were disturbed by the convocation of the first Pan-American Congress in 1889, as they were by Washington's diplomatic muscle-flexing in ensuing years. But London, increasingly concerned about the growing German threat, was interested primarily in cultivating American good will. Thus, in the famous boundary dispute with Venezuela in 1895, the Foreign Office, in the face of a vigorous reaffirmation of the Monroe Doctrine by the State Department, reluctantly recognized that Doctrine. "In British eyes, Latin America was of marginal international importance," one historian has written, "and the price of political disengagement, however visible, was a small one to pay in order to avoid conflict with the United States"

(Smith 1979, p. xiv).⁶ The subsequent, even more dramatic display of authority by the United States in Cuba provoked, therefore, no undue alarm and no change of policy on London's part.

British policymakers, prodded by Washington, gave ground rapidly after the turn of the century, removing diplomatic obstacles to an American-controlled isthmian canal, reducing its West Indies garrison, and in general deferring to the superior military power and hence the political preeminence of the United States in the Western Hemisphere. Sir Edward Grey privately summed up the official British view in August 1910: "These small [Latin American] Republics will never establish decent govt. [*sic*] themselves—they must succumb to some greater and better influence and it can only be that of the U.S.A. We cannot compete with that and must obtain the best terms we can as occasion offers for vested British interests and commercial opportunities" (Calvert 1968, pp. 34–35). The following year Grey confidentially acknowledged that British diplomats had standing orders to avoid "taking a hand in the politics of South America or acquiring political influence" there (Platt 1967, p. 23).

The crisis in American–Mexican relations that erupted in 1913 because of the assassination of President Francisco Madero and the assumption of power by General Victoriano Huerta, created a delicate situation for the Foreign Office. Like most of the major European powers, Great Britain recognized the Huerta regime. Washington's refusal to do so, however, impeded the pacification of Mexico and placed severe strains on Anglo–American relations—a fact that, particularly as European politics grew more unstable, London judged undesirable. "I do not dispute the inconvenience and untoward results of United States policy," Grey informed the new British minister to Mexico, "but . . . His Majesty's Government cannot with any prospect of success embark upon an active counterpolicy to that of the United States, or constitute themselves the champions of Mexico or any of these republics against the United States" (Calvert 1968, p. 225). London therefore supported Huerta only in a formal sense and left political initiatives to Washington.

Berlin's response to American politico-economic expansion was substantially different. German leaders took a keen interest in Washington's Latin American policy, which they saw as an exclusivist one, designed to keep Germany out of the hemisphere. Scorning the Monroe Doctrine, the Kaiser regarded the loss of trade pacts with two South American countries in the mid-1890s as the onset of "a war to the death" between Germany and the United States. He flirted with the idea of a united European front against the United States and its apparent ally, England. The Spanish–American War—an example of "Yankee audacity secretly supported by John Bull," according to Wilhelm—generated a sense of urgency in Berlin, where naval leaders argued that Germany should seize a base in the West Indies. The idea that the Reich needed such a base somewhere in Latin America rapidly became conviction, and in subsequent years German strategic thought focused on the possibility of a conflict with the United States over the Monroe Doctrine. German goals went beyond a simple naval base in the Caribbean to include a formal colony in South America, where the Kaiser envisioned the Reich as the "paramount power" (Herwig 1976, pp. 19–27, 43–68).[7] It was Germany's "duty," he privately explained, to "protect and annex to us" (Vagts 1935, vol. II, p. 1476) the Germans living in South America. Annexation schemes apparently were never transformed into concrete plans, but Pan-Germanists, among them some diplomats in South America, saw southern Brazil as the logical target (Hell 1966).

German reluctance to acknowledge the Monroe Doctrine contributed to what, in American eyes, were threatening gestures in the Caribbean in the early 1900s, such as the famous Anglo–German bombardment and blockade of the Venezuelan coast in 1902–1903, to force the payment of debts. Platt (1962, p. 11) has argued convincingly that the undertaking was in keeping with "traditional practices sanctioned by international law" and after pressure from Washington, the two European powers agreed to submit their grievances to arbitration. The episode aroused strong anti-German sentiment in the United States, however, and led to demands there for fleet expansion and other measures to counter the "German threat" (Vagts 1935, vol. II, pp. 1525–1635). Berlin had specifically assured President Theodore Roosevelt before the incident that reports about German territorial designs in Latin America were "lies and slanders" (Vagts 1935, vol. II, p. 1738). However, the German Admiralty, shortly after the lifting of the blockade, defined German aims in the region as the establishment of a naval station in the Caribbean, a "free hand in South America," and nullification of the Monroe Doctrine (Herwig 1976, p. 86).

Despite discussion of bases in the Caribbean, Germany's politico-strategic attention, as far as Latin America was concerned, seems to have focused increasingly on Mexico in the years immediately preceding the World War. Convinced that sooner or later the United States would dominate its weaker neighbor, and in view of the miniscule German colony and small investment stake there, Berlin had evinced slight interest in Mexico until the Spanish-American War. After that, however, German leaders increasingly viewed that country as a possible future bulwark against American expansion southward. The receptivity of the Díaz regime to German capital and military cooperation encouraged Berlin, but German strategists faced a fundamental dilemma. It seemed obviously in the Reich's interest to assist in the improvement of Mexico's military capabilities and encourage a pro-German, anti-American attitude on the part of Mexico City; yet at the same time such a policy might provoke a confrontation with the United States (Katz 1964). The German minister in Mexico City articulated the somewhat contradictory goals when he wrote in December 1906 that Germany's "sole task must be to avoid friction with the United States all along the line, yet do our best to increase friction between the United States and other countries" (Schiff 1959, p. 572).

A critical factor militating against achievement of Germany's twin aims, not only in Mexico but anywhere else in Latin America, was the European situation. Only a united front on the part of European powers would permit Germany to run the risk of a clash with the United States in Latin America, but there was no hope of such unity after 1905. Realization of that fact encouraged moderation in the *Panther* episode late that year. In response to Brazilian protests and alarmist articles in the United States press about the high-handed manner in which the German warship had landed sailors on Brazilian territory to seize a deserter, Berlin apologized and promised to discipline the ship's officers. Later, during the Washington-Huerta quarrel in 1913–1914, the Auswärtiges Amt recognized the Huerta government, but subsequently informed it candidly that international conditions did not permit an aggressive aid policy vis-à-vis the United States (Katz 1966).[8] German interests in Mexico, Berlin concluded, were simply not important enough to justify undermining cordial relations with Washington (Baecker 1971).

By the eve of World War I, then, whatever broader politico-territorial goals Germany might have been pursuing had proved elusive; indeed, Berlin had gradually acquiesced in American suzerainty over the Western Hemisphere largely because of intra-European politics, which proved an insurmountable constraint (Katz 1966). In Mexico, which would become the focal point of German intrigue against the United States during World War I, Berlin's hopes of developing a preponderant influence over the army had been basically fruitless; in fact, arch-rival France had been more fortunate than Germany in that regard (Schiff 1959). The only political achievement had been not to damage, despite diplomatic support given to Huerta, the anti-Christ of the Mexican revolutionaries, the friendly relations between the two countries. However, even here it could be argued that Germany's success was not a function of her diplomatic skill, but rather of Mexico's antipathy toward Washington.

The First World War and the Interwar Period

The First World War brought vividly to the surface the enduring character of the struggle among the great powers for position and influence in Latin America. Perhaps best illustrative of the phenomenon was the alacrity with which the American business community and the Woodrow Wilson administration undertook a coordinated effort to dislodge European rivals, whose governments were absorbed with the task of waging war (Kaufman 1971). Tremendous advances were made in various fields subsidiary to commerce, such as shipping, communications, and especially banking, an area in which European houses previously had enjoyed a near monopoly (Mayer 1973). In export-import activities proper, United States shippers enjoyed most of the advantages. Their gains vis-à-vis British and German counterparts in the Brazilian market, for example, were striking. German traders could do little to withstand the American onslaught since, even before Brazil broke relations with the Central Powers in 1917, the British blockade and the conversion of the German economy to war production had drastically weakened their position. British business circles and London authorities, alarmed by American advances, took countersteps late in the war, however, dispatching a special trade mission to Brazil in order to reassure that country that Great Britain was still in the export-import business and was looking forward to a normalization of trade (Rosenberg 1978; Healy 1976). American merchants made similarly strong gains in other important Latin American markets, such as neutral Argentina and Mexico, where European competitors faced unique difficulties. In Argentina, a critical source of meat and wheat for the Allies—as Lloyd George publicly acknowledged after the war (Capdevila

1965)—and in Brazil, German merchants were targets of a strong effort by not only American but British rivals as well to eliminate them permanently from the market (Normano 1977; Gravil 1977). In Mexico, they suffered from the general war-related problems, while British traders were hindered by revolutionary turmoil and its attendant friction, which finally provoked a break in relations between Mexico City and London in 1918.

The interwar period saw a resurgence of great power competition, as Germany reentered the Latin American trade with a vengeance in the 1920s and Great Britain struggled to recoup losses. British merchants in Brazil may not have resembled, as an American observer charged in 1919, "hounds with their eyes and tongues sticking out, panting after a price which they believe the Americans want to take away from them" (Tulchin 1971, pp. 47–49, 79–81, 151),[9] but they were concerned about wartime losses and gave vigorous battle to the Germans and Americans.[10] The D'Abernon Mission to Argentina (and Brazil) in 1929 represented an effort to protect Britain's declining position in an important market, even to the extent of abandoning traditional free trade (Gravil 1977; Platt 1967). Germany displayed remarkable resiliency, especially in Brazil. By the onset of the depression, Germany was again the second leading purchaser of Brazilian products and the third leading exporter to the Brazilian market (behind the United States and Britain) (Valla 1972).

The decade of the 1930s witnessed even more intense rivalry, primarily between Nazi Germany and the United States, since Great Britain lapsed into imperial preference and began a relative withdrawal from most of Latin America, except Argentina where she sought through preferential, bilateral arrangements to protect her interests (Smith 1969; Goodwin 1981). German authorities made the region a major target of an aggressive sales drive, launched in 1934 and disciplined according to the needs of Hitler's rearmament program; i.e., it was designed to maximize imports of critical raw materials and exports of industrial goods, through trading methods (compensation and clearing agreements) that obviated the need to make payments in scarce foreign exchange. Washington's adoption of a liberal, reciprocal trade agreements program that same year, in which a special place was reserved for Latin American countries, set the stage for a bitter commercial war. Berlin's endeavor in Latin America was in general a substantial success, most notably in Brazil, which became the Reich's leading trade partner in Latin America and where Germany by 1938 replaced the United States as the major supplier. An indication of the significance of the Brazilian market for the Reich was the fact that it furnished nearly one-third of German imports of cotton that year. With Argentina, too, after a fitful start, Germany established a mutually profitable relationship, as it did with Mexico, emerging in 1938–1939 as the principal buyer of Mexican oil. German successes were watched with alarm and frustration by American and British competitors and met with official protests and complaints about unfair commercial methods; but the advantages of compensation trade were enormous, and consequently there was little inclination to restrict it (Pommerin 1977; Hilton 1975a; Ebel 1971; Volland 1976). President Lázaro Cárdenas of Mexico, for example, was distinctly unimpressed with criticism in the United States and Britain about Mexican oil sales to the Axis. It was "absurd," he told his ambassador in Washington in 1938, for those two countries, "who see not the slightest inconvenience in their nationals' selling it [i.e., oil] to their potential enemies," to decry Mexico's doing likewise (Gomez 1974).

One significant new area of European activity in South America during the interwar period was air communications, which in Germany's case gave her additional commercial advantage. Soon after World War I ended, French, German, and Italian air "missions" became active in a number of Latin American countries, and a small French line began operations in French Guiana in 1919, followed by the establishment of a German-owned company in Colombia two years later. German interests were also responsible for starting mail and passenger service in Argentina and Bolivia in following years. The Argentine enterprise, Aero Lloyd, cooperated with Junkers, the German manufacturer, and in conjunction with a Hamburg shipping company established the Berlin-based Kondor Syndikat in 1924, which in turn laid the groundwork for air traffic in Brazil (Newton 1978). What appears to have been a German-owned, "Brazilian-incorporated successor," the Sindicato Condor, opened the first regular domestic line in Brazil in 1927, linking Porto Alegre to Rio de Janeiro. That same year another German-controlled company, VARIG (Viação Aérea Rio Grandense) began operations in Rio Grande do Sul (Burden 1943, p. 12). Sometime during this period the Sindicato Condor apparently established some kind of as yet undefined link with the newly formed Deutsche Lufthansa, a merger of Aero Lloyd and Junkers, which "swiftly became the chief German aviation medium for promoting economic, political and, after the rise of Hitler, ideological influences abroad" (Newton 1981, p. 77).

Transatlantic service to South America began in 1928, when a French company, Aéropostale, which had started a mail run between Buenos Aires and Natal the previous year, made the inaugural trip linking France to Argentina via Brazil. Aéropostale quickly extended its service to Paraguay and Chile, thus joining most of the Southern Cone to Western Europe. For their part, German interests in the early 1930s established the first all-air lines to South America. The pioneer was the Deutsche Zeppelin Reederei, which opened seasonal airship service between Germany and Brazil in 1931 and maintained it until 1937. In the meantime, Lufthansa began mail flights to Brazil in 1933, giving German exporters a significant advantage over American and British competitors (Burden 1943; Stemmler 1934). The Italians came into the picture in 1939, when the LATI (Linee Aeree Transcontinentali Italiane) company inaugurated passenger service between Rome and Rio de Janeiro. British Airways started preparations for a route to South America in 1937–1938, but the outbreak of war disrupted its plans, which redounded to the advantage of Axis opponents—to the dismay of the 1939 British Foreign Office (Burden 1943).[11]

The only European country that demonstrated a political or strategic interest in Latin America after 1914 was again Germany, and the focal point of its interest initially was again Mexico. The British Admiralty's decision in 1913 to convert the fleet to oil-burning vessels and seek a small contract with the major British oil company in Mexico gave German military planners some reason to be interested in Mexican fields, and plans were developed after the United States entered the war to set them ablaze. Even more important was the fact of Mexico's geographical contiguity to the United States and its deep-rooted antipathy toward that country. This opened up possibilities for creating a diversion on Washington's southern flank, especially in view of the friendly attitude shown toward Berlin not only by Huerta, but later by the Constitutionalists, too. The result was German intrigue with the exiled Huerta and other Mexican opposition figures including, apparently, Pancho Villa, all in an effort to provoke a confrontation between the United States and Mexico. The famous Zimmerman Telegram episode was thus merely the most dramatic and ambitious in a series of efforts to generate a challenge along the Rio Grande that might deter the United States from intervening, at least effectively, in the European war.[12]

In the final stages of the conflict, Western European powers began sending out what appeared to be political signals to Latin American states, especially Brazil. Great Britain, France, Italy, and Belgium raised their legations in Rio de Janeiro to the status of embassies in 1918–1920,[13] but this was more a gesture of recognition of Brazil's stand during the war—and certainly in London's case, another reassurance of commercial interest—than it was a sign of any broader political intent. Several European governments, among them Germany, Holland, and Italy, recognized the Alvaro Obregón regime in Mexico in 1921, two years before the United States did, but that was in keeping with standard diplomatic practice. Those countries, moreover, did not have substantial claims against Mexico, as did France and Belgium, who recognized Obregón only after reaching agreement on the establishment of mixed claims commissions. To protect its own interests in that regard, London sought a reestablishment of relations in 1925 (Estrada 1935).

The major European powers welcomed Latin American participation in the League of Nations, but clearly that was to bolster the prestige of the Geneva organization, which served their purposes, rather than to assist Latin American governments. Indeed, Brazilian observers in the 1920s frequently complained of the disdainful attitude of those powers toward weaker ones (Hilton 1980). Revealing in that sense was the fate of Brazil's campaign for a permanent seat on the League Council. European statesmen, first of all, never really took Rio de Janeiro's candidacy seriously. Certainly the British did not. As Sir Robert Vansittart, the head of the American Department of the Foreign Office—which not only lumped all the Latin American countries together but included the United States as well—recalled in the mid-1920s, British diplomats at the time scorned Latin America, regarding assignments there as "tombstones rather than stepping-stones." The reaction to Brazil's bid for a permanent seat was therefore mildly incredulous. To give Brazil a seat would only cause "great heart-burning" in South America and all the other governments there would claim similar status, said one Foreign Office analyst in May 1925. Consequently, when Brazil, a nonpermanent member of the council, then vetoed Germany's admission to the League in March 1926 because Germany was to receive a permanent place on the council while Brazil was not, European leaders were dumbstruck. "That a South American nation should upset a European settlement of an important European question at Geneva is more than a shock for

Europe," the American ambassador in Berlin correctly noted. Benito Mussolini remarked to a British diplomat that it was "ridiculous" that European policy could be influenced by "exotic and insignificant states," while authorities in London concluded that Brazil would have to be administratively removed from the council since "the League can go on quite happily without Brazil . . . ." Rather than be humiliated, Rio de Janeiro announced its withdrawal from the Geneva organization in June 1926.[14]

The triumph of Nazism in Germany and the subsequent division of the Western world into two ideological blocs, served to make Latin America, particularly countries such as Brazil and Argentina with sizable German communities, a significant field of politico-ideological competition in the 1930s. Berlin cultivated closer relations with the major Latin American powers—it established embassies in Brazil, Argentina, and Chile, for example—and sought in myriad ways to promote anti-communist and anti-American sentiment in the region. The Auslandsorganisation (AO) of the Nazi Party (NSDAP) actively undertook to mobilize support for the Third Reich among Germans in South America, and it has been argued that the Hitler regime pursued territorial aims there (Katz 1966; Hell 1966; Frye 1967; McCann 1973).[15] Certainly American public opinion and policymakers took that possibility seriously, although the historical evidence for it is slender.[16]

At any rate, two things are clear. First, Nazi efforts to establish local bases of political support in Latin American countries, either within the German-speaking community, the domestic fascist movements, or on the part of Latin American governments, produced dubious results. Membership in local branches of the NSDAP was miniscule, and the activities of AO emissaries often caused sharp schisms within the German communities. Relations between German authorities and local fascists, furthermore, tended to be at best ambivalent (Hilton 1972), and in dealing with Latin American governments Berlin was handicapped by a lack of policy unity—the reference here is to the well-known frequent divergence between the AO and the Auswärtiges Amt. In general, as Friedrich Katz has stressed, there was a "deep gap" between goals and means on Germany's part insofar as its search for political influence was concerned (Katz 1966, p. 56). The primary result of Nazi policy, moreover, was to provoke Washington into countermeasures that further impeded German efforts in Latin America (Weinberg 1970).[17] The second noteworthy thing about German policy toward the region in the 1930s is that when a choice seemed necessary, as it did in Brazil in 1938, Berlin refused to allow politics to interfere with commerce, which in itself is an interesting commentary on its aims in South America (Hilton 1975).

The Second World War

Renewed international conflict brought a repetition of World War 1 experiences. In this commercial sphere, the British blockade effectively checked the Reich's advances in Latin America and with Germany once more driven out of the region, the field was left to the British and Americans. The former, of course, faced enormous difficulties. In Mexico the absence of diplomatic relations, which had been ruptured in 1938 because of the expropriation of British oil companies there, greatly hindered British commerce, which concentrated itself largely on Brazil and Argentina. British sales to Brazil dropped substantially, the gain going to Argentina, however, and not the United States, while Britain's percentage share of Brazil's exports remained fairly steady throughout much of the war (Hilton 1975a). In the case of Argentina, although the United Kingdom continued to be her major market, British sales to the La Plata country suffered sharply from American competition.[18] Even Brazil surpassed the United Kingdom as a supplier to Argentina in 1944. In fact, Brazil was now the latter's principal source of imports because of politically-inspired American restrictions on sales to Argentina (Hilton 1975b).[19] Export associations and government authorities agonized over the losses in Latin America and the problem generated considerable discussion in policy-making circles in London, but the outlook seemed bleak. As the Foreign Office lamented in 1943:

> We seem to have little to offer which will compete with the refrigerators and other gadgets which are so attractive to more or less undeveloped and uneducated people. Not only are the United States better placed geographically than ourselves to influence South Americans, and less distracted by other spheres such as Europe and the Dominions which have a prior claim in our case, but the "firepower" which they are able to bring to bear in the shape of credits, facilities, manpower, entertainment, exports (including the all-pervading Hollywood films), in fact of everything, perhaps, except, ultimately, markets, is of an intensity with which we cannot hope to compete.[20]

The example of Argentina during the Second World War is a good illustration of the economic significance of Latin America to Europe, or at least of one Latin American country to a European one. After the United States entered the war, Argentina remained neutral, which led Washington to press London constantly to join it in a policy of sanctions toward Buenos Aires. The British government resisted this because, as the Ministry of Economic Warfare reminded the Foreign Office in November 1942, the United Kingdom was "dependent on the Argentine for many supplies essential to the Allied war effort . . . and Argentine good will was therefore vital." The matter was debated frequently among the various agencies concerned in London, and their conclusion was unanimous: the flow of Argentine meat, leather—Britain was receiving over 30 percent of her imports of those two products from Argentina—wheat, and linseed must not be jeopardized. Six months before D-Day, British military planners warned that, should supplies from the La Plata nation be interrupted, "military operations could certainly not be continued on the scale planned for this year except by means of a severe curtailment of the meat rations of the United Kingdom civilian population." Any sharp reduction in consignments of leather from Argentina, they continued, would produce "a very serious effect on military operational capacity towards the end of 1944."[21] So important was the issue to London that Winston Churchill took it up directly with Franklin Roosevelt.[22]

With respect to strategic interests, the Second World War gave Latin America a new significance. Aside from the obvious importance of the Panama Canal, the area's raw materials, foodstuffs, and minerals were often critical to the Allies; Brazil lay on British convoy routes. The United States began "neutrality" patrols out of ports in the Brazilian northeast in 1941, and started ferrying lend-lease planes and equipment through new bases in that region to British forces in Africa and the Middle East that same year. The LATI run to Brazil during 1940–1941 was Europe's only regular air connection with the Western Hemisphere. The fall of France seemingly raised the possibility of Nazi military intrusion, via Dakar, into northeastern Brazil. Both Holland and France, conquered countries, had colonies in the Caribbean and South America. Also, it proved easier, for technical and "political" reasons, for Germany to communicate by radio with South America than with North America. For all these reasons, Brazil during the period 1939–1942 was the focal point of German military espionage in the Western Hemisphere, an effort that also included Argentina, Chile, Ecuador, Mexico, and other areas, as well, of course, as the United States. For that reason, American and British counterintelligence agencies were also extremely active in Brazil and elsewhere in Latin America combating German espionage (Hilton 1977, 1981),[23] eliminating Axis influence from South American air traffic (Hilton 1981; McCann 1968), and in general seeking to discredit political opponents.[24]

British interest in the politics of Latin America during the World War II era was solely a function of the European crisis, and the necessity of maintaining the entente with the United States was a severe constraint on London's maneuverability. Then too, there was advantage, as far as England's conflict with Germany was concerned, in Washington's preponderant political, economic, and military position in Latin America. Indeed, as the European situation deteriorated rapidly in the late 1930s, British policymakers saw increasing virtue in the Good Neighbor Policy and in American efforts to close hemispheric ranks vis-à-vis the Axis (Hilton 1975a). Intrinsically, the region still held little political interest for Great Britain. Two months after the onset of hostilities in Europe, senior analysts in the Foreign Office "agreed that from the political point of view, the Latin American countries ranked in the lowest order of priority" and that, in trying to juggle the needs of the war economy and export obligations, the reasons for paying attention to certain South American countries, such as Brazil and Argentina, were "mainly strategic," i.e., encouraging those nations to maintain a strict, or better yet, pro-Allied, neutrality. Board of Trade experts also placed Brazil "near the bottom of the list as far as political importance is concerned."[25] The British government, consequently, was little disposed to make exceptions for Brazil in the matter of shipment of consignments of German arms under prewar contracts through the blockade, or in that of sending military observers to the Middle East, or especially in regard to the dispatch of a Brazilian expeditionary force to Europe. In all these cases, London ceded ground only because Washington brought political pressure to bear in their favor. The one instance in which London remained adamant was when American negotiators suggested in 1944 that Brazil be given a permanent seat on the Security Council of the future United Nations (Hilton 1979). In the case of Argentina too, the British government reluctantly deferred to the United States at various junctures because it needed to maintain American good will. As the Foreign

Office explained, regarding Latin America in general, "to appear to challenge American influence in what Americans regard rightly or wrongly as an United States sphere of influence would certainly expose Anglo–United States relations to a strain which they could ill afford to bear."[26]

FROM THE LATIN AMERICAN SIDE

Viewed from Latin America's side of the equation, the varied reactions of governments there to Europe and European events make generalization difficult. World War I, for example, provoked widely different policies in Latin America. In the region as a whole, pro-Allied sentiment, largely because of French cultural influence— "Notre langue est parlée par tous les gens cultivés," wrote the prewar French minister to Brazil in 1918, "et on peut dire de presque tous les Sud-Américains qu'ils ont deux patries: la leur et la France" (d'Anthouard 1920)—was predominant, but Brazil was the only major Latin American country to declare war on the Central Powers. Mexico, Argentina, Venezuela, Chile, and three other countries declined even to sever relations with Germany (Martin 1925; Königk 1935). The Carranza government in Mexico was actually pro-German: it secretly proposed to Berlin in November 1916 a wide-ranging program of collaboration (Katz 1964, 1981), and called publicly for mediation of the conflict by the neutrals; should that fail, said Carranza, Mexico should cut off trade with the belligerent states (Estrada 1935), a move that obviously would have favored the Central Powers. The Hipólito Yrigoyen administration in Argentina apparently was of a similar bent, forming with Mexico a sort of "neutralist alliance." Yrigoyen took Carranza's idea of a conference of neutrals and tried to transform it into a neutralist Latin American bloc directed undoubtedly at the United States (Rosenberg 1975).

Cooperation with Europe in the League of Nations also elicited different responses from Latin American countries. Only nine of them, including Brazil, ratified the Versailles Treaty, and thus became original members of the League; Argentina, Venezuela, and four other states gained such status by quickly endorsing the League Covenant. Mexico refused to join the world organization until 1932, and Argentina withdrew in 1920, not formally affiliating with the League again until 1933 (Kelchner 1930; Perez-Guerrero 1936; Sanz 1965, vol. II). Brazil was the first country to establish a permanent representation in Geneva, and President Arthur Bernardes hailed the country's "double obligation" in international politics, which he explained as a need to follow a "great harmony of action in America and in Europe." In 1926 however, he ordered Brazil's withdrawal from the League when his bid for a permanent slot on the council failed, and told the American ambassador that Brazil now planned "to intensify her relations with the American republics and especially the United States, disassociating herself from European affairs with which she has no natural connection" (Hilton 1980, pp. 352–353; de Melo Franco 1955, vol. III). One prominent Brazilian observer, Barbosa Lima Sobrinho, believed departure from the League would "free us from a European organization where there is little use made of the American nations" (Kelchner 1930).

In the 1930s the issue of League, or European, involvement in hemispheric political questions divided official opinion in South America. Brazil had continued to participate with Geneva in a variety of technical matters, but it steadfastly refused to consider reentry into the League until, as Foreign Minister Afrânio de Melo Franco (1930–1933) repeatedly stated, "that organization has become more democratic in character and has ceased to concern itself exclusively with European affairs."[27] As a disgruntled nonmember of the League and dedicated pan-Americanist, Brazil systematically opposed League mediatory intervention in the Chaco War (1932–1935) between Bolivia and Paraguay,[28] while Argentina championed League efforts to negotiate a truce. During the mid-1930s, Rio de Janeiro was in the vanguard of the movement to strengthen hemispheric peace-keeping instruments and cooperative arrangements vis-à-vis Europe, whereas Buenos Aires staunchly resisted that movement and worked to bolster the prestige of the League of Nations in South America.[29] President Lázaro Cárdenas of Mexico stressed the need for a hemispheric security pact, but at the same time he called for a strengthening of the League (Gomez 1974, vol. I, pp. 203–204).

The impact of the European political crisis of the 1930s on Latin American policies varied from country to country. An active member of the League, Argentina, along with Mexico, supported its response to the Italo-Ethiopian conflict for example, but Brazil bluntly rejected Geneva's request for sanctions against Italy and instead hastily negotiated supply contracts with the Italian army (Volland 1976; Hilton 1979). During the Spanish Civil War, the Cárdenas government became an outspoken supporter of the Republican regime. When the Spanish ambassador requested arms and ammunition shortly after the Franco uprising, Cárdenas ordered his minister of war to ready 20,000 rifles and 20 million cartridges "immediately" for shipment. Mexico subsequently served as a conduit for Spanish arms purchases from third countries, and it consistently opposed the nonintervention policy adopted by the Western European powers, arguing that such a stand actually aided the Axis-backed rebels.[30] The Getúlio Vargas government in Brazil, however, openly sympathized with the Nationalist cause. Less than a month after Franco launched his revolt, Itamaraty sought to persuade other Latin American governments to recognize the belligerency of the Nationalists at the same time that it authorized its ambassador in Madrid to withdraw at his discretion. Rejecting Uruguayan and Mexican proposals for Latin American mediation, Rio de Janeiro continued to stump for recognition of Nationalist belligerency and sent to Franco secret consignments of what he called "great quantities" of sugar and coffee.[31]

The whole episode of World War II itself affected Latin American countries in different ways and elicited, at different stages, policies ranging from strict neutrality, to open favoritism, to belligerency. Brazil maneuvered between the blocs until Pearl Harbor forced a stand in favor of the Allies; its basic loyalty during the period of hemispheric neutrality was to continental solidarity. Argentina, on the other hand, initially favored the Allied cause to the extent even of endeavoring in the spring of 1940 to mobilize hemispheric support for a stronger anti-Axis posture. Rebuffed on all sides at the very height of German victories in Europe, Buenos Aires fell back into a strict neutrality that subsequently became a pro-Axis neutrality. Not until 1944 did Argentina sever diplomatic relations with the Axis (Hilton 1966; Tulchin 1969).[32] Mexico, for its part, followed a policy similar to Brazil's, ultimately cooperating intimately in hemispheric defense and sending an air unit to the Pacific theater.

Despite the differential response of Latin America to Europe, one thing is clear: Europe in the first half of the century was of critical importance to the Latin American economies as a source of loans and investments, and especially as a commercial partner. Argentina, at the first Pan-American Conference late in the nineteenth century, had sharply attacked the idea of a hemispheric trade union, since it would tend to "exclude from the life of commerce that same Europe which extends to us her hand, sends us her strong arms, and complements our economic existence, after apportioning to us her civilization." In ensuing years Argentine spokesmen systematically defended the need to maintain close ties with Europe, since trade was the very lifeblood of the country (McGann 1957, pp. 156, 245, 295). During the 1930s, "only foreign policy issues which touched closely upon the questions of trade in export commodities and the relationship with Great Britain were considered vital to Argentine national interest" (Tulchin 1974, p. 125). At the Buenos Aires Conference (1936) and especially at the Lima Conference (1938), Argentina tenaciously resisted the idea of any hemispheric arrangements aimed at Europe (Hilton 1966).

Brazil, too, had opposed the creation of any exclusively hemispheric commercial union—"Brazil has no interest in divorcing itself from Europe; quite the contrary, it is to its advantage to maintain and develop its relations with her," Itamaraty explained[33]—and the shift of Brazil's diplomatic axis from London to Washington in the early years of the century by no means implied a reduced concern about trade with Europe. Indeed, for President Rodrigues Alves (1902–1906), the function of diplomacy was to produce economic results. He insisted, therefore, according to elder statesman Joaquim Nabuco, that Brazil's diplomats be its "first commercial and industrial agents." Alves' successor, Afonso Pena, keenly desired to attract European capital to Brazil, and Nabuco, one of the architects of the new diplomatic alliance with the United States, argued that a special relationship with the latter would actually encourage European investors, merchants, and immigrants to seek opportunity in Brazil.[34] The revival of German and British trade after World War I was obviously a function in large part of Brazil's own abiding interest in such trade. "From the commercial point of view and considering our urgent export needs," the minister in Berlin aptly noted in 1922, "the reestablishment, in whatever way and as rapidly as possible, of European economic equilibrium is more than desirable."[35] Vargas' careful maneuvering between Washington and Berlin in the 1930s stemmed from conviction that the German market was indispensable to Brazil (Hilton 1975a), and subsequent wartime dependency made Brazilian leaders look forward longingly to a postwar resurgence of the European connection. Foreign Minister Oswaldo Aranha stressed such interest to London early in 1944, and in midyear Vargas, on receiving the new British ambassador, "referred with some emphasis to the commercial relations between Brazil and the United Kingdom, which he was anxious to see greatly strengthened, especially in post-war years." At the end of the year, Vargas publicly hailed the postwar possibilities of attracting European immigrants, capitalists, and traders to Brazil.[36] Perhaps the most vivid proof of Europe's prewar economic significance to Brazil was Rio de Janeiro's intense interest, after the conflict was over, in restoring the Anglo–German connection.

Mexico's dependency on the United States market was overwhelming, but for that very reason Germany and Great Britain were important targets of its commercial interest. Political divergences with both European countries in the 1930s did not facilitate an economic relationship, but Mexican authorities were alert to opportunities. The expansion of trade with Germany was encouraging, for example, and the Mexican legation in Berlin worried that political factors might harm that trade. "The possibilities of German–Mexican commerce are magnificent," the minister commented in 1937. "I do not believe that there are two other countries in the world that complement each other as well in their production as Germany and Mexico."[37]

Europe also remained a crucial supplier of arms to Latin America in the interwar period, a role enhanced by Washington's paternalistic reluctance to engage in the sale of military hardware. Germany's eclipse in the 1920s left the field to French, Swedish, and British competitors, who were the chief exporters of artillery, automatic weapons, and (along with Italy and the United States) airplanes to Latin America.[38] Brazil's experiences with arms acquisitions in the 1930s illustrate the critical significance of Europe. After successive efforts to acquire warships from the United States proved fruitless and even humiliating, the Vargas government in 1936–1937 ordered submarines from Italy and destroyers from Great Britain, and during 1937–1939 it awarded successive contracts to Krupp for hundreds of pieces of artillery and complementary equipment. As Europe's political crisis worsened in 1939, the major preoccupation of the Brazilian army high command was that war would threaten the country's "freedom of trade with European nations," and with hostilities later a fact across the Atlantic, one of the "greatest preoccupations, perhaps the most important one," of army leaders was taking delivery of arms ordered before the war (Hilton 1973, pp. 80–84, 89–90). Germany also provided machinery and technicians for Brazilian military industries in the 1930s (Hilton 1982), and both Germany and France continued to play a noteworthy role in the training of Latin American officers after World War I. France in 1918 sent military and air missions to Brazil, where they remained until World War II; unofficial missions from Germany served in Argentina until mid-1940 (Potash 1969; Atkins and Thompson 1972).

Interesting questions arise about the political aspects of the European-Latin American relationship from the Latin American standpoint. How, for example, was Europe of political use to Latin America? Certainly the Old World remained a source of political inspiration in the interwar period, but its chief role now was to export antiliberal doctrines, such as Marxism and Fascism. The most pervasive impact was probably made by the former. With the funding of the Comintern, Moscow-trained agents from various European countries—Luis Carlos Prestes' German associates in Brazil come to mind—undertook proselytizing missions in Latin America. Fascism, too, left its impact on right-wing movements in some Latin American countries, notably Brazil (Levine 1970; Trindade 1974), where domestic fascists were subsidized financially by the Italian government and received propaganda assistance from German authorities (Hilton 1972). Pan-Hispanism also served as a vehicle for the dissemination of authoritarian principles in Latin America (Pike 1971).

More interesting, perhaps, would be to determine how Latin American governments utilized European ties for national political purposes, such as bolstering their general position or bargaining posture vis-à-vis regional competitors. The Brazilian-Argentine rivalry, for example, was too all-encompassing for it not to influence relations of these two governments with Europe. Brazil's keen interest in the League of Nations before 1926, and its abrupt withdrawal after failing to secure a permanent seat on the council and finding itself about to be removed from that organ, would seem to justify the conclusion of a Foreign Office analyst that year that ". . . it is not so much representation on the council that they [i.e., the Brazilians] are seeking as the prestige of being ranked in the class of the Great Powers to which they do not rightly belong."[39] The importance of prestige to a militarily weak country cannot be overemphasized. "The important thing for Nations like ours is to be seen, participate, reveal their high culture," Nabuco put it early in the century.[40] Since it can be argued that Brazil's general foreign policy strategy in this century has been primarily a function of its rivalry with Argentina, it seems logical that a fundamental reason for its interest in the League was the prestige that accrued to it within the ranks of the South American countries. Could, then, Argentina's reluctance to rejoin the League in the 1920s have been partly a result of the fact that Brazil occupied a place of prominence in the organization? "Jealousy between the two countries is . . . too great for the Argentine to admit [the] claim of [the] Brazilian government to represent Spanish South America [on the Council]," the British ambassador to Buenos Aires reported in March 1926. Criticism by Argentine newspapers and officials of Brazil's claim to a permanent seat and their simultaneous extolling of Argentina's political qualities[41] suggest a zeal to make political capital, in European eyes, out of Brazil's misfortune. In conversation with the British ambassador, the Argentine foreign minister attributed Brazil's action "partly to that country's vanity and sense of its own importance since it took part in the war, partly to its desire to obtain a permanent seat on the Council before Argentina could take her proper place in the League," i.e., before Argentina "might be elected to a permanent seat."[42] When invited by the League secretariat to serve on a special commission to reorganize the council so as to be able to remove Brazil—an invitation intended to be a deliberate slap at Brazil—Buenos Aires quickly accepted, much to the dismay of Brazilian leaders.[43]

It seems clear, too, that Latin American policymakers turned to Europe in search of a counterbalance to the United States, whose political and economic predominance most of them feared. Venezuelan dictator Cipriano Castro, for example, boasted in 1908 that Germany would support him vis-à-vis the United States (Calcott 1968), and Porfirio Díaz in Mexico carefully cultivated European financial interests in an effort to reduce dependency on the United States (Katz 1964; Munch 1977). Most Mexican leaders before World War II, in fact, sought European support in their quarrels with Washington. Jean Meyer has argued, in that regard, that the decision by Plutarco Calles to reestablish diplomatic relations with Great Britain in 1925, coming as it did when Mexican authorities felt "threatened" by the United States, was an effort to split the two stronger powers and generate favorable opinion in England (Meyer 1977, pp. 40–44).[44] Argentina's tenacity in maintaining close relations with Europe undoubtedly was partially linked to her historic resistance to the spread of United States influence in South America. As Sergio Bagú expressed it, Argentina's "tacit alliance" with England allowed Buenos Aires "a heavy dose of audacity" in dealing with the United

States (Bagú 1961, p. 70). During World War II, Buenos Aires' policy of cordiality toward Nazi Germany, and especially the opening of secret arms negotiations with Berlin in 1942, stemmed from the widening political chasm between Argentina and the United States (Potash 1969).

Europe, on the other hand, served Latin America well as a source of leverage for the extraction of concessions from the United States, particularly in times of American–European tensions. A classic example was the response of the Getúlio Vargas government to the American–German trade struggle in South America. Well aware of Washington's anxieties about Nazi machinations in the region, Brazilian authorities astutely and systematically played on those fears in order to stave off American pressures and to secure trade and financial concessions. Later, during the war, Rio de Janeiro exploited Washington's concern about Berlin's possible designs on the northeastern bulge of Brazil and about German–Argentine intrigue to obtain further economic and military assistance (Hilton 1975a; Moura 1980). The Cárdenas government apparently followed an identical policy in discussions with Washington regarding the expropriated American oil holdings. After nationalization of those properties in March 1938, there was immediate fear in American policy-making circles that the Axis would move into the Mexican market. "The action of Mexico . . . brings near to our shores the questions of war, Nazism and Fascism," sometime presidential adviser Bernard Baruch typically warned Roosevelt, while Ambassador Josephus Daniels in Mexico sent alarmist reports in the same vein to Secretary of State Cordell Hull.[45] Cárdenas saw this anxiety, moved quickly to sell oil to the Axis, and then used Axis interest as a wedge between the American government and the oil companies in order to isolate the latter in negotiations for compensation.[46]

Europe, of course, represented not only an opportunity; it was also occasionally a challenge and sometimes a threat to Latin America or to some countries of the region, which led them to seek the solidarity of the United States. Brazil provides probably the best example. At the beginning of the century, Nabuco gave voice to growing conviction in Brazilian policy-making circles when he said that ". . . unhappily I am convinced that if it were not for the 'Monroe Doctrine' Latin America would be as much an object of Europe's intrigues and ambitions as Asia and Africa. . . ." That doctrine, he concluded, was "a gigantic scarecrow that drives away the European eagles."[47] Brazil's effort to forge a special relationship with the United States in ensuing years and decades was primarily a function of rivalry with Argentina, but concern about European intentions in South America remained an underlying impulse and was particularly visible again in the 1930s, a period that generated anxieties in other Latin American countries, too, about European—i.e., Axis—designs on the hemisphere.

Two final and important aspects of the European–Latin American connection from the Latin American point of view that need further study are the uses that Latin American leaders made of Europe (or European interests in Latin America) for domestic political purposes, and especially the "emulative" and "penetrative" linkages between the two general political systems (Rosenau 1969, p. 46). The analysis in this chapter has been primarily of state-to-state relations, which implicitly posits a sort of we-they state of affairs. But as Douglas Chalmers (1969) has reminded us, the interaction among systems takes place along a broad front and at different levels. Suggestive examples are available that either show how European ideas, economic groups, or other agents influenced Latin American policy decisions, or else raise interesting questions about possible influence. For one, Thomas Skidmore (1974) has demonstrated that Brazilian immigration policy bore the heavy imprint of European racial attitudes, and it has also been shown that positivism had a considerable impact on federal educational policies and state allocations of resources in Brazil during the Old Republic (Nachman 1977). Did the French army officers who trained the São Paulo police have any input into decisions on state policy toward the social question? São Paulo's domestic policies, after all, were being geared to its foreign financial obligations, which meant that political stability was a priority goal (Love 1973). The roles played by immigrant groups and associations in local politics could be further studied for linkages. We know that such elements, particularly the labor militants among them, provoked tensions and conflicts with native citizens in Brazil, Argentina, and other countries, and therefore became targets of restrictive laws and other measures of suppression (Maram 1977; Solberg 1969). The nature of the relationship between immigrants and their home governments became a matter of serious concern to Brazilian authorities during both world war eras, leading them to undertake a series of nationalistic measures designed to hasten assimilation of such groups. In Argentina, at least, the immigrant "threat" became a banner for domestic politicians, who made great capital out of the immigrants' economic influence (Cornblit 1967). In heavily dependent economies, foreign economic interests logically played important political roles, willingly or unwillingly. In both Mexico and Brazil, national defense considerations influenced federal authorities to extend their control over foreign-owned railroads. Under radical leader Hipólito Yrigoyen in Argentina, British railroads in the 1920s became "unwilling pawns in the hands of a master politician" (Goodwin 1974, p. 286). Some of the further complexities of linkages involving foreign economic interests have been suggested by recent research on the Argentine experience. Friedrich Katz has shown how private German banks and firms were active agents of German foreign policy in early twentieth-century Mexico; and Joseph Love has done pioneering work on foreign interests and state politics in Brazil (Goodwin 1981; Katz 1981; Love 1980). At the broad national level, foreign military missions obviously had considerable impact on national defense doctrines, military attitudes, army organization, and possibly procurement. Examples similar to that of the Niemeyer Mission to Brazil in 1931, in which British experts wielded direct influence on Brazilian financial policy, may surface from further examination. What these different issue-areas suggest is that, whereas the political dimension of Latin America's relationship with Europe may be secondary to the economic content of that relationship insofar as broad politico-strategic considerations are concerned, the political interaction between the two systems has historically been intense and varied.

NOTES

The author wishes to thank Thomas E. Skidmore, Friedrich Katz, Warren Schiff, and Gerson Moura for helpful suggestions.

1. On the role of German immigrants see Roche (1969) and Brunn (1971).

2. See also Ferns (1960); Goodrich (1964–65); Ferrer (1963).

3. See also Brunn (1969) and Schaefer (1974).

4. Cf. Mitre (1965). For a colorful statement on general French influence in Latin America, see Normano (1941, 78–81).

5. On the impact of positivism in Latin America, see Cruz Costa (1964) and Zea (1943).

6. See also Hood (1977).

7. See also Vagts (1935, vol. II, 1452–1524).

8. On the *Panther* episode, see Vagts (1935, vol. II, 1758–63) and Burns (1966, 103–7).

9. Office of Naval Intelligence to State Department and Commerce Department, 7 April 1919, National Archives (Washington, Record Group 165, document 10672–37).

10. *London Morning Post,* 4 February 1924; *Times Trade and Engineering Supplement,* 20 November 1926; *Oldham Evening Chronicle,* 26 July 1927; *Financial News* (London), 13 August 1927; *Manchester Guardian,* 21 January 1928.

11. Foreign Office memo, 11 September 1939, Records of the Foreign Office (henceforth RFO), A 6503/6503/51.

12. Katz (1981) supersedes all previous work on the subject.

13. Brasil, Câmara dos Deputados, *Mensagens Presidenciaes,* 4 vols. (Rio, 1912–22), IV, 9, 11, 144.

14. Vansittart (1958, p. 20); minute by I. Kirkpatrick, 20 May 1925, RFO W4512/1993/98; U.S. Ambassador (Berlin) to State Department, 18 March 1926, NA, RG 59, 500.C001/345; British Ambassador (Rome) to Foreign Office, 19 March 1926; Medlicott et al. (1966, 540); minute by G. H. Villiers, 13 May 1926, RFO W4139/223/98.

15. On the AO's general effort, see Jacobsen (1968, 90 ff). General statements on Nazi policy in Latin America are Kossok (1961) and Pommerin (1977). Case studies of Nazi activities in Latin America include Kannapin (1966), Kramer–Kaske (1966), Harms–Baltzer (1970), Ebel (1971), and Volland (1976).

16. One target of alleged Nazi territorial interest was Patagonia, a subject that generated heated debate in Argentina in 1939–1940, but the documents purportedly revealing Nazi plans were "almost certainly" forged (Newton 1981).

17. German expansionism was the major impetus behind renewed emphasis in Washington on strategic planning for hemispheric defense (Child 1980).

18. Treasury Office (London), memo, 21 September 1944, Public Records Office (England), RFO AS 5017/78/2.

19. See also Treasury Office to Foreign Office, 22 December 1944.

20. Foreign Office to Ministry of Information, 12 August 1943, PRO A 4801/483/2. See also War Cabinet, Lord President's Committee, joint memo *Commercial Policy in Latin America* by Foreign Office and Board of Trade, 19 May 1943, A 4800/520/51; Ministry of Economic Warfare to Department of Overseas Trade, 31 May 1943, A 5098/281/51.

21. Ministry of Economic Warfare to Foreign Office, 2 November 1942, RFO A 10182/3188/2; 30 October 1943, A 10063/483/2; War Cabinet, Joint Planning Staff, memo *Relations with the Argentine,* 19 January 1944, A 495/4/2; Chiefs of Staff, cited in Foreign Office to British embassy (Washington), 21 January 1944, A 495/4/2.

22. Winston Churchill to Franklin Roosevelt, 14 July 1944, *Foreign Relations of the United States,* 1944, VII, 333.

23. On U.S. interest in Brazil during the war, see also McCann (1973).

24. See, for example, Blaiser (1942).

25. Foreign Office memo, 7 November 1939, RFO A7934/3956/51; Board of Trade to Foreign Office, 18 December 1939, A8930/539/6.

26. Foreign Office to Ministry of Information, 12 August 1943, RFO A4801/483/2.

27. U.S. Ambassador (Rio) to State Department, 9 December 1930, RG 59, 032 Drummond, Eric/34. See, too, British Ambassador (Rio) to Foreign Office, 29 January 1932, RFO 371/15810, A1133/1133/6.

28. See, for example, Ministério das Relações Exteriores (henceforth MRE) to Brazilian minister (La Paz), 29 June 1933, Arquivo Histórico do Itamaraty (henceforth AHI) (Rio), 402/3/2; MRE memo, October 1934, Arquivo Nacional (Rio), Coleção Presidência da República, file 11.587; State Department memo, 7 March 1935, RG 59, 724.3415/4718.

29. Hildebrando Acioly (MRE), memo, 26 August 1936, Instituto Histórico e Geográfico Brasileiro (Rio), José Carlos de Macedo Soares Papers; Foreign Minister José Carlos de Macedo Soares to President Getúlio Vargas, 4 December 1936, Centro de Pesquisa e Documentação de História Contemporânea (henceforth CPDOC), Fundação Getúlio Vargas (Rio), Getúlio Vargas Papers; British Ambassador (Buenos Aires) to Foreign Office, 16 September 1936, RFO 371/20476, W11428/79/98; British delegation (Geneva) to Foreign Office, 24 September 1936, A7726/391/51.

30. Cárdenas to Secretario de Guerra, 18 August 1936; Cárdenas to Ambassador Isidro Fabela (Geneva), 17 February 1937, Gómez (1974); Fabela (1947). See also Smith (1955), and especially Powell (1981).

31. MRE to Brazilian Delegation (Buenos Aires), 17 August 1936; MRE circular, 19 August 1936; MRE to Brazilian Ambassador (Madrid), 22 August 1936, 19 June 1937; MRE circular, 5 April 1937; MRE to missions in Argentina, Chile, and Peru, 29 June 1937; MRE to Brazilian Minister (Asuncion), 8 July 1937, all in AHI; Francisco Franco to Vargas, 29 October 1935, Vargas Papers. On Argentine policy, see Juárez (1963).

32. Recent books on the Argentine question are Francis (1977); Woods (1979). For a general survey of Latin America's response to the European conflict, see Humphreys (1981).

33. MRE circular (draft), n.d. [1899]; MRE, Instructions to Special Mission, 11 July 1889, AHI 273/3/5.

34. Joaquim Nabuco to Rio Branco, April 1904 (draft), Arquivo Nacional, Joaquim Nabuco Papers, microfilm roll 001.11-74, doc. 461; Afonso Pena to Rodrigues Alves, 23 July 1907, Arquivo Nacional, Afonso Pena Papers, caderno 5, p. 37; Nabuco to ? [incomplete draft], n.d. [1907], Nabuco Papers, microfilm roll 001.11-74, doc. 786.

35. Brazilian Minister (Berlin) to MRE, 28 January 1922, AHI 203/1/7.

36. Oswaldo Aranha to Anthony Eden, 29 February 1944, CPDOC, Oswaldo Aranha Papers; British Ambassador (Rio) to Foreign Office, 5 July 1944, RFO AS3778/1130/6; Vargas, speech, 7 December 1944, *A Nova Política do Brasil* (11 vols., Rio, 1938-47), XI, 56-58.

37. Mexican Minister (Berlin) to Mexican Foreign Minister, 11 May 1937, quoted in Volland (1976), 235, footnote 108.

38. Rodríguez (1966, vol. II, 364-65) mentions Argentine arms purchases in the 1920s. On Brazilian acquisitions from Europe, see Hilton (1982).

39. Foreign Office memo, 19 April 1926, RFO 371/11894, W3361/223/98.

40. Nabuco to Graça Aranha, 25 July 1907, Nabuco Papers, roll 001.11-74, doc. 900.

41. British Ambassador (Buenos Aires) to Foreign Office, 11 March 1926, RFO 371/11266, C3142/71/18; 17 March 1926, C3462/71/18; 24 March 1926, 371/11894, W3550/223/98.

42. British Ambassador (Buenos Aires) to Foreign Office, 2 May 1926, RFO 371/11894, W3742/223/98; 3 May 1926, 371/11894, W4840/223/98.

43. MRE to Ambassador Afrânio de Melo Franco (Geneva), 29 April 1926, AHI 274/3/3.

44. Katz (1981) documents Mexican interest in a European counterweight during the World War I era.

45. Bernard Baruch to Franklin Roosevelt, 29 April 1938, Franklin D. Roosevelt Library (Hyde Park), Franklin Roosevelt Papers, Official File 178 (1937–38); Josephus Daniels to Cordell Hull, 30 June 1938, Library of Congress, Manuscript Division, Cordell Hull Papers, box 42, folder 106; 8 July, 22 August 1938, ibid., box 43, folder 107; 9 February 1939, ibid., box 44, folder 114. See also Meyer (1972).

46. See Cárdenas to Castillo Nájera, 4 August 1938, 8 February 1939; Cárdenas to Roosevelt, 28 September 1938, in Gómez (1974), pp. 331, 336–37, 341; Daniels to Roosevelt, 28 March 1939, Roosevelt Papers, President's Secretary's File: Mexico, 1938–43, box 12.

47. Nabuco to President Manuel F. do Campos Salles, 12 July 1900, Nabuco Papers, 4011 001.10674, doc. 293.

REFERENCES

d'Anthouard, Albert François Ildefonse. *La France et les Republiques Sud-américaines*. Paris: 1920.

Atkins, George P. and Thompson, Larry V. "German Military Influence in Argentina, 1921–1940." *Journal of Latin American Studies*, 4 (November 1972):257–59.

Baecker, Thomas. *Die deutsche Mexikopolitik 1913/1914*. Berlin: Colloquium, 1971.

Bagú, Sergio. *Argentina en el mundo*. Buenos Aires: Fondo de Cultura Economica, 1961.

Baklanoff, Eric N. "External Factors in the Development of Brazil's Heartland: The Center-South, 1850–1930," in E. N. Baklanoff (ed.), *The Shaping of Modern Brazil*. Baton Rouge: Louisiana State University Press, 1969, 19–35.

Bastert, Russell H. "A New Approach to the Origins of Blaine's Pan American Policy." *Hispanic American Historical Review*, 39 (August 1959):375–412.

Beyhaut, Gustavo, et al. "Los inmigrantes en el sistema ocupacional argentino," in T. S. di Tella and G. Germani (eds.), *Argentina, sociedad de masas*. Buenos Aires: Eudera, 1965, 85–123.

Blaiser, Cole. "The United States, Germany, and the Bolivian Revolutionaries (1941–1946)." *Hispanic American Historical Review*, 52 (February 1942):26–54.

Brunn, Gerhard. "Deutscher Einfluss und deutsche Interessen in der Professionalisierung einiger lateinamerikanischer Armeen vor dem 1. Weltkrieg (1885–1914). *Jahrbuch für Geschichte von Staat, Wirtschaft und Gesellschaft Lateinamerikas*, 6 (1969):328–35.

———. *Deutschland und Brasilien, 1889–1914*. Cologne: Böhlau, 1971.

Burden, William A. *The Struggle for Airways in Latin America.* New York: Arno, 1943; reprint 1977.

Burns, E. Bradford. *The Unwritten Alliance: Rio-Branco and Brazilian-American Relations.* New York: Columbia University Press, 1966.

Calcott, Wilfrid H. *The Western Hemisphere: Its Influence on United States Policies to the End of World War II.* Austin: University of Texas Press, 1968.

Calvert, Peter. *The Mexican Revolution, 1910-1914: The Diplomacy of Anglo-American Conflict.* Cambridge: Cambridge University Press, 1968.

Capdevila, Arturo. "Primera Presidencia de Yrigoyen," in *Historia Argentina Contemporánea*, vol. 1. Buenos Aires: Academia Nacional de la Historia, 1965.

Cecil, Lamar. *The German Diplomatic Service, 1871-1914.* Princeton: Princeton University Press, 1976.

Chalmers, Douglas. "Developing on the Periphery: External Factors in Latin American Politics," in J. N. Rosenau (ed.), *Linkage Politics: Essays on the Convergence of National and International Systems.* New York: Free Press, 1969, 67-93.

Child, John. *Unequal Alliance: The Inter-American Military System 1938-1978.* Boulder: Westview, 1980.

Cornblit, Oscar. "European Immigrants in Argentine Industry and Politics," in C. Veliz (ed.), *The Politics of Conformity in Latin America.* London: Oxford Press, 1967, 221-27.

Cortes Conde, Roberto. *Corrientes inmigratorias y surgimento de industrias en Argentina, 1870-1914.* Buenos Aires: Universidad de Buenos Aires, 1974.

Cruz Costa, João. *A History of Ideas in Brazil.* Berkeley: University of California Press, 1964.

Dallari, Dalmo de Abreu. "The *Força Pública* of São Paulo in State and National Politics," in H. H. Keith and R. A. Hayes (eds.), *Perspectives on Armed Politics in Brazil.* Tempe: Arizona State University, 1976.

Dean, Warren K. *The Industrialization of São Paulo, 1880-1945.* Austin: University of Texas Press, 1969.

Dulles, John W. F. *Anarchists and Communists in Brazil, 1900-1935.* Austin: University of Texas Press, 1973.

Ebel, Arnold. *Das Dritte Reich und Argentinien: Die diplomatischen Beziehungen unter besonder Berücksichtigung der Handelspolitik (1933-1939).* Cologne: Böhlau, 1971.

Epstein, Fritz. "Argentinien und das deutsche Heer: Beitrag zur Geschichte europäischer militärischer Einflüsse auf Südamerika," in M. Göhring and A. Scharff (eds.), *Geschichtliche Kräfte und Entscheidungen.* Wiesbaden: Franz Steiner, 1954, 286-94.

Estrada, Genaro (ed.). *Un siglo de relaciones internacionales de México (atraves de los mensajes presidenciales).* México: Secretaría de Relaciones Exteriores, 1935.

Etchepareborda, Roberto. *Historia de las relaciones internacionales argentinas.* Buenos Aires: Pleamar, 1978.

Fabela, Isidoro. *Cartas al Presidente Cárdenas.* México, 1947.

Ferns, H. S. *Britain and Argentina in the Nineteenth Century.* Oxford: Oxford University Press, 1960.

Ferrer, Aldo. *La economia argentina: las etapas de su desarrollo y problemas actuales.* México: Fondo de Cultura Económica, 1963.

Fleming, William J. "The Cultural Determinants of Entrepreneurship and Economic Development: A Case Study of Mendoza Province, Argentina, 1861–1914." *Journal of Economic History,* 39 (March 1979):211–24.

Ford, A. G. "British Investment and Argentine Economic Development, 1880–1914," in D. Rock (ed.), *Argentina in the Twentieth Century.* London: Duckworth, 1975, 12–40.

Francis, Michael J. *The Limits of Hegemony: United States Relations with Argentina and Chile during World War II.* Notre Dame: University of Notre Dame Press, 1977.

Frye, Alton. *Nazi Germany and the American Hemisphere 1933–1941.* New Haven: Yale University Press, 1967.

Gómez, Elena Vasques (ed.). *Epistolario de Lázaro Cárdenas.* Vol. 1. México: Siglo Veintiuno, 1974.

Goodrich, Carter. "Argentina as a New Country." *Comparative Studies in Society and History,* 7 (1964–65):70–88.

Goodwin, Paul B. Jr. "The Politics of Rate-Making: the British-Owned Railways and the Unión Cívica Radical, 1921–1928." *Journal of Latin American Studies,* 6 (November 1974).

———. "Anglo–Argentine Commercial Relations: A Private Sector View, 1922–1943." *Hispanic American Historical Review,* 61 (February 1981):29–51.

Graham, Richard. *Britain and the Onset of Modernization in Brazil, 1850–1914.* Cambridge: Cambridge University Press, 1972.

Gravil, Roger. "The Anglo–Argentine Connection and the War of 1914–1918." *Journal of Latin American Studies,* 9 (May 1977):59–89.

Grieb, Kenneth. *The United States and Huerta.* Lincoln: University of Nebraska Press, 1969.

Harms-Baltzer, Käte. *Die Nationalisierung der deutschen Einwanderer und ihrer Nachkommen in Brasilien als Problem der deutsch-brasilianischen Beziehungen 1930–1938.* Berlin: Colloquium, 1970.

Healy, David. "Admiral William B. Capterton and United States Naval Diplomacy in South America, 1917–1919." *Journal of Latin American Studies,* 8 (November 1976):297–324.

Hell, Jürgen. "Das 'sudbrasilianische Neudeutschland'. Der annexionistische Grundzug der wilhelminischen und nazistischen Brasilienpolitik (1893 bis 1938)," in *Der deutsche Faschismus in Lateinamerika 1933–1934.* E. Berlin: Akademie, 1966, 103–10.

Herwig, Holger H. *Politics of Frustration: The United States in German Naval Planning, 1889–1941.* Boston: Little, Brown, 1976.

Hilton, Stanley E. "Argentine Neutrality, September 1939–June 1940: A Re-examination." *The Americas,* 22 (January 1966):227–57.

———. "*Ação Integralista Brasileira*: Fascism in Brazil, 1932–1938." *Luso-Brazilian Review,* 9 (December 1972):9–14.

———. "Military Influence on Brazilian Economic Policy, 1930–1945: A Different View." *Hispanic American Historical Review,* 59 (February 1973):71–94.

———. *Brazil and the Great Powers, 1930–1939: The Politics of Trade Rivalry.* Austin: University of Texas Press, 1975a.

———. "Vargas and the Brazilian Economic Development, 1930–1945: A Reappraisal of His Attitude Toward Industrialization and Planning." *Journal of Economic History*, 35 (December 1975b):754–78.

———. *Suástica sobre o Brasil: A História da Espionagem Alemã no Brasil, 1939–1944.* Rio: Civilização Brasileira, 1977.

———. "Brazilian Diplomacy and the Washington-Rio de Janeiro 'Axis' during the World War II Era." *Hispanic American Historical Review*, 59 (May 1979):222–25.

———. "Brazil and the Post-Versailles World: Elite Images and Foreign Policy Strategy, 1919–1929." *Journal of Latin American Studies*, 12 (November 1980):342–43.

———. *Hitler's Secret War in South America, 1939–1945: German Military Espionage and Allied Counter-Espionage in Brazil.* Baton Rouge: Louisiana State University Press, 1981.

———. "The Armed Forces and Industrialists in Modern Brazil: The Drive for Military Autonomy (1889–1954)." *Hispanic American Historical Review*, 62 (November 1982):629–73.

Hood, Miriam. *Gunboat Diplomacy 1895–1905: Great Power Pressure in Venezuela.* South Brunswick, NJ: A. S. Barnes, 1977.

Humphreys, R. A. *Latin America and the Second World War, vol. 1 1939–1942.* London: Athlone Press, 1981.

Jacobsen, Hans-Adolf. *Nationalsozialistische Aussenpolitic 1933–1938.* Frankfurt a/M: Alfred Metzner, 1968.

Jones, Charles. " 'Business Imperialism' and Argentina, 1875–1900: A Theoretical Note." *Journal of Latin American Studies*, 12 (November 1980):437–44.

Juárez, Joe Robert. "Argentine Neutrality, Mediation, and Asylum During the Spanish Civil War." *The Americas*, 19 (April 1963):383–403.

Kannapin, Klaus. "Zur Politik der Nazis in Argentinien von 1933–1943," in *Der Deutsche Faschismus in Lateinamerika 1933–1934.* E. Berlin: Akademie, 1966, 81–102.

Katz, Friedrich. "Mexiko und die Erdölpolitik in den Jahren 1876 bis 1913," in *Lateinamerika zwischen Emanzipation und Imperialismus 1810–1960.* E. Berlin: Akademie, 1961, 211–33.

———. *Deutschland, Diaz und die mexikanische Revolution: Die deutsche Politik in Mexiko 1870–1920.* E. Berlin: Akademie, 1964.

———. "Einige Grundzuge der Politik des deutschen Imperialismus in Lateinamerika von 1898 bis 1941," in *Der Deutsche Faschismus in Lateinamerika 1933–1934.* E. Berlin: Akademie, 1966, 9–70.

———. *The Secret War in Mexico: Europe, the United States and the Mexican Revolution.* Chicago: University of Chicago Press, 1981.

Kaufman, Burton. "United States Trade and Latin America: The Wilson Years." *Journal of American History*, 48 (September 1971):342–63.

Kelchner, Warren H. *Latin American Relations with the League of Nations.* Boston: World Peace Foundation, 1930.

Kirkpatrick, F. A. *South America and the War.* Cambridge: Cambridge University Press, 1918.

Königk, Georg. *Die Politik Brasiliens während des Weltkrieges und die Stellung des brasilianischen Deutschtums.* Hamburg: H. Christians, 1935.

Kossok, Manfred. " 'Sonderauftrag Sudamerika': Zur deutschen Politik gegenüber Lateinamerika 1938 bis 1942," in *Lateinamerika zwischen Emanzipation und Imperialismus 1810–1960.* E. Berlin: Akademie, 1961, 234–55.

Kramer-Kaske, Lieselotte. "Die Politik der deutschen Faschisten in Kolumbien 1933 bis 1941," in *Der Deutsche Faschismus in Lateinamerika 1933–1934.* E. Berlin: Akademie, 1966, 125–44.

Levine, Robert M. *The Vargas Regime: The Crucial Years, 1934–1938.* New York: Columbia University Press, 1970.

Love, Joseph L. "External Financing and Domestic Politics: The Case of São Paulo, Brazil, 1889–1937," in Robert E. Scott (ed.), *Latin American Modernization Problems: Case Studies in the Crises of Change.* Urbana: University of Illinois Press, 1973, 236–59.

———. *São Paulo in the Brazilian Federation, 1889–1937.* Stanford: Stanford University Press, 1980.

Manchester, Alan K. *British Preeminence in Brazil: Its Rise and Decline.* Chapel Hill: Octagon, 1964.

Maram, Sheldon L. "Labor and the Left in Brazil, 1890–1921: A Movement Aborted." *Hispanic American Historical Review,* 57 (May 1977):254–72.

Martin, Percy A. *Latin America and the War.* Baltimore: Johns Hopkins Press, 1925.

Mayer, Robert. "The Origins of the American Banking Empire in Latin America: Frank A. Vanderlip and the National City Bank." *Journal of Interamerican Studies and World Affairs,* 15 (February 1973):60–70.

McCann, Frank D. "Aviation Diplomacy: The United States and Brazil, 1939–1941." *Inter-American Economic Affairs,* 21 (Spring 1968):35–50.

———. *The Brazilian-American Alliance 1937–1945.* Princeton: Princeton University Press, 1973.

McGann, Thomas F. *Argentina, the United States, and the Inter-American System, 1880–1914.* Cambridge, Ma.: Harvard University Press, 1957.

Medlicott, W. N. et al. (eds.). *Documents on British Foreign Policy, 1919–1939, Series A.* London: HMSO, 1966.

de Melo Franco, Afonso Arinos. *Um Estadista da República: Afrânio de Melo Franco e seu tempo.* 3 vols. Rio: Ed. José Olímpio, 1955.

Meyer, Jean. *Estado y Sociedade con Calles,* vol. 2. *História de la Revolución Mexicana.* México: El Colegio de México, 1977.

Meyer, Lorenzo. *Mexico and the United States in the Oil Controversy, 1917–1942.* Trans. Muriel Vasconcellos. Austin: University of Texas Press, 1972.

Mitre, Jorge A. "Presidencia de Victorino de la Plaza (su Gestión Presidencial)," in *História Argentina Contemporánea.* vol. 1. Buenos Aires: Academia Nacional de la História, 1965.

Mosk, Sanford A. "Latin America and the World Economy, 1850–1914." *Inter-American Economic Affairs,* 2 (Winter 1948):53–82.

Moura, Gerson. *Autonomia na Dependência.* Rio: Nova Fronteira, 1980.

Munch, Francis J. "The Anglo-Dutch-American Petroleum Industry in Mexico: The Formative Years During the Porfiriato 1900-1910." *Revista de Historia de América*, 84 (July-December 1977):135-82.

Nachman, Robert G. "Positivism, Modernization, and the Middle Class in Brazil." *Hispanic American Historical Review*, 57 (February 1977):1-23.

Newton, Ronald C. "The German Argentines between Nazism and Nationalism: The Patagonia Plot of 1939." *International History Review*, 3 (January 1981):76-114.

Newton, Wesley P. *The Perilous Sky: U.S. Aviation Diplomacy and Latin America 1919-1931.* Coral Gables: University of Miami Press, 1978.

Normano, João F. *The Struggle for South America: Economy and Ideology.* Boston: Gordon Press, 1977 (reprint).

Nunn, Frederick M. "Emil Körner and the Prussianization of the Chilean Army: Origins, Process, and Consequences, 1885-1920." *Hispanic American Historical Review*, 50 (May 1970):300-2.

————. "Effects of European Military Training in Latin America: The Origins and Nature of Professional Militarism in Argentina, Brazil, Chile, and Peru, 1890-1940." *Military Affairs*, 39 (February 1975):1-70.

Perez-Guerrero, Manuel. *Les Relations des États de l'Amérique latine avec la Société des Nations.* Paris: A. Pedone, 1936.

Pike, Frederick B. *Hispanismo, 1898-1936: Spanish Conservatives and Liberals and Their Relations with Spanish America.* Notre Dame: University of Notre Dame Press, 1971.

Platt, D. C. M. "The Allied Coercion of Venezuela, 1902-3—A Reassessment." *Inter-American Economic Affairs*, 14:4 (Spring 1962):3-28.

————. "British Diplomacy in Latin America Since the Emancipation." *Inter-American Economic Affairs*, 21:3 (Winter 1967):21-39.

————. *Latin America and British Trade, 1806-1914.* New York: Humanities Press, 1973.

————. (ed.). *Business Imperialism 1840-1930: An Inquiry Based on British Experience in Latin America, 1840-1930.* Oxford: Oxford University Press, 1978.

Pletcher, David M. *Rails, Mines and Progress: Seven American Promoters in Mexico, 1867-1911.* Ithaca: Syracuse University Press, 1958.

Pommerin, Reiner. *Das Dritte Reich und Lateinamerika.* Düsseldorf: Droste, 1977.

Potash, Robert A. *The Army and Politics in Argentina, 1928-1945: Yrigoyen to Perón.* Stanford: Stanford University Press, 1969.

Powell, T. G. *Mexico and the Spanish Civil War.* Albuquerque: University of New Mexico, 1981.

Rippy, J. Fred. *Latin America in World Politics.* New York: Alfred A. Knopf, 1928.

————. "French Investments in Latin America." *Inter-American Economic Affairs*, 2:2 (Autumn 1948):52-66.

————. *British Investments in Latin America, 1822-1949.* Minneapolis: Arno, 1977.

Roche, Jean. *A colonização alemã e o Rio Grande do Sul.* Pôrto Alegre: Editora Globo, 1969.

Rock, David (ed.). *Argentina in the Twentieth Century.* London: Duckworth, 1975.

Rodríguez, Augusto G. "Ejército Nacional," in *História Argentina Contemporánea 1862-1930.* vol. 2. Buenos Aires: Academia Nacional de la História, 1966.

Rosenau, James N. "Toward the Study of National-International Linkages," in J. N. Rosenau (ed.), *Linkage Politics: Essays on the Convergence of National and International Systems.* New York: Free Press, 1969.

Rosenberg, Emily S. "World War I and 'Continental Solidarity.' " *The Americas,* 31 (January 1975):316–27.

———. "Anglo-American Economic Rivalry in Brazil During World War I." *Diplomatic History,* 2 (Spring 1978):131–52.

Sanz, Luis S. "La História Diplomática desde la presidencia de Mitre, 1862, hasta 1930." *História Argentina Contemporánea, 1862–1930.* vol. 2. Buenos Aires: Academia Nacional de la Historia, 1965.

Schaefer, Jürgen. *Deutsche Militärhilfe an Südamerika: Militär-und Rüstungsinteressen in Argentinien, Bolivien und Chile vor 1914.* Düsseldorf: Droste, 1974.

Schiff, Warren. "German Military Penetration into Mexico During the late Díaz Period." *Hispanic American Historical Review,* 39 (November 1959):568–79.

———. "The Germans in Mexican Trade and Industry During the Díaz Period." *The Americas,* 23 (January 1967):279–96.

Scobie, James R. *Revolution on the Pampas: A Social History of Argentine Wheat, 1860–1910.* Austin: University of Texas Press, 1964.

Skidmore, Thomas E. *Black Into White: Race and Nationality in Brazilian Thought.* New York: Oxford University Press, 1974.

Smith, Joseph. *Illusions of Conflict: Anglo-American Diplomacy Toward Latin America, 1865–1896.* Pittsburgh: Pittsburgh University Press, 1979.

Smith, Lois E. *Mexico and the Spanish Republicans.* Berkeley: University of California Press, 1955.

Smith, Peter. *Politics and Beef in Argentina.* New York: Columbia University Press, 1969.

Solberg, Carl. "Immigration and Urban Social Problems in Argentina and Chile, 1890–1914." *Hispanic American Historical Review,* 49 (February 1969):215–16.

Stemmler, M. "Der Luftverkehr nach Südamerika im Dienste des Aussenhandels." *Der Deutsche im Auslande,* 7 (July 1934):150.

Stone, Irving. "British Direct and Portfolio Investment in Latin America before 1914." *Journal of Economic History,* 37 (September 1977):690–722.

Tischendorf, Alfred. *Great Britain and Mexico in the Era of Porfirio Díaz.* Durham: Duke University Press, 1961.

Trinidade, Hélgio. *Integralismo: o fascismo brasileiro na década de 30.* São Paulo: Difusão Européia de Livro, 1974.

Tulchin, Joseph S. "The Argentine Proposal for Non-Belligerency, April 1940." *Journal of Interamerican Studies and World Affairs,* 11 (1969):571–604.

———. *The Aftermath of War: World War I and U.S. Policy Toward Latin America.* New York: New York University Press, 1971.

———. "Decolonizing an Informal Empire: Argentina, Great Britain, and the United States, 1930–1943." *International Interactions,* 1 (1974):123–40.

Vagts, Alfred. *Mexiko, Europa und Amerika unter besonderer Berücksichtigung der Petroleumpolitik.* Berlin: Walter Rothschild, 1928.

————. *Deutschland und die Vereinigten Staaten in der Weltpolitik.* 2 vols. New York: Macmillan, 1935.

Valla, Victor. *Os Estados Unidos e a Influência Estrangeira na Economia Brasileira: Um Período de Transição, 1904–1928.* São Paulo: Coleção da Revista de História, 1972.

Vansittart, Robert. *The Mist Procession: The Autobiography of Lord Vansittart.* London: Hutchinson, 1958.

Volland, Klaus. *Das Dritte Reich und Mexiko.* Frankfurt a/M: Peter Lang, 1976.

Walter, Richard J. *The Socialist Party of Argentina, 1890–1930.* Austin: University of Texas Press, 1977.

Weinberg, Gerhard L. *The Foreign Policy of Hitler's Germany: Diplomatic Revolution in Europe 1933–1936.* Chicago: University of Chicago Press, 1970.

Woods, Randall B. *The Roosevelt Foreign Policy Establishment and the "Good Neighbor": The United States and Argentina, 1941–1945.* Lawrence, KS: Regents Press, 1979.

Zea, Leopoldo. *El positivismo en México.* México: El Colegio de México, 1943.

2

LATIN AMERICA AND WESTERN EUROPE: ECONOMIC RELATIONS THROUGH WORLD WAR II

Werner Baer

The relative importance of Europe's economic presence in Latin America has grown rapidly since the 1950s. Its share as a trading partner has increased substantially and even more notable has been its relative growth as a supplier of direct investment and as a creditor. Is this trend a return to "normalcy," that is, to a situation similar to the one prevailing in the nineteenth century or the first four decades of the twentieth century, when Europe was the dominant outside economic influence in the region? To provide a framework for discussing this question, the first two sections of the chapter give a brief survey of the role of Europe as an investor and trading partner in Latin America, from independence to World War II.

THE NINETEENTH CENTURY SCENE (1820–1914)

In the first century of political independence, the economies of Latin America became part of a rapidly expanding world trading system. In this system there emerged a world division of labor in which Latin America supplied primary products (food and raw materials) in exchange for European manufactures. Trade barriers were kept at a minimum, allowing the logic of comparative advantage resulting in this division of labor to prevail.

For the first part of the period, Britain dominated the scene. France and Germany began to exert their influence later in the century. Other European countries contributed only a small scattering of capital—such as Belgian investment in some public utilities and railways in Argentina and Brazil, Dutch loans to various governments, and Dutch investments in Mexican petroleum—whose overall economic impact was correspondingly minor. The United States came on the scene later than France or Germany, but by the eve of World War II had gained a position second only to that of Britain.

Britain

In the period from 1820 to 1914, Britain invested more long-term capital in Latin America than in any other geographical region. In 1914, Latin America accounted for 20 percent of British overseas investments.[1] Britain not only used its considerable political power to keep Latin American countries from imposing significant trade barriers to interfere with the trading system (Glade 1969), it also allowed a substantial proportion of its savings to flow to the region, in the form of investments that would increase the efficiency of the emerging world economic order. This was an acceptable state of affairs for most of the socioeconomic groups that dominated the newly independent countries and, as Cottrell well stated the matter, ". . . the import of capital led to economic development of an extensive nature and tended to cement, rather than overthrow, existing social structures" (Cottrell 1975, 41).

Early British investments were concentrated in trade and government finance. In the first decades after independence, most of the production of the agricultural export sector in Latin America was owned by nationals or recent immigrants (e.g., coffee in Brazil or wool in Argentina); the commercial aspects of export (finance, shipping) were in the hands of Europeans (at first, mainly the British), who also handled the imports of manufactured goods. The reason for this specialization has been summarized by Platt: ". . . foreign merchants, with their superior contacts abroad, their cheaper credit, great knowledge and experience in overseas markets, had obvious advantages over native Latin Americans in overseas trade. Furthermore, their interest in limiting costs and enlarging profits in the export trades made them progressively inclined to eliminate the native intermediary, which in turn brought them into direct contact, and often conflict, with the Latin American producer" (Platt 1977, 3).[2]

Substantial amounts of British capital went into Latin American government bonds, as the recently independent states had little means of their own for financing their activities. The funds obtained were used to repay debts from the wars of liberation and to meet current government expenditures; only a small amount went into public works that directly or indirectly stimulated production. The loans were thus quite speculative, and by the end of 1827 most Latin American bond issues had gone into default.[3] In addition, many enterprises which had been supported by British capital collapsed. The net result of this early experience was a substantial decline of capital inflow and the general world reputation of Latin America as a high credit-risk area.

The situation changed after 1850, with the acceleration of exports to attend the needs of a rapidly industrializing and urbanizing Europe: coffee (Brazil), wool and meat (Argentina), nitrates and guano (Chile and Peru), etc. The new dynamism of trade and the technological revolution in transportation brought along an intense wave of British investment in the second half of the nineteenth century. British capital flowed to Latin America to build railroads to facilitate the shipment of exportable goods to ports. By buying government bonds, British capital directly and indirectly financed the building and/or modernization of ports; and in the later decades of the century, British capital financed the building of the urban infrastructure (Glade 1969).

An especially intensive flow of capital occurred in the 1890s and the first decade of the twentieth century, reflecting rising trade relations between Europe and Latin America based on the development of low-cost steel, ocean-going steamships, refrigerated ships, and new mining techniques. British capital thus not only continued to go into the already mentioned sectors, but also financed—through either equity participation or bonds—mines, plantations, and meat packing (in Argentina).

Rates of return on British investments in railroads proved to be good, as almost all companies benefited from government subsidies or guaranteed rates of return, and many were exempt from a number of taxes. A similar situation existed in public utilities.[4] Rates of return for bondholders or financial intermediaries were probably even higher, as "the nominal values of outstanding government securities represented foreign legal claims more accurately than they represented the actual foreign financial contributions measured by those claims" (Glade 1969, 217). Platt (1966, 89) gives an apt description of the situation:

> [There was] some justice in the complaining of the Costa Rican Minister of Finance (1895) that, since the Republic only received

about a third of the money for which it had made itself liable, she felt that "she should not in justice be called upon to assume the whole responsibility for a matter in which she has been notoriously defrauded." And the defrauders were not exclusively Latin American politicians and diplomats; indeed, the most successful were the London financiers.[5]

The trade boom in the two and a half decades prior to World War I not only stimulated large increases in British investments; it also resulted in a change of the region's commodity import structure. An increased amount of agricultural and industrial machinery was included, reflecting modernization of certain agricultural areas (like Argentina) and the incipient growth of some domestic manufacturing industries (especially textiles).

A succinct description of British influence on Latin America's economies in the three decades prior to World War I appears in Cottrell (1975). In the case of Brazil, he puts it this way:

[British dominance] over the Brazilian export sector was increased by inter-company links. English export merchants had financial interests in the shipping lines and railways, and consequently exerted pressure for better port facilities, the construction of which was financed by British capital. The bulk of the liabilities of the British-owned banks were local deposits, but they were lent primarily to the alien mercantile houses, railway companies, urban service companies, dock companies and contractors. The majority of Brazil's imports came from Britain and were handled by English export-import houses [42–43].

The case of Argentina was similar:

[The] landed plutocracy, though it did not invest in the new railway companies, shared a common interest with British capital in the growth of agriculture. . . . Argentinian railways in 1919 were controlled by three British financial and management groups formed through interlocking directorships. The railways had substantial interests in land and mortgage companies, meatpacking, warehouses, dock companies, and urban tramways. The lines were run by British nationals, as were the associated enterprises, together with expatriate families such as the Robertsons, Parishes, Fairs, and Drabbles. The Argentinian middle classes provided local figurehead directors, but their main energies were absorbed in the professions and politics, with most ministers of public works having been at some time a member of the legal department of a railway company [42].[6]

Until the last two decades of the nineteenth century Britain remained Latin America's chief trading partner and supplier of capital. Though the economic presence of France, Germany, and the United States was increasingly felt in the three decades preceding World War I, these countries did not successfully challenge Britain's dominance.[7]

France

France's economic presence, though felt in many parts of Latin America throughout the nineteenth century, was never as overwhelming as that of Britain. Considerable sums were invested at times in government securities—for example, a sale of Haitian government bonds as early as 1825; French subscriptions to Peruvian government securities in the 1850s and early 1860s; and of course, substantial sales of the Maximilian Mexican government's bonds in France (Rippy 1948a; Glade 1969).

There was also considerable French migration to Latin America. It has been estimated that during the period from 1840 to 1940 over 300,000 Frenchmen migrated there, especially to Argentina, Brazil, Uruguay, Chile, and Mexico, establishing themselves as traders and bankers and bringing with them substantial sums of capital. Many also brought along technical skills and founded some of the earliest manufacturing enterprises (Rippy 1948a).

French capital was also involved in some infrastructure investments (such as railroads) and in real estate, but for the most part shunned public utilities. Although individual French-owned mercantile houses were small, they multiplied rapidly in the latter part of the nineteenth century, and their capitalization by 1900 was estimated at close to a half-billion francs. French capital was also in the forefront in maritime operations between Europe and Latin America (Rippy 1948a).

Many French investments came to sad endings in Latin America. One example was the considerable amount invested in the Mexican securities of the Maximilian regime (already mentioned), which were repudiated by subsequent governments and only assumed in part by the French government. Huge losses were also suffered from investments in the largest single French investment project, which failed— the attempt by the Universal Interoceanic Company to build the Panama Canal. As Rippy (1948a, 57) put it: "Sad losses of little French investors resulting from the failure of this canal enterprise . . . were almost typical of a very considerable portion of French investments in Latin America." Frenchmen generally did not fare much better in rail-road investments and "only French promoters and construction com-panies obtained big profits from railways in Latin America, if any such profits were ever made by Frenchmen" (63). And, although in some projects huge returns were obtained, "the losses of many little Frenchmen far outweighed the gains of the fortunate few in Latin America" (64).

Surprisingly, the many disappointments did not stop the French from investing capital in the region. Between 1900 and 1914, the nom-inal value of French holdings in Latin America tripled, and in 1914, the region accounted for 13 percent of French foreign investments.

Germany

Germany's early capital flow to Latin America accompanied German immigrants, who settled in Argentina, Chile, and southern Brazil, and established themselves as traders, bankers, and small-scale manufacturers (Rippy 1948b). Much of this capital lost its iden-tity as its owners or their descendants became naturalized. The rate of German investment increased in the last years of the nineteenth cen-tury and the first decade of the twentieth century. As the British were already dominant in railroads and public utilities, German capital was mainly invested in government bonds (especially in Argentina, Brazil, Chile, Mexico, and Venezuela), banking establishments, insur-ance, some mining, and plantations. Although by 1914 Germany was the fourth largest investor in the region, its capital was much less con-centrated sectorally than that of its major rivals. On the eve of World War I Latin America accounted for 16 percent of Germany's foreign investments and amounted to about US $900 million.

The United States

Although there were small amounts of U.S. investment activity in Latin America in the middle of the nineteenth century, the huge flows that made the United States the second largest foreign investor in Latin America by 1913 began only in the last two decades of the nineteenth century. Most funds went at first to Mexico, Cuba, and Central America, and only gradually was there a movement further south. Much of the U.S. capital went into mining, some to railroads, plantations, and public utilities. In contrast to British investments, the relative importance of railroads and government securities was much smaller. By 1890 U.S. investments were estimated at $250 million, growing to $320 million in 1897, and $1.6 billion in 1914.

Overall Trade Picture

Although Latin America's trade relations were dominated by Britain in the first half of the nineteenth century, the second half was characterized by increasing geographical diversification. As Latin America's export sectors boomed, an increasing amount of luxury goods were imported, especially from France, whose exports to the region increased more than fourfold between 1848 and 1860. By the same token, as Europe's urbanization/industrialization process increased in the second half of the nineteenth century, Britain's share of Latin America's exports declined. For example, an increased amount of Brazilian coffee and Colombian tobacco went to the Hanseatic cities, and Argentinian wool to French ports (Safford 1974).[8]

The dynamic expansion of the 1880–1913 period was characterized by substantial changes in the commodity composition of imports. Previously, consumer goods (especially textiles) were dominant. But as Latin American countries built railroads, as some modernized agriculture evolved in a number of areas, and as some domestic manufacturing industries were created, imports of equipment and industrial fuels increased.[9] In this period, Britain's dominance was seriously challenged by Germany and, later on, by the United States. Britain did maintain a general lead in Latin America's import trade, especially in South America. This was due in part to "long-established credit and marketing relations; the predominance of British banking . . . heavy investments in mining and railways, which brought the purchase of British equipment in these fields." However, it "was unable to keep up with Germany and the United States in sales related to technologies developed after the era of steam. The Germans dominated the chemicals trade, and shared that in electrical equipment with the United States" (Safford 1974, 591).

By the end of the nineteenth century Latin America's trade relations had fallen into two distinct patterns. One group of countries exported mainly to the United States—i.e., those specializing in minerals and tropical agricultural goods. However, the same countries imported manufactured goods not from the United States but from Europe. Other countries in Latin America's temperate zone (e.g., Argentina) exported to Europe, but relied on imported machinery (especially agricultural machinery) from the United States. The former countries developed balance of trade surpluses with the United States and deficits with Europe; the latter had trade deficits with the United States and surpluses with Europe. Thus, a triangular trade relationship gradually emerged, to decline only when various political crises brought with them increasing obstacles to multilateral settlements of accounts (United Nations 1955).

THE EVE OF WORLD WAR I THROUGH THE IMMEDIATE AFTERMATH OF WORLD WAR II

The tables in Appendix A give some indication of Europe's presence in Latin America in 1913. Britain was still the dominant investor (43.5 percent), followed by the United States (20 percent), France (14.1 percent), and Germany (10.6 percent). British capital was concentrated in Argentina, Brazil, and Mexico, accounting for over 50 percent of total British investments in the region in 1880, and over 74 percent in 1913. In 1888, almost 90 percent of British investments were in government bonds and railroads together (with government bonds predominating). By 1913 there was a shift away from bonds, toward increased investment in railroads (46 percent), and new interests in mining and public utilities (20 percent). French capital was even more geographically concentrated in Argentina, Brazil, and Mexico (89 percent). It was not so concentrated in type of investment, however, with nearly 43 percent in things other than government bonds and railways in 1913 (including real estate and industry). Germany concentrated much of its capital—which was mainly in trading, banking, and industrial activities—in the same countries.

By 1913, about 70 percent of U.S. capital in Latin America was in Mexico (53 percent) and Cuba (16 percent), with an additional 11 percent in Chile—and was concentrated in mining (43 percent), agriculture (19 percent), and railroads (14 percent).

During World War I the inflow of European capital came to a halt. There was little reduction, however, in Europe's capital stock in the region, with the exception of the sale or confiscation of some German holdings and the acquisition of Latin American citizenship by the owners of others (United Nations 1955).

Nor did the investment position of Europe in Latin America change much in absolute terms during the 1920s. Although some British investments declined due to amortization of bonds and the sale of some assets, this was counterbalanced by new issues of government securities on the London market.[10] German investments remained strong in chemicals, pharmaceuticals, and in a number of manufacturing industries, trade, and aviation. French investments declined somewhat, due in part to the depreciation of the franc, which led to an increase in the repatriation of securities without a corresponding flow of new French capital into the region.

There was a large inflow of capital from the United States during the war years and during the 1920s, which resulted in a substantial growth of the U.S. relative position in the region and a corresponding relative decline for Europe. From 1914 to 1919 the value of U.S. investments in Latin America increased by 50 percent, and from 1919 to 1929 it doubled. Most of the growth of U.S. investments in Latin America was in government and private bonds, and went mainly to Argentina, Brazil, Chile, Colombia, and Cuba.

The 1930s, of course, were dominated by the Great Depression, which led to widespread defaults on the external government debt of Latin American countries.[11] This, combined with widespread use of exchange controls to alleviate balance of payments problems, virtually froze the investment stocks held by Europe and the United States in Latin America and shrank foreign investment flows into the region to insignificant levels.[12] Thus, throughout the 1930s the relative positions of Europe and the United States changed little.

After World War II, however, the European presence declined substantially. Although outstanding debt problems were settled, most European countries were in no position to make new loan commitments. Thus, Europe's role as a creditor declined. There was also a substantial amount of European disinvestment in public utilities, which were sold to the governments of the region.[13] In the case of Britain, the repayment of debts and the sale of assets resulted in an investment decline of 227 million pounds sterling in the period 1946-50.[14] By 1950 the United States was well established as the dominant foreign investor in the region, accounting for over half of total foreign capital. Similarly, in trade relations half of the region's exports and imports were taking place with the United States by 1950, with Europe's share of Latin America's trade having dwindled to a little over 20 percent.

DISCUSSION

From the description above, it is clear that Europe's dominant economic presence in the nineteenth and early twentieth centuries in Latin America was closely associated with the region's role as a primary products supplier to the industrial centers. Although this specialization resulted in rapid growth rates in periods of export booms, it is not clear how the gains from this trade were apportioned. There is still a need for research on the distribution of the trade benefits between Latin America and its trading partners. Since a substantial share of trade was in the hands of Europeans, a simple terms of trade analysis will not suffice to establish that distribution. In addition, the gains that went to nationals from trade did not produce long-term development benefits commensurate with their magnitude, since wealth and income were highly concentrated, leading to the compiling of nonproductive assets and/or spending on conspicuous consumption.

Further studies are also needed to determine the full economic implications of large-scale European bond financing throughout the nineteenth and early twentieth centuries. It remains to be determined, for example, what percentage of government expenditures—both current and capital—was financed by foreign borrowing. The motivation for borrowing may have been based more on an inability to raise domestic revenues through taxation than on the need to cover balance of payments deficits. Given the high interest rates and the discrepancy between the nominal value and the actual financial contribution made by government bonds sold in Europe, Latin America paid in real resource transfers for its administrative and socioeconomic backwardness.

It is interesting to note that from the European side, economic relations with Latin America were in private hands (i.e., both trading and lending institutions were privately owned). On the Latin American side, in contrast, the role of government was substantial (either as the recipient of the privately raised loans or as the guarantor of the rate of return on investments). The early-established bad reputation of Latin American countries as debtors was exploited by both European financial agents and their allies in Latin American governments, to create a situation which made it possible to squeeze huge rates of return out of loans. When defaults or bankruptcies occurred, the losers were usually the small European investors. The winners were the European intermediaries and some Latin American government officials.

In sum, Latin America had to pay a high price for its economic relations with Europe. It received limited benefits from its trade specialization and from the high price it paid for European savings. At the same time, it became saddled with a type of infrastructure which was more effective in linking its economies to trade than in expanding and diversifying its internal market. A long-term positive element was the number of instances when migrants moved simultaneously with capital. This resulted in the emergence of a number of commercial and financial growth poles which gradually became "nationalized" as subsequent generations adopted local citizenship.

THE NEW EUROPEAN PRESENCE

What are the differences or similarities between the new European presence in Latin America in the 1970s and 1980s and its presence there prior to World War II? Let us briefly compare various types of links.

Direct Investment

The growth of direct European investment since the 1950s has been concentrated in the manufacturing field; infrastructure investments are nonexistent. Whereas the old investments in infrastructure were meant to facilitate trade, the latter-day investments were designed to establish import-substituting industries. As such, their intent was to decrease the necessity of trade. However, a number of studies have shown that perfect import substitution was never attained and that a new post-import-substituting dependency emerged in Latin America instead, as the various countries relied increasingly on imported raw materials and capital goods for their industrial development.

Risk and Returns on Investments

From the available evidence it would seem that direct investments of Europeans in Latin America in the nineteenth and early twentieth centuries had a very high rate of return relative to the risks involved. The large investments (with a few exceptions) were fairly secure, because there were government-guaranteed returns and no risk of international payments restrictions or nationalization without compensation. Obviously, these risks are much greater in the present age. It is difficult under modern conditions of interdependence and multinational operations to ascertain the returns to investments, however, because they consist not only of the officially-allowed profit remittances, but also of hidden repatriation of profits through transfer pricing and payments for technology.

International Debt

The present-day international debt of Latin America is different in a number of ways from its previous debt picture. One difference is that, once concentrated in the government sector, it is currently divided among government, state enterprises, private domestic firms, and multinationals. Another is that, whereas previously the debt was held by many small European savers, it is currently divided among multinational agencies, the U.S. and European governments, with a large and growing portion held by multinational banks as they recycle petrodollars. Defaulting is no longer a major problem and debt crises are usually resolved by debt renegotiation through consortia of international lending banks, often coordinated by such international agencies as the International Monetary Fund. Greater international financial sophistication and competition, moreover, make it next to impossible to have the type of financial fraud that occurred so often in the nineteenth century.

Yet another difference is the phenomenon of world inflation. The greater economic stability in pre-World War I days meant that Latin American debtors could not look forward to having their real obligations reduced by inflationary forces. In the last twenty years, however, there have been periods when world inflation, combined with relatively low interest rates, has led to a redistribution of wealth from the creditor to the debtor countries. This has been less true since the second half of the 1970s, however, now that a larger proportion of loans for Latin America is made by private banks recycling petrodollars at high interest rates.

Finally, in the nineteenth and early twentieth centuries most of the loans made were not tied to sales, either of a particular company or country, whereas a large portion of credits made at present are so tied. To the extent that such tie-ins exist, the countries of Latin America have less flexibility now than previously to buy from the cheapest source—though this must be balanced against the much more numerous buying options that exist today.

There are advantages and disadvantages to both equity and debt financing. From the point of view of the recipient country, equity investment has the disadvantage of foreign control over part of the country's productive structure and the possibility of secret remittances of profits. It has the advantage that remittance of profits can be controlled in times of balance of payments crises. Debt financing's disadvantage is that the servicing has to take place no matter what the state of the balance of payments (unless a refinancing is negotiated); its advantage is that control over the resources of the economy remains in the hands of nationals.

Before the Great Depression, payment restrictions due to balance of payments problems did not exist, and direct investments in infrastructure involved control of the economy to the extent that the investment itself shaped the structure of the economy and that the tariffs allowed on the infrastructure implied a certain type of international income distribution. Also, given the structure of the Latin American economies in the nineteenth century, debt financing did not provide more flexibility than equity financing. The present situation is complex, given the interrelationships of different units of multinationals, and the fact that these firms also engage in debt arrangements among parent and subsidiaries. There is the possibility, however, that the Eurocurrency market and the recycling activities of multinational banks did give Latin American governments and state firms a greater degree of flexibility, at least for a certain period of time.

The nineteenth century, as we have seen, was characterized by extreme dependence on Great Britain, with some measure of diversification being achieved only in the years immediately prior to World War I. This was maintained in the 1920s, but as a result of the Great Depression and World War II, the region developed a heavy dependence for its trade and source of investment funds on the United States. The resurgence of the European (as well as the Japanese) connection with Latin America in the 1970s and 1980s and the geographical diversification of economic relationships it brings with it may well provide a greater degree of stability and bargaining power than was possible in previous eras.

APPENDIX A

Table 2.1.   British Investments in Latin America (In Percentages)

	1870	1880	1890	1913	1928	1939	1949
Geographical Distribution							
Argentina		11.3	36.8	35.8	34.7	38.0	12.3
Brazil		21.7	16.2	22.4	23.6	23.1	30.4
Mexico		18.2	14.1	15.9	16.4	15.3	25.0
Peru		20.1	4.5	2.6	2.1	2.6	4.5
Chile		4.7	5.6	6.4	6.3	7.6	8.0
Cuba		—	6.3	4.4	3.5	3.0	4.3
Uruguay		—	6.6	4.6	3.3	—	—
Remainder		24.0	9.9	7.9	10.1	10.4	15.5
Total		100.0	100.0	100.0	100.0	100.0	100.0
Total in Millions							
of Pounds Sterling	85	179	426	999	1,211	1,128	560

Sectoral Distribution	*1880*		*1913*		*1930*		
Government Bonds	68.6		31.0		21.0		
Railways	19.2		46.0		55.0		
Mining and Public							
Utilities	—		20.0		9.0		
Banking and Shipping	—		3.0		—		
Other	12.2		—		15.0		
Total	100.0		100.0		100.0		

Source: Compiled from various tables in Rippy (1959).

Table 2.2.   Foreign Investments in Latin America: 1913

Origin	U.S. Dollars (In Millions)	Percent
Britain	3,700	43.5
France	1,200	14.1
Germany	900	10.6
United States	1,700	20.0
Other	1,000	11.8
Total	8,500	100.0

Source: United Nations (1955, 6).

Table 2.3. French Investments in Latin America (Percent Distribution)

	1902	1913	1938	1943
Geographical Distribution				
Argentina	28.4	23.9	35.3	39.2
Brazil	21.4	41.8	29.6	26.0
Mexico	9.2	23.9	20.1	11.8
Uruguay	9.1	2.1	2.7	3.4
Chile	6.9	2.5	3.8	3.1
Colombia	7.6	—	—	—
Remainder	17.4	5.5	8.5	16.5
Total	100.0	100.0	100.0	100.0
Total in French Francs				
(In Billions)	3.2	8.4	11.3	12.2
Total in US Dollars (In Millions)	—	1,200	450	306
Sectoral Distribution				
Government Bonds	29.5	30.9		
Railways	4.9	26.3		
Other	65.6	42.8		
Total	100.0	100.0		

Source: Compiled from tables in Rippy (1948a).

NOTES

I have benefited greatly from the critical comments of Barbara Stallings and Pedro Malan on an earlier version of this chapter.

1. A large proportion of the data used in this article is based on the work of Rippy (1959). Although these have been subject to considerable criticism (the latest can be found in Platt 1980, 4, footnote 5), none to date has made a systematic analysis of the supposed weakness of his data, and it is not clear that alternative numbers would change the picture substantially. For example, Feis's (1965) data, adapted from Paish's earlier work, show British Latin American investments in 1914 to have amounted to 756.6 million pounds vs. Rippy's estimate of 999 million pounds. Feis's data, however, include only long-term, publicly issued British capital. The relative distribution of capital among individual Latin American countries is similar, although not identical, whichever set of estimates is used.

2. Another succinct description of the role of trading firms can be found in Glade (1969, 205):

[They] provided the crucially important links to overseas markets at a time when the domestic economic environment was falling into disarray. They also were the channels through which foreign capital financed the movement of export goods from Latin America to overseas consuming centers and which, indirectly, contributed to the financing of local production. . . . By 1822 . . . there were substantial numbers of British traders in the Platine region—39 British-owned mercantile houses in Buenos Aires alone, with other British shopkeepers located in provincial cities. Most of the foreign commerce was in their hands.

3. Rippy (1959, 17–18) gives a vivid description of the period. He found that:

inhabitants of the British Isles indulged in a wild speculation spree in the early 1820's, investing large sums in the bonds of foreign governments and in the securities of hundreds of joint stock companies organized for operation at home and abroad. Clever salesmen, scheming attorneys, and gamblers of every description swarmed through the business streets, subsidized journalists, induced members of Parliament to grant company charters, and peddled engraved paper. Poor and rich alike were soon scrambling for bonds of young and unstable governments and the stocks of almost every conceivable economic enterprise. . . . British losses from their Latin-American ventures . . . were heavy [and] only stock-jobbers, merchant-bankers, advertisers, and managing staffs too shrewd to risk their own funds profited from the orgy. Latin-American governments largely wasted the proceeds of their bond sales and gravely injured their credit.

4. According to Rippy (1959, 32–33), "Latin American governments usually guaranteed a return of 7 percent on a stipulated portion of the investment. Capital invested in public utilities likewise brought good returns as a rule. Gas plants and waterworks were sometimes guaranteed a yield of 7 percent on a large part of their capital, and tramways were also likely to be profitable."

5. Glade's (1969, 217–18) discussion on the matter is also most enlightening:

[T]he nominal values of outstanding government securities represented foreign legal claims more accurately than they represented the actual foreign financial contributions measured by those claims. The discounts at which Latin American governmental obligations were placed in the European markets were often heavy and the charges exacted by European investment banking houses were quite high. For example, the Peruvian bond issue of 1870 gave British investors securities nominally worth £12 million (bearing a stated interest rate of 6 percent) at a price of 82.5, while the £15 million, 5 percent issue of 1872 was taken by the British public at 77.5. . . . On the other hand, if part of the creditors' claims were fictitious in origin, so were the debtors' promises to pay. Debt obligations were often scaled down considerably during the renegotiation of defaulted claims, new bond issues were exchanged for interest obligations long in arrears, and many of the bond emissions subscribed abroad ultimately had to be written off altogether.

6. Diaz-Alejandro (1970, 60–61) notes that:

An atmosphere of resentment against foreign investors and the liberal system created since 1862 developed shortly after external capital began to flow into the country. Criticisms were levied first against specific features of that system, [and] gradually spread to a general condemnation of British-Argentine ties. . . . Railroads, meat-packing plants, and public utilities were accused of making exhorbitant [*sic*] profits by taking advantage of oligopolist [*sic*] and oligopsonist power. . . . Although some of the accusations against foreign investors were based more on emotional first-generation xenophobic nationalism than on facts and economic reasoning, the cavalier contempt with which most investors treated even sensible inquiries about their activities accentuated the bitterness of Argentine resentment. As late as 1934, a British meat-packing company attempted to smuggle out of the country (under the marking of corned beef!) records of its Argentine activities which had been subpoenaed by the Senate under a law upheld by the Argentine Supreme Court.

7. Platt's recent article (1980) throws considerable doubt on the adequacy of existing data on British foreign investments in the nineteenth century. He points out that prior to 1870 a considerable amount of the loans contracted in the London money market was obtained from non-British sources, and that therefore, data on British overseas investments might be substantially overstated. Though this may somewhat change Britain's relative importance, none would deny that it was the dominant foreign investor in the nineteenth century in Latin America. British capital's political importance is shown by the many descriptions of British representations on behalf of its investors throughout most of the nineteenth century (see, for example, Feis 1965; and Jenks 1973).

8. Reviewing the trade of Latin America in the nineteenth century, the Steins (1970, 152–53) stated that:

[O]ne fear of Spanish and Portuguese merchant oligopolists during the last colonial decades did fail to materialize. English, French, and United States merchants could not completely dominate the national economies of Latin America down to the retail level. Instead, at the wholesale level a division or specialization developed according to the origin of imports, and allowed Iberians to share foreign trade with the newcomers. Iberians were reduced to their traditional products, wines, and food specialities [*sic*]; the French concentrated on products destined for consumption by high income groups, wines and liqueurs, fine textiles, glassware, jewelry, and furniture. Predictably enough, the English controlled the lion's share of imports of iron and steel equipment, hardware, and especially cotton and woolen textiles. Unlike the French, the English concentrated on sales of relatively mass consumption goods stressing uniform quality and low prices. By the middle of the century, the circle of large-scale importers had been widened by—as in the colonial past—foreigners who effectively dominated the supply and price of imports and exports and exchange flows.

9. Safford (1974, 591) notes that:

in 1850, 63 percent of Great Britain's exports to Latin America consisted
of textiles and only 18 percent of metals and machinery; by 1913 textiles
represented only one-third of British exports to Latin America, and
metals and machinery were up to 27 percent. . . . In 1867 less than 4
percent of Chilean imports consisted of agricultural and industrial machinery and tools; by 1908 their share had risen to nearly 20 percent. In
Argentina the change came dramatically. Before 1900 two-thirds of its
imports were for unproductive consumption; after 1905 more than half
the imports were classified as investments in production.

10. The United Nations study (1955, 7) notes that:

in consequence . . . of the drop in Europe's exports during the war several countries, notably Argentina, accumulated an export surplus that
was financed through short-term credits to European countries and continued to grow for several years after the war. The United Kingdom re-
sumed lending to Latin America on a reduced scale in the 1920's.

11. In reference to the defaults, the United Nations study (1955, 10) found
that:

following widespread defaults on external government bonds, action
was taken over a period which did not end until the early 1950's to adjust
obligations through such steps as funding, reducing or cancelling arrears
of interest, scaling down interest rates and extending the period of amortization.

12. In the case of Argentina, however, Diaz-Alejandro (1970, 265) notes that:

[A]lthough after 1930 the capital inflow fell drastically, a modest stream
of foreign direct investment was maintained, helping the 1933–1943
industrialization. The expansion of rubber manufactures was almost
wholly due to the establishment during the early 1930s of subsidiaries of
well-known foreign tire firms. Foreign manufacturing firms established
in the 1920s and even earlier, continued to expand. Ford and Chevrolet
assembled automobiles in Argentina during the 1920s and continued
their activities there in the next decade. By the late 1930s there was growing interest by many foreign firms in more complex manufacturing activities including iron and steel.

And in a footnote on the same page, he notes that ". . . immigrants fleeing the
deteriorating European scene, many of them taking along their capital . . . played an
important role in the expansion of the textile industry during these years."

13. The United Nations study presents a list of the most important investments
sold to governments of the region. They include French and British railways in Ar-

gentina, British railways in Brazil, British railways, tramways, and waterworks in Uruguay (United Nations, 1955, 11).

14. For an interesting discussion of British disinvestment in Argentina, see Diaz-Alejandro (1970, 120).

REFERENCES

Cottrell, P. L. *British Overseas Investment in the Nineteenth Century.* London: The Macmillan Press Ltd., 1975.

Diaz-Alejandro, Carlos F. *Essays on the Economic History of the Argentine Republic.* New Haven, Ct: Yale University Press, 1970.

Feis, Herbert. *Europe, The World's Banker 1870-1914.* New York: W. W. Norton & Company, Inc., 1965.

Glade, William P. *The Latin American Economies: A Study of Their Evolution.* New York: American Book Company, 1969.

Jenks, Leland H. *The Migration of British Capital to 1875.* New York: Barnes & Noble, 1973.

Platt, D. C. M. "British Portfolio Investment Overseas before 1870: Some Doubts." *The Economic History Review,* 33:1 (February 1980).

———. "British Bondholders in Nineteenth Century Latin America: Injury and Remedy." In Marvin D. Bernstein (ed.), *Foreign Investment in Latin America: Cases and Attitudes.* New York: Alfred A. Knopf, 1966.

———. "Introduction." In D. C. M. Platt (ed.), *Business Imperialism 1840-1930.* Oxford: Clarendon Press, 1977.

Rippy, J. Fred. *British Investments in Latin America, 1822-1949.* Minneapolis: University of Minnesota Press, 1959.

———. "French Investments in Latin America." *Inter-American Economic Affairs,* 2:3 (Winter 1948a).

———. "German Investments in Argentina." *The Journal of Business of the University of Chicago,* 21:1 & 2 (January & April 1948b).

Safford, Frank. "Trade (1910-1940)." In Helen Delpar (ed.), *Encyclopedia of Latin America.* New York: McGraw-Hill Book Company, 1974.

Stein, Stanley J. and Stein, Barbara H. *The Colonial Heritage of Latin America.* New York: Oxford University Press, 1970.

United Nations. *Foreign Capital in Latin America.* New York: Department of Economic and Social Affairs, 1955.

3

EUROPE'S REDISCOVERY OF LATIN AMERICA

Gerhard Drekonja Kornat

As Rafael Gutíerrez Girardot (1976) has put it so well, ever since the colonial period, Latin America has been an active but exploited partner in the capitalist world. Its actions have tended to echo decisions made by the central powers, and, although ruled by the law of progress, Latin America has limped along behind. In the nineteenth century this took the form, as described in chapter 2, of dominating European influence in the investment and trade of Latin American countries. As the twentieth century progressed, European influence in these areas was steadily dislodged by the United States, whose position became increasingly consolidated up to and into World War II.

By 1945, both Latin America and Europe had become important parts of the American system of influence and interest. For the next ten years, Latin America and Europe continued as regional subsystems largely independent of one another. The late 1950s, however, saw the beginnings of a new era in European-Latin American relations.

The objective of this chapter is to trace through the series of events that have produced the new era and to discuss their implications. The events of the last two decades can usefully be addressed in three parts—the first is the contribution made by the interaction of the European Economic Community and Latin America; the second is the phenomenon of Gaullism; the third is Europe's cultural policy toward Latin America and recent ideological transfers. The next three sections discuss each in turn. The chapter ends with an assessment of the current situation and a question for the future.

THE EUROPEAN ECONOMIC COMMUNITY AND EUROPEAN INTEREST IN LATIN AMERICA

The Treaty of Rome was signed on January 1, 1958, binding the six founders of the European Economic Community (EEC) to the creation of a common market and a political union headquartered in Brussels. Latin America set great hope on Brussels on the assumption that Europe, as another regional subsystem within the American alliance, would offer some kind of preferential treatment in its own political interest.[1] It was soon clear that this hope was unrealistic. The Latin American "contact group," which established itself in 1963, discussed a few points with Brussels but was never allowed to touch on real political issues. Italy's special interest in Latin America initially led to some insistence on initiatives in this respect. However, for the most part, the first ten years of relations between Latin America and the EEC showed little evidence of anything more than the traditional European view of Latin America as an export market seen in a Third World context.[2]

A political initiative on the part of the Latin Americans began finally to change this situation. A new generation of Latin Americans interested in foreign policy, whose efforts were coordinated by Gabriel Valdés, a Christian Democrat in charge of the Chilean Ministry of Foreign Affairs (1964–70), was able to use the Comisión Especial de Coordinación Latinoamericana (CECLA) established in 1963 as a vehicle for dialogue with the EEC. As the first collective bargaining entity representing the subcontinent, in 1970 CECLA produced the *Carta de Buenos Aires*, a document voicing Latin America's demand for an economic and political dialogue with Brussels (Valdés 1974).[3] The document was a success, at least in the short run, helped undoubtedly by the fact that, in the previous year, Brussels had also called for an effort to encourage neglected relations with Latin America.[4] 1971 was designated as the first "Latin American Year" for the EEC.

A much celebrated "mechanism for dialogue" was established, which provided for at least one yearly meeting between Latin American ambassadors and their counterparts at the Charlemagne Building. The political nature of mutual relations was accepted by Brussels, and Ralf Dahrendorf (who as a member of the "Commission" was essentially the Minister of Foreign Affairs for the EEC) enhanced relations by visiting Brazil, Argentina, Chile, and Peru in the fall of 1971. Beginning with Argentina in 1971, Brussels simultaneously initiated negotiations with several Latin American countries concerning the establishment of bilateral, nonpreferential trade agreements. Brussels also demonstrated an interest in the integration scheme adopted by the Andean Group, which had a structure similar to its own, thus offering the potential for a special dialogue with Lima.

However, the good fortune of several farsighted statesmen handling Latin American affairs in Brussels was not to last for long. Dahrendorf clearly saw contact with Latin America as a matter of politics and outlined prospects for autonomy through cooperation with the EEC (Dahrendorf 1971). However, his views failed to carry the day in Brussels. 1971 was also the last "Latin American Year" for the EEC, and a year or so later Brussels created a global Third World policy for the EEC, thereby depriving Latin America of its last hope for special status. Preferential treatment (the Lomé Agreement) was granted only to former colonies of the EEC countries. Against the backdrop of a relative decline in Latin American trade with Brussels, by the late 1970s mutual relations had been limited to:

- Nonpreferential bilateral trade agreements with Argentina (1971), Brazil (1973), and Uruguay (1973)
- Agreements for economic cooperation with Mexico (1975) and Brazil (1980)
- Bilateral agreements with Argentina (1963) and Brazil (1965) concerning the peaceful use of atomic energy
- Technical assistance in integration (with the former Associación Latinoamericana para Libre Comercio [ALALC], the Andean Group, the Central American Common Market, and the Latin American Integration Institute [INTAL] in Buenos Aires)
- Export promotion
- Technical and financial aid.

And what of the political nucleus of this cooperation? What had happened to the autonomy, which, according to theory, should have materialized as a result of interaction between two regional subsystems tied to a larger whole?[5] Europe, after having experienced a tremendous economic expansion during the 1960s and having dedicated itself to a strong foreign policy in the early 1970s, abandoned these initiatives and began to put its economic interests ahead of all else as a result of the global economic crisis beginning in 1973.[6] Its resource vulnerability led it to follow increasingly where Washington led. Latin American foreign policy whose *autonomia periférica* (Jaguaribe 1979) had first peaked around 1972–73 also began to change as the *tercermundistas* lost ground to the *occidentalistas.*

In the end, only marginal improvements were made. For tactical reasons, Brussels renewed its dialogue with Latin America at the end of the 1970s and established contact with the Sistema Económico Latinoamericano (SELA) in Caracas.[7] In 1980, a more ambitious attempt to formalize relations with the "democratic" integration group—the Andean Pact—failed with the Bolivian coup d'etat of July 1980.[8] Since then, dialogue concerning a future global agreement between the EEC and the Andean Group has been suspended. The political crisis surrounding the Andean Pact has led to silence between Brussels and Lima. Meanwhile, Argentina is concerned about growing EEC restrictions on agricultural imports and is reconsidering an extension of its 1971 bilateral trade agreement. A Venezuelan observer sums up the situation thus:

> Ahora bien, cuál fue el papel desempeñado por Europa? Sin duda, no asumió un papel protagónico ni independiente, sino que basicamente fue un *partenaire* de los Estados Unidos en sus relaciones con América Latina, como segundo socio comercial, segundo centro financiero y segunda zona proveedora de tecnología y de inversiones directas. No se perfiló, o al menos no suficientemente, una concepción política y una estrategia económica que se diferenciara con nitidez de la de los Estados Unidos [Vacchino 1981, 2].

Latin America's young critics began to see the situation as a growing divergence of interests between the two subcontinents. Latin America wanted to force the political question, while Western Europe—where individual countries neither were superpowers nor possessed sufficiently ample internal markets—wanted to keep the issue economic. This was already clear by 1973 and has become even more so since then.

Prior to 1973, Latin America was a major, although not decisive, customer for Europe. Latin America was an important supplier of raw materials and proved to be a profitable area of operations for private Western European investment. However, the Federal Republic of Germany was the only European country to give investments in the region any priority. By the end of the 1970s, Bonn had concentrated 64 percent of all its private investments for developing countries in Latin America. France, Italy, and Great Britain (economically, politically, and ideologically the "hard-core" countries) remained more diversified.[9]

European interest in industrial exports and investment continued after 1973, of course, but Europe was now clearly identifying with First World interests. The Middle East became of the utmost importance because of its oil. At the same time, Western Europe's security needs forced it to rely on Washington's (nuclear) arms umbrella more than ever before. In this context, Europe—characterized by its status as a medium power with limited internal markets, resource vulnerability, and growing economic difficulties—had little room for a "special relationship" with Latin America. Instead, a set of global rules was developed for the Third World, offering relatively expensive concessions in the areas of export agreements, financial aid, and institutional cooperation (i.e., Stabex, Lomé). The "old order" of 1945, which after all had provided Europe with considerable gains, turned out not to have undergone drastic revision. Thus, a number of overlapping and contradictory elements remain with regard to Western European interests:

- Industrial export interests continue to dominate at a global level and are reinforced by free trade ideologies.
- Strategically, Western Europe continues to be characterized by Western Bloc interests.
- A number of special overlapping interests remain at the national level, which have as their common denominators the search for partial autonomy and defense of the status quo (life style, material well-being, social market economies, party democracy, etc.).

It should be noted, however, that these elements are increasingly antithetical to the political-ideological-humanistic demands of Western European parties, trade unions, churches, and political ideologies. These contradictions, which have continued to grow since 1973, have served to raise the level of antagonism between these actors. Attitudes have become increasingly polarized. One faction favors a "stability alliance" between Western Europe and Latin America—emphasizing exports, European transnational business activity, investments, safe and secure supplies of raw materials, and Western Bloc interests. The other faction advocates an ideological focus, which would reflect and reinforce demands for human rights, democracy based on popular support, the New International Economic Order, and social justice.

The impact and success of these transatlantic cross-currents will be an important factor in determining whether Europe's economic orientation continues to dominate in the years ahead, or if persistent Latin American demands for a political dialogue will eventually be heard.

GAULLISM: A GESTURE OR SOMETHING MORE?

Gaullism is a metaphor for France's effort to create its own maneuverability within the American system, particularly with regard to foreign policy and military matters, under the presidencies of Charles de Gaulle (1959–1969) and his successor Georges Pompidou (1969–74). Paris began the Gaullist experiment after having tackled the Algerian situation and its decolonization problems. De Gaulle first sought a fresh approach to French foreign policy, and secondly a new view of the Third World and an alternative definition of France's role on the international scene.

De Gaulle's concept of a powerful Europe, one capable of acting on its own,[10] seemed ideal to Latin Americans who during the early 1960s had also begun their first intellectual experiments with a semi-autonomous foreign policy. They still placed great hope in Europe, and under the circumstances, De Gaulle's two trips to Latin America in 1964 seemed extremely symbolic.[11] It could even be said that France took the offensive in Latin America at this particular juncture (see Goldhamer 1972), as De Gaulle played with the principle of *latinité*—a concept (as clearly opposed to *hispanidad*) that emphasized similar cultural traditions and the vision of a great destiny for all "latin" nations.

Though still very much oriented toward Paris, however, the Latin American elite were honest enough to realize that their own reality could scarcely be explained within the context of Malraux or Proust. Once the initial enthusiasm had passed, reaction was mixed. Latin Americans would of course have liked to have given De

Gaulle's *latinité* real political substance and used it as the basis for an alliance among the medium powers within the American system. But their interest cooled when it became evident that De Gaulle had little more in mind than a *beau geste*. Since De Gaulle really had no intention of subordinating French economic and cultural interests to *latinité*, the gesture was never followed by practical offers. In 1973, when Argentina (in the midst of the second wave of Peronism) took the Gaullist metaphor literally and gave it a decidedly anti-American turn on the basis of a *geopolítica de la liberación*, De Gaulle's heirs assumed a noncommittal attitude (Moneta 1979).[12] When Chile's Christian Democratic President Eduardo Frei made his pilgrimage to Paris, he at least had De Gaulle's rhetorical support in his quest for independence. Yet even this was later denied to a left-wing Peronist Argentina. It had become quite clear that France, rather than accepting Latin America as a serious ally, only sought a tactical advantage.

With hindsight, this should not, perhaps, have been surprising. Back in 1966, when atomic testing was begun, France had little regard for the protests of South American countries bordering the Pacific. One of history's ironies is that, at the same time (1967–68), France was beginning to sell the first Mirages to Peru—thereby making her first inroad (via arms technology) into the U.S. sphere of influence. Brazil, Colombia, Venezuela, Argentina, and Ecuador were subsequently clients for French combat planes and tanks. In this context, everyone understood that there could be no question of either *latinité* or any specific European-Latin American cooperation. Despite initial expectations, therefore, De Gaulle's Latin American initiative also proved a disappointment.[13]

But again, perhaps not. Régis Debray and *Les Temps Modernes* may have done more for the Gaullist design than the statesmen at the Elysee by attempting to eliminate the bipolarity via cooperation between Latin American and European clientele states within the American system. In 1981, with François Mitterrand as French President and Régis Debray as novelist turned presidential advisor, the Gaullist heritage has reappeared in a socialist context. Not all Latin American countries acclaimed the Franco-Mexican alliance of the summer of 1981 when both countries recognized the armed opposition in El Salvador. However, all of Latin America definitely understood that finally a Western European nation was prepared to dissent from Washington on the basis of an alliance with a strong Latin American partner.

CULTURAL POLICY AND IDEOLOGY TRANSFER

There is an important cultural and ideological facet to all this which should not be ignored. It has been part of the scene ever since the myth of the good savage gained currency during the nineteenth century.

In 1959, the United States was forced to revise the organizational structure of its Latin American sphere of influence as a result of the Cuban Revolution. This led to an ambitious initiative known as the Alliance for Progress, which, despite its failure as a whole, did produce some lasting effects. Through the empirical social sciences and working within the framework of a science policy begun in the 1950s, the United States succeeded in creating an elite corps of technocrats designed to dislodge "corrupt" oligarchs from the newly-established planning offices, land reform agencies, and development projects. Having regained its strength, Europe was urged to take part in this enterprise. Yet, the Old World wasn't as concerned about Fidel Castro as Washington was. Only Bonn, the United States' most loyal European ally within the American system, broke off relations with *La Habana*. Otherwise, Europe offered Latin America a series of cultural policies, but little else.

The difference in attitudes between Europe and Washington was striking. Whereas the United States provided intense training in the reform-oriented social sciences, European countries offered only their own traditions and cultural values. France, working within the scope of Gaullism, mobilized a well-organized and well-financed chain of Alliance Française institutes, which provided Latin Americans with an opportunity to read Proust in the original—just as before. The Federal Republic of Germany opened its cultural doors via the Goethe Institutes, where pupils took cram courses in German,[14] Great Britain, with its overseas bureaus of the British Council, made only a modest attempt to exert its influence, since the teaching of English was already dominated by the more aggressive and better-equipped U.S. centers. Rome, with its overbureaucratic Dante Alighieri Institutes, played a similar role.

In other words, Europe offered whatever cultural elements it happened to have in stock: language study, literature, self-representation. Often these efforts were directed more toward Europeans living abroad than toward Latin Americans themselves. Dozens of *colegios alemanes* financed by Bonn insisted on conveying a traditional image of a Germany that had little bearing on the new reality of the Federal

Republic in the 1970s. Consequently, in 1972–73, with prompting from the social liberal coalition, Bonn took advantage of a redefinition of priorities and froze financial aid to German cultural programs in Latin America (where older Germans did not agree with Bonn's current view of the world).

The best thing to be said about Europe's cultural policy in Latin America is that it did little harm, due to its inefficiency. In any event, its effect was limited when compared with the massive United States science policy, which produced thousands of PhDs and a new corps of elite technocrats.[15]

An exchange of experiences through informal channels established between Latin America and Europe did, however, prove much more effective. In the early 1960s, the Old World, left with the obsolete theories of archeologists and anthropologists, at a time when it had embarked on development policies, was forced to train its own experts. This gave way to the establishment of a variety of Latin American institutes referred to previously. Yet Latin America could not be understood in terms of European history and civilization. Europe's young "latinamericanists" were therefore eager to use tentative solutions coming from within the region itself, the foremost of these being the concept of *dependencia*. Its attractiveness obviously had something to do with the revolutionary approach. A popularized version of this theory reached Europe's academia around 1970, where it was quickly accepted and still holds a prominent place today. We might even go so far as to say that the theory of dependency monopolized European discussions on Latin America, to the extent that other variations and schools were excluded.[16] Unfortunately, as pointed out by Steger (1981), Europe's enthusiastic reception of the theory of dependency overlooked the concept's most basic element: an insistence on the structural impossibility of solving Latin American problems with European revolutionary logic.[17]

Psychologically it would have been difficult for Europe, which controlled Latin America along commercial and technological lines, to play a recipient role. This made it convenient for Europe to offer ideologies, the reception of which seemed to confirm Latin America's passivity. Two variations of this "ideology transfer" appeared after World War I: the Christian Democratic and the Social Democratic movements.

The Christian Democrats were responsible for Europe's first offensive move in Latin America since 1945. They are historically credited with the reconstruction of war-torn Western Europe and were able to provide an ideological incentive by adapting the formula of "reconstruction" to one of "development." This initiative was first evident in the form of reading material for young intellectuals who, having outgrown conservatism, and prior to the invasion of U.S. empiricism, devoured Toynbee, papal encyclica, Luigo Sturzo, Oswald van Nell-Breuning, Ludwig Erhard, and French philosophers of any stripe. The fact that Maritain finally surpassed Maurras as a favorite among Latin American readers is due to the influence of strong European political father-figures like Adenauer, de Gasperi, and Schumann who gave postwar Europe its democratic stamp. Maritain's Christian Humanism and Gabriel Marcel's Christian Existentialism, both specific European responses to a new beginning after World War II, proved to be fascinating to Latin America's national Catholics, partly because their message was so abstract.[18]

Latin America's fledgling Christian Democratic political movement, however, got its chance only when the United States needed an alternative revolutionary formula to play against the Cubans. Chile's "Revolution in Liberty," which achieved a sensational victory under Eduardo Frei in the 1964 elections, was the movement's first test. In order for Frei to win the elections, solid organizational work had to be done, so as to adjust a rather abstract Catholic social doctrine to the requirements of a cadre party within a Third World context. Italy's Christian Democratic Party, spiritually supported by the European and North American Catholic Church, saw this as an opportunity for a modern-day mission and provided organizational support. The Catholic University of Louvain assumed the task of familiarizing Christians in general and young theologians in particular with the tools of (Christianized) positivism and the empirical social sciences, thereby enabling them to work among the *marginados* as caretakers of the body as well as the soul. Some extraordinary tactical work was done by the Belgian Jesuit, Roger Vekemans, who built the multi-financed Centro para el Desarrollo Social de América Latina (DESAL) in Santiago, Chile, whence he spread the gospel of European cooperativism. The result was Latin America's Christian Democratic *comunitarismo*, which achieved some important inroads during the late 1960s and early 1970s (i.e., Rafael Caldera's victory in the 1968 Venezuelan elections; a strengthening of the Catholic cooperativist movement in Central America). Yet, from an operational point of view, in Latin America *comunitarismo* was no rival to Marxist ideology. Put to the test, Christian Democratic youth sided with Christian radicalism and were prepared to sacrifice the formal elements of democracy.[19] While Europe merely sustained a "dialogue" with the Marxists, young Latin Americans in the Christian Democratic movement succeeded in collaborating with the *Fidelistas,* Marxists, and Trotskyites. In 1965–66, it was Louvain-trained Camilo Torres, Latin America's most famous guerrilla priest, who led the way in this respect.

In this sense, 1970 marked a turning point for Latin America's Christian Democratic movement. The Unidad Popular triumphed in the Chilean elections with the unhesitating support of the radical Mapu Christian Democrats.[20] Latin America's Christian Democratic movement never recovered from this turn of events. After 1970, only the anticommunist and antifidelist CD-centrist parties survived. And they appear to be unable to achieve a decisive breakthrough despite improved organizational cooperation.

The Social Democrats were the successors to the Christian Democrats as a leading political force in Western Europe. Although organized as early as June 1951 at Frankfurt-am-Main as the Socialist International (SI), the contact of Western Europe's Social Democratic movement with Latin America was, for several years thereafter, quite sporadic and sometimes so orthodox that even potential allies were attacked. (For example, Peronism was labeled a *dictadura totalitaria.*)[21] A real transfer of ideology was offered to Latin America only after Western Europe's Social Democratic parties had established themselves in government and settled a series of urgent local matters. The Austrian Hans Janitschek, a former Secretary General of the SI (1969–76), was instrumental in getting things started by establishing contacts leading to a meeting between Social Democratic party leaders from Europe and Latin America in Caracas in May 1976. In the years that followed, the SI succeeded in building a tight network of affiliate parties.[22] The Socialist International's Latin American initiative, which had lent a Social Democratic turn to the Gaullist design, developed into one of Europe's most successful political/ideological efforts since the end of World War II. Nevertheless, a certain degree of mistrust remains among Latin Americans, who are uncertain as to how far Europeans will go toward risking Washington's disapproval.[23] After all, Western Europeans are still the United States' most reliable allies in the strategic field.[24]

THE CURRENT SITUATION AND A QUESTION
FOR THE FUTURE

Twenty years of interplay—clichés, generalities, understandings and misunderstandings, half-hearted attempts at dialogue, gestures, and the transfer of ideology—have fostered what is today the sharpest dissent ever witnessed within the Atlantic Alliance regarding Latin American affairs. Heirs to the European Christian Democratic transfer of ideology to Central America finally challenged the stability of the American system, thereby receiving the support of the Socialist International. This in turn caused alarm in Washington.[25]

The cases of Nicaragua, El Salvador, and Grenada in 1981 are proof that the European–Latin American encounter after World War II has been plagued by too much improvisation, too much emotion, too many and too diverse ideologies. To begin with, Europe failed to take account of the fact that Latin America's importance as an active partner on the international scene has increased tremendously since 1973. At that time, the international system suddenly became an "energy social system"[26] as a result of cooperative action on the part of oil-exporting countries (whose OPEC organization would not exist in its present form were it not for the tenacious efforts of the Venezuelan Juan Pablo Pérez Alfonzo). Nation-states and geopolitical competition regained status, Western Europe lost maneuverability, and Latin America's *poder negociador* increased substantially. Certainly by the mid-1970s, if not before, Latin America should have been much more important to Europe than as a mere market for goods and ideologies. But London, Brussels, Paris, Bonn, and Rome still had no clear understanding of the transformation that had taken place.[27] It was up to Latin America's new foreign policy to make full analytical use of the sudden change and to diagnose Western Europe's "strategic dependency."[28] The logic inherent in this process should have encouraged Europe to adopt a more balanced approach toward cooperation with Latin America, a continent rich in raw materials and energy resources. However, Europe continues to focus on her traditional way of doing business.

Europeans have been successful in establishing some remarkable inroads into what had previously been strictly U.S. territory in Latin America (Lagos 1979). The transfer of arms technology is one example which, by the late 1970s, was dominated almost exclusively by Europeans (including Israel). European firms consolidated their positions in Argentina, Brazil, and Mexico, in certain fields of selected technology. Their influence was also felt in Central America with regard to politics and ideology. And last but not least, Western Europe managed to break Washington's monopoly in the nuclear sector. The atomic agreement signed in 1975 between Brasília and Bonn might have caused even more dissent in the Atlantic Community than it actually did were it not for the fact that Brazil was forced to pull back partially on these projects for financial, administrative, and managerial reasons. Even so, the example proves the point that Europe is still not fully prepared to recognize the inevitable implications of what is happening. While Bonn's representatives initiated atomic cooperation with Brazil as good (i.e., normal) business, their Latin American counterparts interpreted it as an eminently political initiative, an expansion of *autonomia periférica*, which seemed appropriate for applying Gaullist principles in a Latin American context.[29]

Today, Latin Americans are much more self-confident in their behavior toward Europe, and are prepared to collect on old debts. Despite their adherence to "Christian civilization," the former automatic alignment with Europe can no longer be guaranteed.[30] During the 1980s Latin America will give the Old World credit only where credit is due. Europe must be prepared to offer substantial concessions in terms of finance, commerce, politics, and diplomacy if it is to profit from relations with Latin America.[31]

Will a social democratic Western Europe make a difference? Particularly with France under Mitterrand, who might "social-democratize" the Gaullist tradition? On the one hand, a prominent Latin American observer, Constantine V. Vaitsos (1981), remains pessimistic. He sees the danger of Western Europe's resource vulnerability, export necessities, growing economic difficulties, unemployment, and the ever-increasing contradictions existing between countries of the North imposing restrictive attitudes, regardless of the political parties in power:

> Within this framework, the emergence of progressive political forces close to or within the power structures of Western Europe, have shown themselves to lend support and political weight in favour of some important internal causes for change in developing nations. Yet, in the external sector (which is intimately related to the internal changes in the Third World), the nature of Western Europe's own interests might mitigate against any serious contri-

bution for economic development in developing nations, regardless of what parties find themselves in power in Europe.

On the other hand, however, the Franco-Mexican alliance of the summer of 1981 in favor of El Salvador's opposition forces is basically what Latin America's intellectual avant-garde has been hoping for ever since 1945: a political alliance between Latin American and medium Western European powers, aimed at weakening the rigid structure of the American system. Only time will tell whether this initiative is successful in increasing the (limited) autonomy of the regional subsystems centering, respectively, around (1) Brussels, Bonn, Paris, Rome, and (2) Mexico City, Caracas, Brasília, Buenos Aires, and—why not?—Havana.

NOTES

1. This was consistent with international theory which forecasted a strengthening in the trend toward autonomy as a result of interaction between regional subsystems (Kaiser 1968).
2. On the early relationship between Latin America and the European Common Market, see Drekonja (1974).
3. As Valdés wrote in 1970 (123): "Europa es el fruto más perfecto del hombre occidental; América Latina es el inmediato desafío al hombre occidental."
4. Comunicación de la Comisión al Consejo, "Las Relaciones con los Paises Latinoamericanos" del 29 de Julio de 1969.
5. Disappointment must be measured against expectations. After all, Britain, France, and Germany "are middle powers in a global system characterized by loose bipolarity, detente, and tendencies toward multipolarity" (Rosenau 1976). Not even Latin America's rich mineral and energy resources motivated a stronger interest on the part of Brussels (see Wionczek 1981, 2).

The idea of a complementary relationship based on cooperation between Europe and Latin America is tempting, even more so if founded on democracy. Orrego (1981, 53) states "Probablemente, lo más interesante que tiene la idea de mirar a nuevas formas de cooperación entre Europa y América Latina, es que comienza a dibujarse, al menos en la imaginación, la perspectiva de una relación diagonal entre los dos continentes, que se aparta de las formas tradicionales de vinculación vertical u horizontal." However, I see no evidence of it.
6. In so doing, it adopted a defensive position and lost its taste for cooperation with Latin America, which had become decidedly *tercermundista* in terms of the North–South dialogue. See the case study by Manfred Nitsch (1982).
7. SELA issued Resolution No. 44 of 1979 calling for a *qualitative* improvement in relations between the two regions and threatened asymmetrical countermeasures if Latin American demands were not heard ("America Latina ante la CEE" 1979).

8. This was actually an attempt to adapt the ASEAN cooperation model to South America.

9. All authoritative texts on the relationship between Europe and Latin America reflect this phenomenon, and authors inevitably lament the relative decline in trade between the two regions, which effectively keeps Latin America in a position of secondary importance.

10. Such a situation, in which the classical bipolarity was replaced with new power centers, was exactly what Johan Galtung (1972) hoped to avoid.

11. De Gaulle's Mexico visit took place in March 1964. Visits to Venezuela, Colombia, Ecuador, Peru, Bolivia, Chile, Argentina, Paraguay, Uruguay, and Brazil were made in September/October 1964. See Schwarzbeck (1976). The fact that De Gaulle enjoyed enormous prestige, even among radical students, is demonstrated in a 1965 interview/study done in Colombia. De Gaulle is at that time rated far ahead of Castro, Nasser, and Frei. See Latorre (1980).

Conservative Latin America always remained Francophile and Gaullist. "Nos interesa Francia, avanzada Latina," says the editorial of *Vision* dated March 20, 1981: "El ejemplo francés es particularmente interesante para los latinoamericanos, desde el momento que Francia es el más avanzado de los paises latinos: en ella, en cierto modo, miramos nuestro propio futuro."

12. In Peronist writings of the early 1970s, Europe as a political alternative appears as a recurrent theme. As an example, see Ceresole (1972) and Uriburu (1970). The topic is introduced again in a European version by Lietar (1979). The Belgian author sees Latin America as the last and only logical area for significant European diversification. A massive resource and technology transfer is advocated through European transnational firms in order to create a strong interdependence between Western Europe and Latin America, with mutual benefits for both.

13. The handy formula of *latinité* was of little use in resisting the "American challenge." In 1978–79, it was energy-rich Mexico that assumed a "Gaullist" profile, while President Giscard d'Estaing rather modestly traveled to Mexico City as a customer (see "Lopez Portillo Stakes His Claim" 1980).

14. From the mid-1970s on, a further function of their duties has been to deny the existence of the Herder Institutes (the cultural arm of the German Democratic Republic).

15. To a certain degree, Latin America's new technocrats, capable of handling the modern social sciences, became "the functional equivalent of a ruling class." This, at least, is the result of a study on the impact of international development agencies in developing countries. See International Legal Center (1977). The excellent chapter on Colombia was written by Fernando Cepeda.

16. Darcy Ribeiro, author of *The Process of Civilization*, barely passed through this barrier. Orlando Fals Borda's "action research" was used only by outsiders. (Orlando Fals Borda's thesis on "sociologia subversiva" was amply discussed during 1969/1970/1971 in the journal *Aportes* edited in Paris by Luis Mercier Vega. *Aportes* made some important contributions toward budding Latin American Studies in Europe, giving them a more professional nature.) And the work of an important Peruvian philosopher, Augusto Salazar Bondy ("Para una Filosofía de Valor") was totally ignored. After 1970, Europe became more receptive to the Latin American literary boom: Gabriel Garcia Márquez, literary metaphysicians from

Buenos Aires to Mexico City, the manifold authors of "dictator" novels, and, finally, just about every more or less suitable and translatable author were all marketed by European publishers.

17. Régis Debray stumbled into this trap, as he later recognized in "La Critique des Armes." Had he clearly understood *dependencia* he might have spared himself, and Latin America, his disastrous focus theory.

18. Jacques Maritain's decisive influence on Catholic thinking in Latin America is confirmed by Frei (1977). See also Williams (1967). On the Charles Maurras reception in Latin America, see *Le Monde Diplomatique en Español* (November 1980). On the formation of the European Christian Democracy, see Meyeur (1980). See also Velasco (1967).

19. Darcy Ribeiro feels that this was inevitable (1971, 209):

La Democrácia Cristiana de Chile, aunque tenga algunas potenciali dades reformistas, es principalmente un esfuerzo de restauración del patriciado con un nuevo ropaje. La de Venezuela, todavia más tibia, apenas aspira ser un partido de tecnócratas capaces de conquestar algunas ventajas en el trato con los norteamericanos.

20. Yet the Unidad Popular exceeded the limits to Latin American reformism granted under the American system, and the Christian Democratic ideology imported from Europe became the "Kerenski" formula, reference to a hateful pamphlet by Fabio Vidigal Xavier da Silveira, *Frei el Kerensky Chileno*. The Spanish version was printed in Argentina (Editora Cruzada, 1968) and widely distributed to decision makers in Chile and throughout Latin America.

21. See "Mensaje a los Trabajadores de América Latina" (1955) in Guensche and Lantermann (1979).

22. For this, it was organizationally framed by the ILDIS Institutes of the Friedrich Ebert Foundation of the Federal Republic and inspired by Willy Brandt's international prestige. Some occasional "headhunting" for associates was unavoidable. See "Latin America: Socialist Headhunters" (1978). The list of Latin American members and associate members of the London-based Socialist International is in "La Socialdemocrácia en América Latina" (1980).

23. The fact that the Development Fund of the European Community was considering cofinancing the construction of a jet airport on revolutionary Grenada led to a clash of opinions with Washington in April 1981. Washington feared that Cuba would take advantage of the new Port Salines airport as a "bridge" to Africa.

24. No wonder Latin Americans occasionally denounce European double-crossing and several Latin American Labour parties have refused to be enlisted as SI allies. See Quijano's violent denunciation (1976).

Leading Latinamericanists of the Soviet Union discuss the role of the Socialist International in Latin America in "Socialist International" (1978). In Brazil, Luis Inácio da Silva, better known as "Lula," keeps the Partido dos Trabalhadores outside the social democratic camp and leaves this "European connection" to Leonel Brizola's Partido Democrático Trabalhista.

25. In Washington, European partners are expected to guard the flank, not provoke controversy. See Grabendorff (1980).

26. See Klausner (1979). According to the author, 1973 and the years following witnessed a metamorphosis in the international system favoring nation-states that, if they possess energy resources, are gradually assuming control of the transnational petroleum distribution network.

27. The Iran crisis finally shook Western Europeans out of their complacency. Fearing other "Iranisations," Bonn began a complete revision of its cultural policies. On this point, see Mols (1980).

28. "Strategic dependency" is the dependence of advanced capitalistic countries on foreign sources for the supply of cheap, critical minerals essential to their economies and national defense (Muñoz 1980).

29. In this respect, Brazil's military government even went so far as to modify the "Brazilian model." *Distensão* and *abertura* appeared; scientists who had emigrated after 1964 were called back and rehabilitated; and European experiences were introduced to free Brazil's system of higher education from its unilateral fixation with U.S. standards (Freitag 1979). The fact that such forceful strategic moves are usually met with evasive tactics on the part of the Europeans naturally brought about trouble in the end. In discussing the basis for a new foreign policy, Latin Americans have created the concept of *clase media de las naciones* (Orrego 1979), or even more unconditionally, that of *paises intermedios* which is a hispanic adaptation of the NICS-concept (Newly Industrializing Countries) whose followers want to independently force their way into the OECD group.

30. Willy Brandt discovered this when his "report" was dismantled and criticized during two Latin American evaluation seminars in Canela (Brazil), August 1980, and in Villa de Leyva (Colombia), October 1980. There is a basic mistrust of the Brandt Report among Latin Americans. They fear being coopted into the First World via the NICS-concept and through the Latin American monetarists, the "Uncle Toms" of the subcontinent. See "El Informe Brandt y América Latina" (1981). The fact that the Brandt Report, though credited with the best intentions, could be interpreted as a delaying, maneuvering tactic directed against Latin America as part of the Third World demonstrates that Latin America's best brains are on the verge of losing their patience.

31. Costa Rica's ex-President Oduber (a member of the SI) cannot hide his doubts about renewed European interest: "The European countries that made us poor and then abandoned us are again turning their attention to our Caribbean Basin, and seek it as an alternative to the Middle East to guarantee their way of life. As the Middle East and Persian Gulf crises become more acute, our territories will become more and more an area fought over for the advantage of others, but never for our own development" (Oduber 1981).

Gabriel García Marquez (1981) is also unsure about European interest in Latin America. He feels it will be easier to establish a dialogue with the people of a partially "hispanoamericanized" United States than with the arrogant Europeans:

> Durante la década de los sesenta, los intelectuales europeos se colocaron en la primera línea de la solidaridad con nosotros, nos desbordaron con un alborozo idealista que sin embargo no resistío el primer embate serio de la realidad. Su análisis tenía, y sigue teniendo un rezago colonial: sólo ellos se creen depositarios de la verdad. Para ellos sólo es bueno lo que

ha probado serlo en su propia experiencia. Todo lo demás es extraño, y por consiguiente, inaceptable y corruptor.

REFERENCES

"América Latina ante la CEE: Bases para una Relación de Nuevo Tipo." *SELA en Acción. Boletín Informativo*, 5 (February 1979): 3–12.

Castillo Velasco, Jaime. *Las Fuentes de la Democracia Cristiana.* Santiago: Ed. del Pacifico, 1967.

Ceresole, Norberto. *Geopolítica de la Liberación.* Buenos Aires: Ediciones Corregidor, 1972.

Dahrendorf, Ralf. "Möglichkeiten und Grenzen einer Aussenpolitik der Europaischen Gemeinschaften." *Europa-Archiv*, 26:4 (April 1971).

Drekonja, Gerhard. "América Latina y las Comunidades Europeas: Política Comercial o Política Exterior?" *Revista de la Integración* (INTAL-Buenos Aires), 8:16 (May 1974): 41–69.

"El Informe Brandt y America Latina: La Lucha Contra el 'Tio Tom' Latinoamericano." *Desarrollo y Cooperación*, 1 (January 1981): 18.

Frei, Eduardo. *América Latina: Opcíon y Esperanza.* Barcelona: Pomaire, 1977.

Freitag, Barbara. *Escola, Estado e Sociedade.* São Paulo: Coleção Educação Universitária, 1979.

Galtung, Johan. *The European Community: A Superpower in the Making.* Oslo: Univositäts-forlaget, 1972.

Goldhamer, H. *The Foreign Powers in Latin America.* Princeton, NJ: Princeton University Press, 1972.

Grabendorff, Wolf. "Die Beziehungen der USA und Westeuropa zu Lateinamerika: Gemeinsamkeiten und Unterschiede." *Zeitschrift für Lateinamerika* (Vienna), 17 (July 1980): 19–29.

Guensche, K. L. and K. Lantermann. *História de la Internacional Socialista.* Mexico: Ed. Nueva Imagen, 1979.

Gutiérrez Girardot, Rafael. *Horas de Estudio.* Bogotá: Instituto Colombiano de Cultura, 1976.

International Legal Center (ed.). *The Impact of International Organizations on Legal and Institutional Change in the Developing Countries.* New York, 1977.

Jaguaribe, Helio. "Autonomia Periferica y Hegemonia Céntrica." *Estudios Internacionales* (Santiago de Chile), 12:46 (April 1979): 91–130.

Kaiser, Karl. "The Interaction of Regional Subsystems: Some Preliminary Notes on Recurrent Patterns and the Role of Superpowers." *World Politics*, 21:1 (October 1968): 84–107.

Klausner, Samuel A. "The Energy Social System." *The Annals of the American Academy of Political and Social Science* (Philadelphia), 444 (July 1979): 1–22.

"La Socialdemocrácia en América Latina." *Le Monde Diplomatique en Español*, 2:23 (November 1980): 15.

Lagos, Gustavo (ed.). *Las Relaciones entre América Latina, Estados Unidos y Europa Occidental.* Santiago: Instituto de Estudios Internacionales de la Universidad de Chile, 1979.

"Latin America: Socialist Headhunters." *Latin America Political Report* (London), 12:50 (December 1978): 397–98.

Latorre, Mario. *Politica y Elecciones*. Bogotá: Universidad de los Andes, 1980.

Lietar, B. *Europe + Latin America + the Multinationals*. Farnborough: Westmead, 1979.

"López Portillo Stakes His Claim as Latin America's DeGaulle." *Latin America Weekly Report* (London), 8 August 1980.

Marquez, Gabriel García. *El Espectador* (Bogotá), 13 September 1981.

Meyeur, J. M. *Des Partis Cátholiques a la Démocratie Chretienne*. Paris: A. Colin, 1980.

Mols, Manfred. "The Relationship of the Federal Republic of Germany with Latin America." Mainz: October 1980 (paper).

Moneta, Carlos J. "La Política Exterior del Peronismo: 1973–1976." *Foro Internacional* (México), 20:37(2) (October/December 1979): 220–76.

Muñoz, Heraldo. "Strategic Dependency and Foreign Policy: Notes on the Relations Between Core Powers and Mineral-Exporting Periphery Countries." *Vierteljahresberichte* (Bonn), 80 (June 1980): 165–81.

Nitsch, Manfred. "Los intereses de los paises ricos y el desarrollo del Tercer Mundo: La República Federal de Alemania." *Estudios Internacionales*, 14:54 (April/June 1982): 224–53.

Oduber, Daniel. "Toward a New Central American Dialogue." *Caribbean Review* (Miami), 10:1 (Winter 1981): 10–13.

Orrego, Francisco (ed.). *América Latina: Clase Media de las Naciones?* Santiago: Instituto de Estudios Internacionales de la Universidad de Chile, 1979.

Orrego Vicuña, Francisco. "Europa y América Latina: Hacia un Rol Internacional Complementario?" *Estudios Internacionales* (Santiago de Chile), 14:53 (February/March 1981): 3–16.

Petras, James F. "La Socialdemocrácia en América Latina." *Le Monde Diplomatique en Español*, 2 (June 1980).

Quijano, Anibal. "La Doble Táctica de la Actual Ofensiva Imperialista." *Economía* (Quito), 67 (December 1976).

Ribeiro, D. *El Dilema de América Latina*. Mexico: Siglo XXI, 1971.

Rodriguez Plata, Horacio. *La Inmigración Alemana al Estado Soberano de Santander en el Siglo XIX*. Bogota, 1968.

Rosenau, James N., et al. *World Politics*. New York/London: The Free Press, 1976.

Schwarzbeck, Frank. "Frankreich und Lateinamerika in der Gaullistischen Era." *Vierteljahresberichte der Friedrich Ebert Stiftung* (Bonn), 66 (December 1976): 253–74.

"Socialist International in Latin America." *América Latina* (Moscow), 4:20 (Winter 1978): 88–137.

Steger, Hanns-Albert. "Gesellschaft und Kultur in Lateinamerika." In Otto Molden (ed.), *Dialog Westeuropa-Lateinamerika*. Wien: Fritz Molden, 1981, 114–27.

Uriburu, E. J. *El Plan Europa: Un Intento de Liberación Nacional*. Buenos Aires: Ediciones Corregidor, 1970.

Vacchino, Juan Mario. "América Latina y la Europa Comunitaria: Alcances y Perspectivas de las Relaciones Recíprocas." *Comercio Exterior* (Mexico), 31:2 (February 1981): 123–33.

Vaitsos, Constantine V. "From a Colonial Past to Asymmetrical Interdependences: The Role of Europe in North–South Relations." In EADI Conference, "Europe's Role in World Development," Milan, September 1980.

Valdés, Gabriel. "América Latina y la Política del Nuevo Mundo: El Papel de la Comisión Especial de Coordinación para Latino-américa, CECLA." In H.H. Godoy y D. Uribe Vargas (eds.), *Política Mundial Siglo XXI*. Bogota, 1974.

———. *Conciencia Latinoamericana y Realidad Internacional*. Santiago de Chile: Ed. del Pacifico, 1970.

Velasco, Jaime Castillo. *Las Fuentes de la Democracia Cristiana*. Santiago de Chile: Ed. del Pacifico, 1967.

Williams, Edward J. *Latin American Christian Democratic Parties*. Knoxville: University of Tennessee Press, 1967.

Wionczek, Miguel S. "Las Relaciones entre la CEE y América Latina en el Contexto de una Crisis Economica Global." *Comercio Exterior* (México), 31:2 (February 1981): 145–52.

4

WESTERN EUROPE AND LATIN AMERICA: LESSONS OF THE LAST TWO DECADES FOR THE FUTURE

Roberto Russell

The idea of a triangular relationship between the United States, Western Europe, and Latin America is not new. As early as 1965, Giuseppe Saragat, then President of Italy, after visiting Latin America, called it the continent "of Europe's future" and characterized its process of development "despite crises, mistaken directions and errors [as carrying] within itself the germs of a future on which depends . . . not only the destiny of the continent but also that of the world." In Saragat's view, it was "not utopian to predict a partnership that will unite Europe and North America with the South American countries."[1] Both before and after these words were spoken, similar views were put forth in numerous speeches, official documents, and academic works—envisioning bright futures, "natural" alliances, and common destinies. My purpose in this chapter is to focus on the experience of the last two decades with respect to one side of the triangle: the connection between Western Europe and Latin America.

Inevitable rhetoric aside, it is clear that the relationship between the two regions has been a relatively important part of the international picture. In later sections of the chapter I discuss particular facets of it in some detail. Before I do so, however, it is useful to establish a framework for discussion by giving a brief overview of the international system of which the ties between the industrialized countries and the developing world are a part, the recent changes that have taken place in it, the trends portrayed by these changes, and their probable consequences for the structure of the world political and economic order to come.

THE GLOBAL CONTEXT

From the point of view of European–Latin American relations, the most important change that has taken place over the last two decades has been the proliferation of political world power. This has been caused by the relative erosion of North American hegemony in the international capitalist system, accompanied by the rise of Germany and Japan, and the emergence of China. Added to this has been the new phenomenon of countries moving from an underdeveloped or developing status into the so-called international middle class, with their own ideas of playing a differentiated role in world relations and diversifying their sources of capital goods, technology, and financing.

A second factor of major importance has been the increasing politicization of economic issues over the 1970s. Not only have economic issues assumed an increasingly important role in their own right. This trend has also been in part a logical consequence of the disappointment felt by many leaders of the developing world with the neoliberal doctrine which left world allocation of resources in the "invisible hands of the market" (Russell and Carballal 1979).

A third factor has been the growing interdependence of countries that make up the industrialized world (among them some in the Southern Bloc) accompanied by a relative reduction in the weight of the Third World in the international economic system. As a consequence, the developed countries increased their share in world exports from 60 to 64.5 percent between 1950 and 1977. According to CEPAL (1980, 27 and 29), "factors that have contributed strongly to this have been the integration processes, the reduction or elimination of tariff and nontariff barriers for manufactured products and the operations of transnational corporations. The developing countries, for their part, have greatly diminished their share of world trade, in both exports and imports, with the proportion of their exports in world trade dropping from 31.7 to 25.8 percent during the same period [1950 to 1977], and that of their imports falling from 27.1 to 22.7 percent."

Within the group of developing countries, Latin America is the region that has lost the most ground. The importance of primary products in the total of Latin American exports (around 80 percent), together with their sharp drop as a percentage of world trade, is the principal reason for the drastic decline of Latin American participation in world trade between 1950 and 1977, as regards both exports (from 10.4 to 4.4 percent) and imports (from 9.0 to 4.9 percent).

In the case of Western Europe, the important increase in interzone trade helps explain the decreasing proportion of total imports coming into Europe from the developing regions. Interzone trade increased from 33.1 percent of the total trade of Western Europe in 1955 to 43.7 percent in 1975. For the European Economic Community (EEC), the percentage of intercommunity trade in total imports grew continually from 40.5 percent in 1963 to 57 percent in 1972, stabilizing from then on at 56 percent.

Yet another factor of some importance is the essentially internal crisis within the industrialized world, bringing with it electoral demands for important modifications in the structure of both the political and economic systems. As a consequence of this crisis, a debate that goes beyond the boundaries of the political parties and groups has arisen between two lines of thought: one defensive, opposed to adjustment and in favor of protectionism; the other, which can be termed offensive (following Ferrer 1980, 1337), "prepared to face the challenge of change, to recover a strong growth rate, and to promote the politico-institutional transformations that will free the forces of growth."

Accompanying all this has been a new aggravation of East–West tensions. Its fundamental causes have been events such as the Cuban intervention in Angola, the crises in Iran, Nicaragua, and Afghanistan, accompanied by the United States' return to policies of containment in a new cold war context. The policies of world order and of global interests that characterized at least the theoretical ideas of the Carter administration apparently have been rejected.

Finally, there has been a weakening of the interimperial system and a resurgence of the importance of the nation-state and of separate national identities. As Galbraith has recently said (1981, 12–13), in this decade the clock will be stopped at the "hour of the nationalities."

Within this overall context, the industrialized world of the North has been following a strategy of gradual incorporation on an individual basis into the existing order of its eventual challengers from the South. The Southern Bloc, at the same time, has become increasingly differentiated. To both these developments we now turn.

"LOW PROFILE" IN THE NORTH; DIFFERENTIATION IN THE SOUTH

The dominant position in the industrialized world at present with respect to dealing with the Third World is that which seeks to generate a system of selective bilateral alliances with the countries making up the international middle class, and at the same time to break up the unity of the South by not accepting them as a legitimate bloc in international negotiations. This "low profile" attitude is essentially explicable by the continuity in the North of two basic assumptions (Russell and Carballal 1981).

- That the national interest can effectively be served without having to develop a general negotiating capacity between the North and the South as blocs.
- That the current international economic system is adequate to solve the problems that concern the underdeveloped countries.

It is clear that the belief in an open liberal system of trade is increasingly difficult to reconcile with the short-term problems faced by the industrialized countries. This is what has given rise to the ambivalence of the social and political demands internal to the northern countries (mentioned earlier) which waver between liberalization and opening up, on the one hand, and protectionism, on the other; between global collective interests in the long term and maximization of individual opportunities in the short term; between the search for a more equitable new international order and the maintenance of national or sectoral interests (Comeliau 1980).

To match the lack of a regional European or North American policy toward Latin America, there is an analogous lack of a regional Latin American policy toward the Northern Bloc. The reasons for its absence are, however, different.

With respect to the Southern Bloc, the lack of a regional policy can be traced to the different levels of development and potential of the developing countries. Because of this, the stance and policies of different countries vis-à-vis the developed world differ in major ways. Thus, within the Southern Bloc there are substantial differences related to the nature of the ties with the industrialized world, to the order of priority of the demands that constitute the North–South agenda, to the manner of negotiating with the countries of the North, and to the degree of affinity with the systems of values of the developed societies. Furthermore, if one bears in mind that the countries making up the so-called international middle class (in particular, Brazil, Argentina, Venezuela, Mexico) have achieved conspicuously high levels of growth within the current economic system, one can understand their lack of interest in modifying it to acquire the forms desired by the more radicalized, less well-off countries. Their wish to become part of the system, in a privileged although subaltern position, fits perfectly into the strategy of cooption implemented by the industrialized countries and also has a fundamental internal correlation. Most of the countries in this international middle class are led by authoritarian governments or by governments which, though democracies in a formal sense, are able to control the mobilization and participation of the populace in the political process.

The international conditions noted above have also created, in recent years, a propitious climate for the countries that have entered the "middle class" to seek out forms of connection among countries that are no longer regional, much less global, in nature. Thus, these countries have become increasingly receptive to the idea of establishing some form of preferential alliance or connection with other intermediately developed countries. As has aptly been pointed out: "[Latin America] has not had a very fortunate experience with integration and is too heterogeneous to adopt a common regional position in world negotiations. In fundamental matters, it is more probable that Venezuela will join forces with the OPEC than with its own neighbors; that Brazil will do the same with the new more advanced semiindustrialized oligopolists rather than with the poor countries of the region" (Malan 1980).

In the case of Brazil, its policy of "responsible pragmatism" and of "nonautomatic alignment," and the need to strengthen its position in areas where unilateral or bilateral means are insufficient, leads it to adopt positions in solidarity with the countries of the Third World (especially in the "weak forums") as a tactical measure for obtaining individual advantages, rather than as a strategy to strengthen the South as a bloc. Mexico is also showing a deliberate wish to reinforce its connections with the intermediate countries: "We intend to establish more important contacts in the political field with a group of countries we can consider or qualify as medium powers, irrespective of the side to which they belong," said Foreign Minister Jorge Castañeda, in a recent statement; he gave as examples of medium powers Yugoslavia, Sweden, Algeria, India, Brazil, and perhaps Roumania.[2]

In Argentina, the position has been less explicit (perhaps less concrete) so far, but the policies that have been implemented, the course of the country's relations abroad, and the objectives established by its leaders on the economic levels reflect a basic affinity with proposals of this type.

Together with this tendency to effect selective alliances among groups of medium countries, one can perceive a strong general favoring of bilateral instruments, starting from the specific weaknesses and advantages of each country, as a means for achieving a more advantageous entry into the international economy.

RELATIONS BETWEEN WESTERN EUROPE AND LATIN AMERICA

After World War II, the close alignment of Latin America with the United States and the priorities given by Europe to regional integration and to relations with other areas of the world prevented the development of significant interregional ties with Latin America. European interest in the region was concentrated almost exclusively on trade and investment—political matters together with those of military security taking second place, and being restricted to the achievement of certain specific national objectives (e.g., a German diplomatic offensive designed to prevent recognition of the government of East Germany by the Latin American countries, or French or Italian attempts to reestablish their cultural prestige and get Latin America to reorient itself toward Western Europe). The conflict with the Soviet Union in the area, for example—which only came on the cold war map with the events in Guatemala in 1954, and only became important with the Cuban revolution—and the preservation of Latin American alignment with the capitalist orbit, was left exclusively to the United States.

In the mid-1960s, according to Goldhamer (1972, 24),

[t]he developing East–West detente [and the] Soviet interest in establishing diplomatic and economic relations with the Latin Republics, while rejecting Castro's and Guevara's guerrilla strategy for Latin American revolution, together with the failures of the latter, provided further justification for Europe's almost exclusive concern with investment and trade in Latin America and its tendency to find somewhat dated both United States pre-

occupation with security issues and its political future in the region. In any event, the Saragat–Fanfani triangular policy and similar lines of thought in Europe and the United States viewed Soviet and Latin American national revolutionary influences as more liable to be blunted by a diversified Western influence than by a dominant and sensitive United States presence.

The first contact of Europe as a region with Latin America, effected by the EEC, was on March 19, 1958, a little less than three months after the implementation of the Treaty of Rome. From this point on the contacts multiplied until, on June 18, 1971 (as mentioned in chapter 3), the EEC accepted the proposal of the member countries of CECLA in the 1970 Buenos Aires Declaration to maintain a more systematic cooperation between both regions, establishing to this end a mechanism for dialogue between Latin America and the EEC. In spite of this rapprochement, which was (as also noted in chapter 3) the high point of the planned relationship, and despite other commercial agreements signed by the EEC with several Latin American countries shortly thereafter (Argentina 1971, Uruguay 1973, Brazil 1973), the relationship between the two regions as such deteriorated from then on, and no new channels for potential cooperation have been developed.

From the European side the following may be noted.

- An increasing interdependence on the part of the European countries, among themselves and with the other industrialized nations, to the detriment of their ties with the Southern Bloc.
- The development of protectionist policies as a result of difficult internal economic situations, this time "of an industrial nature with systems that are daily more sophisticated" and which complicate "the process of diversification of exports" undertaken by Latin America (SELA 1979, 58).
- The "common foreign tariff . . . with its even more prejudicial corollary of restrictive formulas" (Instituto Italo–Latino Americano 1979, 67).
- The common agricultural policy which produced a steady decrease in the relative importance of the imports of agricultural products.
- The policy of preferential agreements as specified in the Lome I and II Conventions,[3] the Mediterranean Basin Convention (global scheme of the Mediterranean), the special agreements with certain Arab countries, the European free trade zone with the countries of Western Europe that are not a part of the EEC, and the agreements

for certain products such as those in existence with India, Pakistan, and Bangladesh. All these are discriminatory and restrict the access of Latin American products to the European market.

From the Latin American side, the following contribute to the problem.

- The lack of a foreign policy at the regional level, which prevents the region from developing and making a firm commitment to a common strategy.
- The different levels of development of individual countries, which prevent them from adopting continental positions of solidarity and, as a consequence, encourage the trend we have already pointed out toward the unilateral search for new forms of entry into the international system.

With the intensification of the international economic crisis from 1975 on, Europe has started a policy of rapprochement with new regions of the developing world (Asia, the Arab Middle East, and Latin America), with the objects of keeping and enlarging markets for its products[4] and investments, and assuring itself alternative sources of supply for raw materials, especially minerals and oil.[5]

In this context, the enlarging of sales of European products in the markets of the Third World, above all in the countries under its "zone of influence," is considered among other factors as one of the most relevant means to alleviate the difficult economic situation. To this end it is essential to create or reactivate the demands stemming from these countries. In this sense, according to the Brussels European Committee:

> The idea is to inject during a determined period of three, four or five years, massive financial currents—in the nature of 10,000 million dollars per year—into the countries of the Third World that represent, for Europe, the strongest potential markets and thus contribute toward a reactivation of world economy [Dubois and Ramadier 1980, 21].

In keeping with these renewed interests, Europe has again started on a policy of new contacts with Latin America, with the intent of breaking the impasse. Among the most significant of these are agreements for economic cooperation—which go beyond merely commercial matters—signed with Mexico in 1975 and Brazil in 1980; the start of conversations with the Andean Group regarding an international agreement applying to trade, economic, industrial, technological, and financial issues; strengthening of official ties with SELA, with the Secretariat for Central American Integration (SIECA), and with the countries of Central America; and inauguration in Caracas in 1978 of the new headquarters of the Commission of European Communities' Delegation for Latin America.

Contacts have also increased in the political arena. Thus, European social democrats, for example, during the international congress on decolonization, autodetermination, and freedom for Latin America and the Caribbean (held in March 1981 in Aruba), decided to place Latin America first on their scale of political interests in the developing world.[6]

However, generally speaking, the results of this European policy of rapprochement with new Third World regions, and with Latin America in particular, have not been encouraging thus far. Apart from the global factors leading to the current stagnation of negotiations between the industrialized and the developing worlds, several internal factors affecting the countries of Europe are having an unfavorable influence on European–Latin American relations. According to Wionczek (1981, 149), "the inability of the EEC to develop a general framework of policies in the developing world may well be the consequence of the varying national political interests and characteristics among its members, of the disturbing state of relations between the EEC and the United States, and of the recent internal economic conflicts of the EEC. These complex factors must be borne in mind when the future of relations between the EEC and Latin America is considered."

CONCLUSION

Among the several possible alternatives for the world order in the 1980s, the one that will apparently predominate—not without conflict—may be called controlled administration of the interdependencies (symmetrical and nonsymmetrical). The greater weight of this "administration" will obviously fall on the industrialized countries; the greatest threats to its "control" will come from the Third World (Perez Llana 1979).[7] This administration of the interdependencies presupposes, on the part of the developed countries, a concerted strategy to overcome their internal economic crises and the effective coordination of policies toward the Socialist world and the developing countries. It also presupposes, as regards the international middle class, the concession of a differentiated treatment to the intermediate countries in commercial, technological, and financial matters and their gradual integration into the capitalist system, although it is not quite clear in which category they will have access to the "club of the rich."

It must also be recognized that Western Europe integrates part of the industrialized world, and as such, it must give priority to responding to the basic interests of the industrialized world. The relations between Western Europe and Latin America, therefore, must be pursued within the overall framework of the relations between the industrialized countries and the Third World.[8]

The evolution of the industrialized countries, with which Latin America maintains the bulk of its foreign relations,[9] has a special influence on the process of economic development of the region. It is important to point out this influence without trying to extract from it a simple cause-and-effect relationship, because obviously there are other internal and external factors that influence the process. What I am trying to stress is that in this world of nonsymmetrical interdependencies the course of events in the industrialized world inevitably affects the current situation and the future development prospects of Latin America. This becomes particularly important when it is borne in mind that, during the 1970s, there was a profound transformation in Latin America's position in the international system and, in particular, an intensification of its connections with the capitalist developed world.

As a consequence, the achievement of the export goals called for by the economic growth of Latin America will greatly depend, especially at first, on access to the markets of the industrial countries. "And this will, in turn, depend on the evolution of foreign demand from these countries and especially on considered policies to further the elimination of the well-known restrictions of every kind that inhibit access to their markets and on policies of restructuring their internal economic activity which encourage basic conditions for a new expansive presence in the world economy on the part of the developing countries" (CEPAL 1979, 23).

Intraregional cooperation and the expansion of reciprocal trade are also essential conditions in this process, although they must not be "considered as a substitute for greater ties with the industrialized countries. Both strategies must be conceived as complementary objectives, especially during . . . the next decade" (CEPAL 1979, 10).

None of this will be easy. As noted, Western Europe does not have a global policy for Latin America. In recent years it has been possible to perceive a trend toward bilateral ties—between the EEC and particular Latin American countries—which generally pursue specific short- and medium-term objectives. Latin America, for its part, does not behave like a unitary actor in international politics. Regarding relations with the developed world, it presents, particularly in the "soft forums," a relatively homogeneous front, but there is an increasing trend at the level of the greater powers of the region to favor a policy that—without causing them to lose the solidarity of the rest of the countries of the continent—makes possible their "prosystemic insertion" into the bloc of the developed countries (agreed cooption).

It should be noted, however, that, although relations between Latin America and Western Europe have undergone persistent deterioration during the last 20 years in quantitative terms, Latin America's relevance for Europe—particularly in the context of generalized crisis in which competition has become sharper among the industrialized countries for the markets and sources of supply of raw materials in the Third World—should also be evaluated from a qualitative point of view. There is fertile ground for the promotion of concrete initiatives in the economic, political, and cultural fields. The well-known complementary positions of both regions—Latin American dependence on basic supplies and imports of capital goods and technology, essential for the furtherance of the process of productive transformation and its industrialization plans; its need to diversify its foreign relations to prevent excessive influence on the part of the United States; its enormous growth potential and the current and future importance of its markets—are the key aspects that make Latin America an area of undoubted importance for Europe.

The possibilities for cooperation exist and cannot be denied. But for Europe to be able to give renewed impulse to its relations with Latin America, it must be in a position to overcome:

- The "defensive nationalism" (unconvincing from the theoretical point of view predominating in Europe itself) arising from the "common agricultural policy" and the "new industrial protectionism."
- The "discriminatory regionalism" arising from the policy of association with the ACP countries and with the Mediterranean Basin.
- The "metropolitanism of domination" arising from the place of Europe in the world capitalist center (and in its system of rules,

solidarities, and conflicts), which leads it to two types of strategic confrontation: with the Communist countries (for world domination) and with the peripheral countries (for the establishment of a new international order) (Vacchino 1981, 132).

It may be a hard fact to face, but there is nothing on the horizon to suggest that any of these three barriers can be substantially overcome. On the contrary, current trends are working against improvement in the relations between the two regions.

European interests—in spite of the contacts between political parties and groups from Europe and Latin America in recent years—continue to be essentially economic and are concentrated on the more important countries due to the attraction offered by their ample markets (both real and potential) and their abundant natural resources. It is important to keep this geographical concentration in mind, since:

[i]t is often affirmed that Latin America is going through a period of industrialization, that Latin America has increased its participation in the world trade of manufactured products when, in reality, it is the greater relative weighting of countries like Brazil and Mexico that distorts the growth figure on the regional level. In the economic relations between Latin America, the United States, and Western Europe, it is exactly countries like Brazil, Mexico, and Venezuela that stand out most and which are of the greater importance to the more advanced countries [Muñoz 1979, 84].

Finally, the prospects for the evolution of a world economy are not encouraging, and in spite of the undoubted strength of the arguments of the defenders of the theory of "mutual interests" regarding the salvation of "almost everybody" on the long term in an "adjusted" order, the "defensive" positions are those that prevail at present.

The developed world has a notorious incapacity either to find concrete answers to its internal challenges, or to assimilate and understand the changes that are happening in the heart of the Third World. The interests of Western Europe in Latin America are clear, but in spite of them, Europe (and the industrialized world in general) does not seem to understand clearly what their external interests are.

Latin America—and especially the major countries of the region—can play a fundamental role in the process of reformulating the existing order. In addition, the increasing importance of countries like Brazil, Mexico, Venezuela, and Argentina in the international system endangers the stability of any adjustment that is effected without contemplating their basic demands and interests.

Latin America is still prepared to enter the current system without questioning its basic laws. However, for this to happen the developed countries must be prepared to adopt less defensive internal attitudes to international cooperation and to accept the incrementalist demands brought up by Latin America in the North–South negotiations. If Western Europe (and the North) reacts with ambiguous and dilatory answers, however, Latin America—in spite of the process of growing differentiation of the Southern Bloc mentioned above— could lean toward a more radicalized attitude; that is, toward strengthening its ties with the rest of the Third World.

It would seem evident, therefore, that the relations between Western Europe and Latin America can only improve to any substantial degree with the adoption of measures agreed on by both sides which allow for the internal recovery of the developed countries and at the same time for the reformulation of the rules of the game of current international economic order. Traditional recipes created for traditional situations will only serve to produce partial and temporary palliatives. Wionczek (1981, 152) puts it well.

> It is difficult to conceive that Latin America or any other under-developed continent, or all of them together, can provide the necessary stimulus for the economic recovery of the industrialized countries, carrying all the burden of such recovery, supposing this should happen. On the contrary, the internal economic recovery of the industrialized world, accompanied by progress in negotiations on the principal questions between the North and the South, offers much wider possibilities for cooperation between Latin America—rich in potential resources and markets—and the European Community.

It is precisely in the field of North–South negotiations that Europe can serve as a liaison to achieve a better understanding with the United States, because it shares a series of demands with the developing nations that enable it to appreciate better some of the South's positions. As Manfred Nitsch (1980, 5) so well observes, "it is at the European level that understanding can be achieved vis-à-vis the demands of the Third World for control of the transnational corporations in order to increase their negotiating position and to effectively control their own economies."

The job of constructing a more equitable international order that will, without doubt, contribute toward recreating and consolidating a system of shared values is, I believe, an effort worth making. I also believe, unfortunately, that the current trends in the relationship between Western Europe and Latin America, as well as those between Latin America and the United States, are not very promising, at least for this decade.

NOTES

1. "Corriere Della Sera" Milan, 25 September 1965, 1, quoted in Goldhamer (1972), 57–58.

2. *Le Monde Diplomatique* (June 1980), 21–22.

3. Since a large quantity of the ACP countries are within the "European zone of influence," the Lome I and II Conventions should be seen from a political perspective. After the signing of Lome II, spokesmen for the community declared: "Beyond the obligations, the progress, and the innovations the new regulations will contain, the essential part continues to be the confirmation of a political option and of a type of interregional relations of a group of industrialized countries—Europe— and a group of developing countries—ACP." "El nuevo convenio de los paises de Ultramar, Comunidad Europea," *Boletín mensual* (September–October 1979), 4, cited by Vacchino (1981), 128.

4. Armaments should be included in manufactured products; Britain, France, and West Germany supplied over one-half of the major weapons imported by Latin America during the 1970s. Latin America is West Germany's largest market, accounting for about 75 percent of its sales of major weapons during the 1970s. See Latin American Bureau (1981), 7–8.

5. The degree of the EEC's overall dependence on its supplies of raw materials is 75 percent, compared with 90 percent for Japan and only 15 percent for the United States. In regard to oil, it is estimated that the minimum Latin American reserves come to 490 billion barrels and the maximum to 1,225 billion. European interests in Latin America will increase to the extent that the crisis in the Middle East worsens.

6. The endeavors to extend the influence of European Social Democracy in Latin America began in April 1976 at a meeting of Western European and Latin American political leaders, effected in Caracas. At the meeting there was discussion about the new possibilities that were opening in the region, and bases were set out for reinforcing contacts with the Latin American political forces favorable to this trend. Christian Democracy has assumed a more conservative attitude, closer to that of the United States. Regarding the action of Social Democracy in the region, see Petras (1980).

7. Regarding the different alternatives of world order, see Perez Llana (1979).

8. With regard to the developing countries, Europe's interests are concentrated in the first place on the ACP countries and on the Mediterranean Basin, although it will have to open new fronts during the 1980s. A detailed analysis of the relations between the EEC and the first signers of Lome II shows us that, beyond the particular agreements granted, the structure of the ties between both regions is maintained within the classic "colonial" patterns. The EEC imports primary products from the ACP countries and provides them with manufactured products. Furthermore, since 1978 the EEC trade balance has been slightly in surplus, to the detriment of ACP countries to the extent of over 900 million units of account; and the participation of ACP countries in the EEC imports dropped from 7.4 to 6.8 percent of the EEC's total imports. It should also be noted that only one African country, Nigeria, has an important quota of EEC imports and exports, which shows a deep imbalance in the exchange of trade with the other countries. In 1977, 50 percent of EEC imports from the ACP countries came from three of them: Nigeria (oil) 28 percent, Ivory Coast 12 percent, Zaire 10 percent, while 50 percent of EEC exports to these countries went to three of them: Nigeria 37 percent, Liberia 7 percent, and Ivory Coast 6 percent. Primary products are still the essential part of European imports from ACP countries: 95 percent in 1976. On the relations between Europe and ACP countries, see Dubois and Ramadier (1980), 27.

9. In recent years, the value of all Latin American exports has been distributed as follows: nearly two-thirds to the developed countries, somewhat under 20 percent to Latin American countries, slightly over 10 percent to socialist countries, and 5 percent to other developing areas.

REFERENCES

CEPAL. "América Latina y la Nueva Estrategia Internacional del Desarrollo, Enunciación de Metas y Objetivos." CEPAL Document L. 210 (December 1979a).

———. "Como puede Europa Occidental contribuir al logro de las metas de desarrollo de América Latina?" CEPAL Document R. 201 (October 1979b).

———. "The Economic Relations of Latin America with Europe." CEPAL Document, E/CEPAL/G. 1116 (October 1980).

Comeliau, Christian. "North South Relations—Some Recent Views." Paper presented at Second International Conference on Latin America and the World Economy, OAS, Torcuato di Tella Institute, Buenos Aires, 26–29 August 1980.

Dubois, Jean Pierre and Paul Ramadier. "Un balance limitado de las relaciones entre la CEE y sus socios del Tercer Mundo." *Le Monde Diplomatique en Español*, 2:18 (June 1980).

Ferrer, Aldo. "Notas para una Teoría de la Independencia." *Comercio Exterior,* 30:12 (December 1980).

Galbraith, John Kenneth. *Clarín* (Buenos Aires), 5 April 1981, 12–13.

Goldhamer, Herbert. *The Foreign Powers in Latin America.* Princeton, NJ: Princeton University Press, 1972.

Instituto Italo-Latino Americano. "Memorandum: Algunas Reflexiones sobre las *relaciones* CEE-América Latina." *Integración Latinoamericana*, 34 (April 1979).

Latin American Bureau (London). "The EEC and Latin America." Seminar Notes, 1981.

Malan, Pedro. "Los Países Latinoamericanos y el Nuevo Orden Economico Internacional." *CEPAL Magazine* (April 1980).

Muñoz, Heraldo. "Las relaciones económicas entre la periféria latinoamericana, Estados Unidos y Europa Occidental." In Gustavo Lagos (ed.), *Las Relaciónes entre América Latina, Estados Unidos y Europa Occidental.* Santiago: Instituto de Estudios Internacionales de la Universidad de Chile, 1979.

Nitsch, Manfred. "Los intereses de los países ricos y el desarrollo del Tercer Mundo: La República Federal de Alemania," paper presented at the International Seminar on the Report of the Brandt Commission, held at Canela, Brazil, August 7-9, 1980.

Perez Llana, Carlos E. "Alternativas de Ordenamiento Mundial." *Mundo Nuevo*, 2:3 (January/March 1979): 38-46.

Petras, James F. "La Social Democracia en América Latina." *Le Monde Diplomatique en Español*, 2:18 (June 1980).

Russell, Roberto and Teresa Carballal. "América Latina. Hacia que Neuvo Orden Economico Internacional?" In Luciano Tomassini and Eduardo Hill (eds.), *América Latina y el Nuevo Orden Economico Internacional.* Santiago: CPU, 1979, 139-64.

———. "El Nuevo Orden Economico Internacional: Tendencias Observables en el Norte y en los Países Mayores de América Latina." *Estudios Internacionales*, 14:53 (January/March 1981).

SELA. "Relaciones entre América Latina y Europa." *Integracion Latinoamericana*, 4 (March 1979): 57-63.

Vacchino, Juan Mario. "América Latina y la Europa Comunitaria." *Comercio Exterior*, 31:2 (February 1981).

Wionczek, Miguel S. "Las relaciones entre la CEE y América Latina en el contexto de una crisis economica global." *Comercio Exterior* (México), 31:2 (February (1981).

5

BRAZIL TURNS TO WESTERN EUROPE: CHANGING PERSPECTIVES

Walder de Góes

The aim of this chapter is to discuss the essence and evolutionary trends of Brazil's foreign policy, underscoring the characteristics of national and international factors and trying to identify their interaction.

The first section studies the diversification of Brazil's dependence on foreign trade, the different answers given by Carter and Geisel to the crisis of U.S. hegemony, and the strategic objectives of Brazil's position before the world. The second section discusses the political, economic, and social situation of Brazil and analyzes the impact of domestic affairs on the country's foreign policy.

The third and last section tries to identify, in a more direct way, the evolutionary trends of Brazil's foreign policy stemming from internal factors linked to the international order.

RECENT ECONOMIC AND POLITICAL TRENDS IN BRAZIL'S FOREIGN POLICY

My thesis in this section of the chapter is threefold. First, the diversification of Brazil's economic relations with other countries took place at the expense of exchange between Brazil and the United States and despite the political aspects of U.S.-Brazilian bilateral relations. It was caused fundamentally by the relative fragmentation of world power associated with the decline in U.S. leadership, the increase in intercapitalistic competition, and the development of Brazil.

Second, the United States and Brazil reacted very differently to the crisis in U.S. hegemony. The Carter administration responded with a defensive policy of nonproliferation and human rights. The Geisel administration, on the contrary, responded with an offensive policy of opening new fronts, which ended in an attempt to obtain nuclear technology from Germany. The confrontation strengthened existing, although latent, anti-American feelings in Brazil. In the South American countries, the trend toward integration and "regional nationalism" was intensified. Third, although Brazil's foreign policy is responding to the need to capture external resources, which are essential to face the current economic crisis, Brazil's internal policy is to give the military control of strategic decisions within a context of detente with respect to authoritarianism, and a strengthening of Brazil as a potential world power. Each of these three points is discussed in turn.

Diversification of Brazil's Economic Relations with Other Countries

Substantial changes have taken place in the last two decades in three different indicators of Brazil's economic relations: foreign trade, foreign investment and reinvestment in the Brazilian economy, and Brazil's foreign debt. Despite the different degree of dependence (and of autonomy) in each of these sectors, they all point to a process of increasing diversification in foreign economic relations.

Trade

The U.S. market share of Brazil's foreign trade has been declining consistently over the last two decades. In 1959, Brazilian exports to the United States accounted for 46.1 percent of the country's total sales[1]—a proportion that had shown no change in trend over the previous six years. In the years between 1959 and 1975, however, the proportion decreased progressively. Although the decrease averaged 1.5 percent per year over the period, it was much sharper over some periods than others. The decreases were sharpest between 1960 and 1961 (4 percentage points), 1963 and 1964 (4 percentage points), 1968 and 1969 (7 percentage points), and 1971 and 1973 (from 26.1 to 18.1 percent). Starting in 1974, the trend stabilized to a substantial degree, with the U.S. share of Brazilian sales only dropping from 18.1 to 17.3 percent by 1980.

The timing of the sharpest declines is important, because they did not bear any systematic relationship with the political climate. For example, after a long period of automatic alignment of Brazilian policy with that of the U.S. State Department (1945–60)—a period that corresponds with the East–West Cold War—the beginning of the decline of U.S. leadership gave Brazil ample space to set the basis for a vigorous policy of independence through the Jânio Quadros administration (1961). In 1962, 1963, and 1964, U.S.–Brazilian relations deteriorated considerably because of the leftist and clearly anti-American orientation of the João Goulart administration. In 1960 and 1961, Brazilian sales to the U.S. market fell drastically, as they did again in 1963 and 1964, when sales also declined sharply.

The next two periods of sharp decline, however, mark the realignment of Brazil's foreign policy with that of the U.S. State Department, in spite of which Brazilian exports to the United States continued to decline. During 1965–69 the Castelo Branco administration's policy led to Brazil's participation in the inter-American forces operating in the Dominican Republic. During 1971–73 the Garrastazu Médici administration's Brazilian–American relations were characterized by orthodox anti-Communism and great emphasis on national security. However, Brazilian sales to the U.S. market declined from 26.1 percent to 23.3 percent, and finally to 18.1 percent.

The total absence of direct or indirect causal bonds between the political and economic aspects of U.S.–Brazilian relations makes it clear that there was a structural transformation in economic exchange patterns between the two countries, which continued in times of political confrontation as well as in times of political agreement.

The flow of Brazilian imports from the U.S. market confirms the conclusions drawn from export data, showing that the replacement of chronic U.S. deficits with chronic Brazilian deficits can also not be attributed to the politics between the two countries. The U.S. share of Brazilian imports decreased from 34.8 percent in 1959 to 17.7 percent in 1980. Between 1959 and 1968 (as well as during the preceding decade), the U.S.–Brazilian balance of trade showed a consistently positive balance for Brazil; during the period 1968–69 it turned consistently negative.

It is interesting to note that while commercial relations between Brazil and the United States were decreasing sharply in the last two decades, Brazilian trade with countries of the European Economic

Community (EEC) was not.[2] In 1959 the EEC shares of total Brazilian imports and exports were 27.4 percent and 24.4 percent, respectively. In 1980 the figures were 27 percent and 15.3 percent. During the 1959–80 period, Brazilian exports to the EEC ranged from a minimum of 26.6 percent to a maximum of 37.4 percent and their imports from the EEC ranged from a minimum of 15.3 percent to a maximum of 32 percent.

The U.S.–Brazilian and EEC–Brazilian experience differed not only in the trends, but also in the effect of political relations on it. Historically, economic relations between Brazil and the United States have always been affected by the political currents between the two countries. Therefore, the structural decline in trade must be interpreted as taking place in spite of the moments of intense activity in bilateral political matters—which were simply not long enough to change the structural trend.

With respect to Western Europe, the situation is reversed. Trade between Brazil and the EEC has been politically encouraged—not, however, for political purposes. Brazil's interest in depoliticizing its foreign economic relations coincides with the position of Western Europe, which does not impose political demands on Latin America.

Foreign Investment, Reinvestment, and Debt

The diversification of Brazilian changes in the structure of foreign investment, reinvestment, and debt in Brazil tell the same basic story as is told by trade. In 1950 the United States and Western Europe had investments or reinvestments in the Brazilian economy amounting to US $103 million each. By December 1980, the United States had US $5.2 billion invested or reinvested in Brazilian capital stock; the analogous figure for Western Europe had risen to US $8.2 billion. Although the lack of reliable statistics on the evolution of Brazil's foreign debt renders comparisons over time difficult, the changes since 1970 are substantial enough to show a clear and similar pattern. In December 1971, 61 percent of Brazil's foreign debt had originated in U.S. financial institutions, versus only 27 percent for the EEC. By December 1980, data on Brazil's foreign debt indicate that 40 percent was payable to U.S. financial institutions, versus 44 percent to financial institutions in EEC countries.

Although the center of gravity with respect to credit and investment sources has shifted, there has been much less general diversification than in the case of trade. Data obtained for December 1980 indicate that countries other than the United States and Europe invested or reinvested a total of only US $3.9 billion in Brazil (with US $1.7 billion coming from Japanese institutions). Similarly, only 16 percent (US $53.8 billion) of Brazil's foreign debt was payable to nations other than the United States and the EEC (also mainly to Japan).

Brazil's Trade Relations with the Third World

Although Brazil's foreign investment and foreign debt are still held largely by the United States and the EEC countries, Brazil has been able to diversify its foreign trade such that Third World countries are now substantially represented. Historically, Brazil's commercial relations were oriented toward Western Europe until World War I, and toward the United States during the period between the wars and until the end of the 1950s. Third World countries played only a marginal role in Brazil's foreign trade. In 1960, for example, Brazilian sales to the Third World represented only 9.6 percent of the country's total exports. That rate increased to 18.1 percent in 1973, 24.1 percent in 1977, and 38.6 percent in 1980. It is important to note that in 1980 15.6 percent of Brazil's exports were destined for LAFTA (Latin American Free Trade Association) countries—only 1.7 percent less than the U.S. share of that market. This accelerated development of Brazil's trade with LAFTA countries is recent. In 1950, Brazilian exports to that market accounted for 7 percent of total sales. In 1963 the figure had increased to 9 percent. In the 13 years after 1950, therefore, there was an increase of only 2 percentage points. In the six years between 1973 and 1980, in contrast, there was an increase of over three times as much (6.6 percentage points). The accelerating trend began during the Geisel administration's economic deceleration, which (helped by the aftermath of the 1973 oil crisis) restrengthened the search for complementarity between the Brazilian economy and those of the LAFTA countries. Geisel's foreign policy gave added stimulus to intracontinental relations, and at the time of confrontation with the United States under Carter (when Brazil sided with Argentina and Chile) served as a factor increasing political unity in the Southern Cone of the continent.

However, from the perspective of evaluating the structural transformation of trade relations between Brazil and Western industrialized countries, the most significant aspects of commercial relations between Brazil and Third World countries transcend quantitative issues and concern the *quality* of exchange. In the past, the Third World (and especially LAFTA) played only a marginal role in Brazil's foreign economic relations. That was the result of the low level of complementarity between the economies of Brazil and those of other Third World countries. The oil crisis and its consequences, such as the ban on imports imposed by developed countries and the economic crises suffered by them, forced economies like Brazil's to make additional efforts to export manufactured goods to less modernized markets. Consequently, trade expanded, and its structure changed. In 1973 only 38 percent of Brazil's exports to the Third World was manufactured goods. In 1978 this share had already increased to 67 percent— with the share held by certain types of manufactured goods even greater. Examples include vehicles and transportation materials (77 percent), electric machines and equipment (45 percent), chemical products (50 percent), and textiles (24 percent).

In addition to becoming an exporter of manufactured goods to the Third World, Brazil has become a seller of services and provider of technology to Third World countries, because the intermediate technologies assimilated by the Brazilian economy are readily adjustable to the low level of technical development of most Third World countries. The following construction projects are being implemented by Brazil at a total cost of US $3.6 billion: dams and hydroelectric plants (Paraguay, Uruguay, Venezuela, Ecuador, Algiers, and Peru), ports (Uruguay), highways (Mauritania and Saudi Arabia), railways (Iraq), paving and leveling (Nigeria), popular facilities (Algiers), sanitation works (Costa Rica), telecommunications (Nigeria), agriculture and animal husbandry (Nigeria, Ivory Coast, and Costa Rica), and training of technical personnel (Nigeria).

Although the qualitative change in Brazil's foreign trade is best epitomized by its exports to the Third World, it in fact characterizes the entire export capacity of the country. Back in 1970, primary products accounted for 75.1 percent of total sales abroad. That rate had decreased to 42 percent by 1980. Over the same period, the share of industrialized products increased from 24 percent to 56.5 percent.

Although this qualitative change in the structure of Brazil's foreign trade obviously reflects important changes in the entire international system, it occurred in the specific context of Brazil mainly because of special transformations in the Brazilian productive system. In other words, the changes that occurred redefined the different forms of economic complementarity between Brazil and other countries. On the one hand, because of the modernization of Brazil's productive system to a higher degree than that attained in other Third World countries, the Brazilian economy became complementary to the economies of *these countries*. On the other hand, the evolution of the Brazilian productive system from its emphasis on primary products to emphasis on industrialized products took place at a faster pace than the evolution of the developed economies from the industrial stage to the tertiary or postindustrial stage. Thus, the Brazilian economy became less complementary to those of the affluent countries and more complementary to those of the Third World—an explanation that is supported by its general pattern of international commercial transactions—with the single exception of Western Europe. The reason for this becomes clear when it is remembered that industrial progress has turned Brazil into a country which, despite its (still high) exports of primary and manufactured goods, now imports mainly the modern technology that is essential to increase the autonomy of its economic development and modernization.

The United States has always strongly opposed the transfer of advanced technology to other countries. The Western European countries, on the contrary, in order to become more competitive in relation to the United States, have shown great flexibility. It is within this context that the loss of complementarity between the economies of Brazil and the industrialized countries was reflected more in Brazil's economic relations with the United States than in its trade with Western Europe. Following the economic recovery after World War II, Western Europe was able to move more freely in the international scene, precisely when its economic strengthening stemming from the decline in U.S. leadership enabled it to enter markets formerly dominated by the United States, such as Brazil. The end of the Cold War, the strengthening of the Federal Republic of Germany and Japan, persistent deficits in the U.S. balance of payments in the 1970s, reorganization of the Arab world, cartelization of world oil supplies, loss of the U.S. monopoly in new technology (especially in nuclear technology), decolonization of Africa, and the Vietnam War all combined to eradicate the U.S. position of total dominance over Latin America. The entire region, and Brazil in particular, became an area of relatively decentralized power, which allowed increased capitalistic competition in the political and economic environment of Latin America. Thus, the new international participation of Brazil, which reflects an internal economic transformation, can only be understood in the context of the relative fragmentation of world power, which increased competition among the affluent countries for goods which are scarce within their own boundaries and which are the most important patrimony of the Third World.

Nuclear Proliferation and Human Rights

The disagreement in nuclear policy between Brazil and the United States dates back to 1951, the time of the Cold War and of United States domination of Brazilian policy. In January 1951, President Eurico Gaspar Dutra established the National Research Council,[3] after passage of a law that banned exports of thorium, uranium, and any compound minerals, except from government to government and "after having heard from the appropriate agencies." The "appropriate agencies," according to the law proper, were the National Research Council and the National Security Council, which were charged to act in accordance with the "theory of specific compensations"—the basic tenet of which was that Brazil would not sell radioactive minerals to other countries except on the basis of agreements with governments that were willing to transfer to Brazil the necessary technology for the development of nuclear energy. That same year, Admiral Alvaro Alberto da Mota e Silva, president of the National Research Council, began to develop Brazil's National Atomic Energy Program. The theory of specific compensation was, of course, contrary to the spirit of the MacMahon Act, adopted by the United States during the Truman administration, which turned U.S. nuclear energy activities into a government monopoly, imposed the death penalty for violation of nuclear secrets, and banned exports of nuclear technology.

At the time these events were taking place, in all other respects—politically, economically, militarily, and culturally—Brazil followed the lead of the United States. It fell to the government of Getúlio Vargas (1951–54), which regained power only a few days after passage of the Dutra Act establishing the Brazilian National Research Council, to deal with the conflict created by Brazilian confidence in U.S. leadership, on the one hand, and the resistance of the United States under the MacMahon Act on the other hand, to transfer the knowledge necessary for the implementation of Brazil's National Atomic Energy Program. This tension, within a policy of detente, is generally agreed to have been the nucleus of the controversies that were to give a nationalistic tone to the Vargas administration. The issue opened in

1951 would permeate the military and have deep civilian implications—which were already manifest with respect to the government's monopoly on oil and would extend to the internal debate on the exploration of other natural resources, to the military agreements signed with the United States, and to the Korean War.

The confrontation came over the Brazilian interest in gaining nuclear technology and the U.S. determination to acquire radioactive minerals from Brazil. Convinced that the MacMahon Act was a definitive obstacle to U.S. scientific aid, the president of the Brazilian National Research Council, with President Vargas's personal authorization, traveled to Germany in 1952. Although Germany was still under Allied occupation, he established contact with German physicists, among them Otto Hahn, and contracted for the manufacture and shipment to Brazil of three ultracentrifuges, destined for experimental production of nuclear fuel from thorium, abundant in Brazil. At the time of this mission, Germany was governed by Harvey Smith, an English brigadier general. Smith, by request from U.S. High Commissioner James Conant, had the equipment confiscated and prevented its export to Brazil—even though at the same time the United States was expressing its intention to obtain Brazilian radioactive minerals, especially monazite (the main source of thorium), found principally in Brazil and India. Since Brazil refused to export this mineral, in compliance with the theory of "specific compensations," the U.S. State Department, in a secret letter sent to the Brazilian Ministry of Foreign Relations, threatened to impose economic sanctions and gave Brazil the choice of shipping 15,000 tons of monazite or sending troops to Korea. Faced with this situation, the government decided to violate the regulation of "specific compensations" established by the National Research Council and make the shipments of monazite.[4]

The issue of the ultracentrifuges and its corollaries is useful as a case model to explain the nature of Brazilian dependence on the United States during the Cold War, which eventually promoted the growth of latent anti-American feelings in Brazil. This, and other cases revealing U.S. hegemony after 1960, can be interpreted as part of a U.S. policy of systematic resistance to the development of Brazil, stemming from the assumption of colonial dependence whose elimination, in the opinion of successive generations of Brazilian elites, was a prerequisite to internal development. Theories such as those formulated by the ISEB (Instituto Superior de Estudos Brasileiros,

1955–64) are based precisely on this idea of cultural decolonization, and represent currents of thought prevalent to varying degrees in Brazilian governments clearly dedicated to the establishment of national plans (as was the case during the administrations of Juscelino Kubitschek, Jânio Quadros, and Ernesto Geisel). At the same time however, anti-Communism has become a feature of the political culture of Brazil and a connective tissue of the governing agreements, giving shape and content to the integration of Brazil into the Western system. Thus, the anti-Americanism of the elites tends to collide with the need to recognize that the economic, political, and military leadership of the United States is a guarantee of the Brazilian invulnerability to communist expansion.

For this reason and because there is no resolution of such a contradiction, an independent foreign policy (known as "pragmatism") was partially implemented during the Kubitschek administration and stressed by Presidents Quadros and Geisel. Pragmatism translates into an attempt to erase the boundary line between ideological commitments and national interests to be defended in the arena of international relations. Thus, the pro-Cuba and pro-Eastern Europe policy of Quadros originated from the need to open new commercial avenues under the allegation of a need to gain new markets,[5] as did the Geisel administration's recognition of the pro-Soviet government of the Popular Movement for Angolan Liberation and establishment of diplomatic relations with Communist China, after breaking them with Formosa. Pragmatism is thus an attempt to make concrete national interests viable through expansion and diversification of economic relations with other countries, without discussing or questioning issues of ideological alignment in foreign policy, which respond to Brazil's wishes of integration to the Western system and which are implicit in the formulation and implementation of Brazil's foreign policy.

In this sense, pragmatism is a conceptual solution aimed at detaching a strongly anti-Communist national policy from an ideologically flexible foreign policy. The history of the Brazilian administrations after the 1964 military intervention shows how this ideological flexibility in foreign policy has fluctuated, depending on the specifics of the internal state of affairs in Brazil.

Under the administration of Castelo Branco, who succeeded a president overthrown with U.S. cooperation (which tempered anti-American feelings for a while), Brazil's foreign policy was oriented toward automatic alignment with the United States. During the Garrastazu Médici administration, the high rates of economic development and social mobility also allowed foreign policy committed to anti-Communism, in the sense that no ideological concessions were required in order to acquire foreign goods. The Geiscl administration, however, immersed in the crisis following the sudden increase in oil prices that inhibited international trade, formulated a foreign policy free of ideological blockades. It increased trade with Eastern Europe, recognized Peking after breaking relations with Formosa, entered Africa through Angola and Mozambique, and expanded relations with Western industrialized nations by capitalizing on the contradictions between Western Europe and the United States. The Figueiredo administration, immersed in an even more serious economic crisis, continues and even strengthens the foreign policy of the Geisel administration by trying to establish better economic relations with other Third World countries.

The events of the last three administrations give authenticity to the story according to which, under President Médici, Brazil was the smallest of the rich countries (and for that reason it ignored the Third World); under President Geisel, it was the largest of the poor countries (and therefore it tried to join the Third World); and under President Figueiredo, it is an underdeveloped country (and therefore it thoroughly understands the legacy of the Third World).

The Carter administration's mistake was to rely too simplistically on the assumptions that Latin America was the most unarmed region of the world, of little strategic and political importance to the United States, and could therefore be used as a low-cost testing area for its policy of nuclear nonproliferation, human rights, and reduction of international transfer of armaments (Hirst 1980). The strategic and political assumptions were not wrong. In reality, the political and strategic factors of Latin America mean little to the United States. In addition, the regional armed forces are concerned with issues of internal security and have become a weak auxiliary instrument of U.S. military power. In recent years, in fact, the only reason that the United States has had to attach any value to Latin America was the implantation of Communism in Cuba, which led it to take additional care in Central America and the Caribbean. The United States has only had a Latin American policy in times of acute localized tensions. The mistake was the conclusion drawn from these assumptions.

Why did the test fail in matters of human rights, nuclear nonproliferation, and transfer of armaments? In the case of Brazil the reasons are clear, regardless of matters pertaining to internal issues of

U.S. policy and to the relations of the United States with Western Europe. The testing action undertaken in Brazil was launched when the country, under adverse economic conditions, was implementing its independent foreign policy at a point in its history when the crisis of U.S. international leadership coincided with the relative autonomy of Brazil. Gradually slackened through time, U.S.–Brazilian relations were not a relevant consideration for the Brazilian armed forces. Brazilian foreign trade, now widely diversified, gave the country a sense of independence never experienced before. Furthermore, the economic relations between the two countries—as far as trade, investments by firms, and credit were concerned—did not constitute an arsenal of the Carter administration. Having passed the stage of government-to-government aid, relations between the United States and Brazil were now conducted on the basis of equality in political, strategic, and economic affairs. From an economic standpoint, the Carter administration had only one weapon—the imposition of retaliatory measures under the Trade Act. But the implementation of such measures in any concrete way meant internal difficulties for the United States and in any case would not significantly affect an economy that now imported only 17.3 percent of its goods from the U.S. market.

Carter's objectives were never attained because Brazil had become a relatively diversified power. The "big stick" could not be backed up by a U.S. policy able to qualitatively change, expand, or consolidate the bonds of loyalty between Brazil and the United States. The decline of United States hegemony and the fragmentation of world power, followed by East–West detente and the new status of Brazil, and the anti-American feelings of the Brazilian elite (especially in the military) gave the Geisel administration enough strength to oppose, with support from West Germany, the pressure exerted by the Carter administration in matters of nuclear nonproliferation. Furthermore, the pressures of the Carter administration coincided with a special time in Brazil's internal policy. The Geisel administration was trying to strengthen the weakened basis of legitimacy of the Brazilian military regime with examples of independence of its internal policy at a time when anti-Communism did not provide enough justification for military protection and when the commitments to democracy and economic development could not be completely rescued. Thus, the U.S. pressure in matters of nonproliferation stirred anti-American feelings and turned the foreign policy of resistance into a factor of legitimacy for a regime in crisis.[6]

Nuclear nonproliferation failed because of its own base and the environment in which it was implemented. On the one hand, this policy did not seem to be an expression of concern for world peace but a reflection of U.S. strategic and economic interests. As pointed out by Hirst (1980):

> [T]he Brazilian nuclear program became a point of debate and concern in the U.S. not at the moment of its formulation or at the beginning of its implementation, but at the moment when its continuity implied breaking the sales monopoly of U.S. industries. . . . This claim was intended to curb reductions in exports of the U.S. nuclear industry, which in 1974–75 had experienced a decrease from 70 percent to 40 percent in its share of the international market. This decrease reached an extremely lucrative area of foreign trade and affected the interests of a large and powerful industrial sector. In 1974, income from this sector reached US $1.5 billion and it is foreseen that by 1985 it will reach US $3 billion.

On the other hand, the U.S. nonproliferation policy made its appearance at a time when U.S. hegemony was experiencing its sharpest decline, and when the situation characterized by the world strengthening of Western European capitalism and diversification of Brazilian trade was being defined.

The human rights policy failed for the same reasons; it was understood and judged in Brazil, even by the liberal nuclei of the political system, as an instrument for imposition of the nuclear nonproliferation policy. The inconsistency of this human rights policy was even more visible when it was applied to some countries and not to others where U.S. economic and/or strategic interests were of utmost importance. Furthermore, the breaking of military agreements in 1976 by Brazil's initiative rendered U.S. pressure completely useless. Thus, as pointed out by Soares de Lima and Hirst (1980), "the failure of the U.S. government in the application of pressure to implement its policies clearly explained the crisis of U.S. dominance in the continent." It should be pointed out in this connection that the pressure exerted by the Carter administration strengthened the Brazilian military regime by exacerbating existing anti-American feelings, especially among the armed forces, reinforced unity in the South American countries, and gave a new momentum to Brazil's diversification. It is important to note that, in this sense, the establishment of a new political understanding in South America opened the way for the Brazilian–Argentine agreement for the construction of the Itaipú hydroelectric plant and facilitated the development of intrazonal trade; Brazilian exports to LAFTA increased from 9 percent in 1973 to 15.6 percent in 1980, while the growth observed during 1960–73 was only 2 percentage points. At the same time, a greater effort was made in economic diplomacy to explore possibilities of cooperation with Africa, Asia, and Eastern Europe, and to give priority to trade with EEC countries, over trade with the United States.

Brazil's Foreign Policy

Grabendorff's thorough study of Brazil's foreign policy (1979) observes that Brazil's entry to international circles represents an intermediate step between the First World and Third World. Such a representation illustrates both its present economic situation and its efforts to take advantage of the ambiguity created by the fact that Brazil is not a rich country but not a poor one either. Its practical viability emerges from the relative fragmentation of world power, the decline of U.S. dominance, and the increase in intercapitalistic competition associated with the development of Brazil and the diversification of its foreign dependence. Seen in this light, the pragmatic tactics of changing loyalties in Brazil's foreign policy appears as an instrument to obtain modern technology from European industrialized countries, and to establish trade relations with the Third World without detrimental effects to Brazil's financial relations with the Western financial system.

This rationale for Brazil's foreign policy explains that Brazil and the United States have different concepts of the Western world.[7] The United States considers the Third World—Latin America included—as an appendage of countries with little international responsibility, archaic political systems, and a historical experience almost incompatible with U.S. patterns. This judgment, which reflects a certain nostalgia for the big-stick policy, justifies the authoritarian position of the United States in intervening in internal affairs of Third World countries and trying to control their fate. Western Europe, in contrast, understands the particular aspects of the political systems in the

Third World and relates to these countries on a more equal basis—as demonstrated in the case of Brazilian relations with Western European nations by the frequency and nature of the dialogue between their elites, including government authorities, and by the better access that Brazil has to modern European technology. Under these circumstances, Brazil sees no reason to give first priority to its relations with the United States and is encouraged to have closer economic and political relations with Western European countries.

Such a policy allows Brazil to show its understanding that the West—even though it comprises developed, underdeveloped, and developing countries—is an indivisible entity with its own ideological and cultural identification. By adopting a loyal attitude to these commitments, Brazil can show lack of discrimination against countries or blocs within the Western system, while still pursuing the processes of economic and political exchange in accordance with tradeoffs, studied case by case. It is in this way that the dynamic flux of Brazilian foreign policy shows itself in the search for modernization of the domestic productive structure on the basis of Western European technology and in increasing its foreign trade by selling increasingly sophisticated goods and services to the less developed countries of the West, which are not absorbed into the markets of the industrialized countries.

At the same time, this position is in line with the objective of legitimizing the country's political system in international circles, emphasizing that the system's recent progress is not based on classic democratic models but on the establishment of a regime of limited popular participation. Based on these assumptions, it is understood that the political and economic systems of Brazil, even in the case of advantageous relations with the United States, exhibit a trend to reach a stable and satisfactory level of complementarity with the developed countries of Western Europe and to an affinity with the less developed countries of the Western system.

Grabendorff's analysis, although contrary to Brazil's official version, offers a consistent explanation of Brazil's foreign policy. It should be added that a "pendular" policy such as he describes does not cause a dichotomy, because it works in a continuum of hierarchies and preferences within the West. It gives first priority to underdeveloped and developing countries, second to developed European countries, and third to the United States. Such a hierarchy reflects interest in economic exchange, but it also reflects political preferences destined to legitimize the Brazilian regime internationally. And in internal affairs, the pendular policy is bound to give the military the necessary control, because without it, Brazil will not be able to ensure that it is perceived as a potential world power.

An argument of Brazilian diplomacy which originated in military circles should be remembered here: that Brazil does not need to have a totally democratic regime to be a harmonious part of the Western system. The West is not considered as an aggregate of countries with uniform political systems or in relation to the freedom of its citizens or the decision-making process of its governments. On the contrary, different countries have different political systems.

In the case of Brazil, the lack of pluralism in the political system is attributed to specific historical conditions and justified by the need to defend itself against internal and foreign enemies and to give continuity to policies aimed at the transformation of the country into a world power through technological revolution. Because the Western European countries have shown flexibility in the transfer of technology and have not demanded an extensive democratization of Brazil's political system, they appear to be better partners than the United States.

The Third World became the first priority in foreign policy because it has political systems similar to the Brazilian system and because it is a buyer of manufactured goods and services. In an attitude quite different from that exhibited by both Western Europe and the Third World, the United States has been strict in transfers of technology, has made unbearable political demands, and has closed its market to modern Brazilian production. Furthermore, the Brazilian military are convinced that Carter's policy of human rights, which called for the democratization of the Brazilian regime, tried to create a climate of freedom in Brazil to facilitate acceptance of United States influence and to guarantee the success of the nuclear nonproliferation policy.

This description of the logic that serves to orient Brazil's foreign policy validates another observation made by Grabendorff: that Brazil's foreign policy seems to be conditioned by the impression that the country is exposed to a war situation on two fronts. The first front is an undeclared war between the North and the South. The second is a civil war represented by the fact that the chaotic forces within the society itself are trying to eliminate the "forces of law enforcement," as the military are known, which represent the best organized factions of the dominant elite. The first aspect of Grabendorff's observation has already been discussed. With respect to the second, in general, Brazil's foreign policy is always to legitimize the military regime existing in the country. This phenomenon was evident during the last visit of Chancellor Helmut Schmidt to Brazil in April 1979, for example. As I pointed out at that time (Góes 1979):

> At present, we only have evidence wrapped in shadows but in the future it may be possible to prove this hypothesis: by giving unprecedented importance to the relations of Brazil with the Federal Republic of Germany, especially through an agreement on nuclear technology between the two countries, Geisel launched a foreign policy strategy which is closely linked to national policy objectives. . . . Geisel's policy toward Germany will have originated in clear reasoning. First of all, a priority partnership with the U.S. was not very profitable. The Americans took advantage of Brazil's dependence to gain in commercial relations and to make transfer of technology increasingly difficult. It would then be necessary for Brazil to diversify its foreign relations, by making a daring entry to the space opened by the contradictions of the Western world. In the second place, the excessive degree of dependence of Brazil on the U.S. was politically eroding the Brazilian regime, which could be accused of installing a military autocracy to defend U.S. interests. At a moment of great political isolationism of the regime, it would be necessary to introduce a new factor for legitimation. The answer was easy: anti-Americanism would be that factor. There would be two goals: diversification of foreign relations to increase commercial and technological gains, undertaken in a way which would allow legitimation of a regime which had lost its old foundation and needed new oxygen. . . . The diversification of foreign relations and the calculated assembly of an anti-American mechanism would need a strong object or symbol. The nuclear agreement between Brazil and Germany was the great discovery. It fully illustrated the greater European flexibility in the transfer of technology and, what is most important for this analysis, it would offer the military and the anti-American feelings a formal basis for cohesion, giving body to the project of turning Brazil into a world power. It was very simple: if the goals developed by the military on the basis of the doctrine learned at the Escola Superior de Guerra were met, and if the military were given an instrument to strengthen their institution and sufficient authority to enforce their policy, they would not have a thing to claim from the Presi-

dent. Under these circumstances, Geisel considered Germany a very important partner. Germany became the second most important partner from an economic standpoint, in trade and investment matters, and the agreement turned it into an ally that would allow Brazil to have an internal policy which was simultaneously anti-Communist and anti-American. That is, without knowing it, Schmidt was for Geisel a valuable ally in foreign and domestic policy matters.

DOMESTIC AND FOREIGN POLICY: CHANGING PATTERNS

Political Readjustment of the Armed Forces

The policy of domestic detente initiated by the Geisel administration is marked by a paradox: it is based on the most authoritarian leadership of the armed forces since 1964. Today's generals (the high hierarchy) are the colonels who, in 1964, were in charge of police and military investigations and took the place of the police in fighting subversion. Their vision of the world is faithful to this past, and by virtue of their status in the military, if not by class background, they constitute a segment of the economic and political elite. The intermediate hierarchy (from lieutenant to colonel), however, constitutes a middle class segment. Both segments are united under common values, to the extent that the common ideology of the group—anti-Communism, widespread nationalism, commitment to the overriding importance of national security, and awareness of the need to defend the interests of the group—results in homogeneity, and the principles of hierarchy and discipline reinforce the encouragement given to cohesion. However, the two segments have divergent connections with their social counterparts outside the military. Thus, both segments live the dialectics of dual loyalty. External connections corrode the functional nature of the values, but the culture of the group leads to internal cohesion.

This equilibrium is only disrupted in times of acute social tension, when the corrosive impact of external connections of the two segments is greater than the force of the elements that serve as a basis for internal cohesion. Even in these cases, the control system available to the high hierarchy (the policy of wages and tradeoffs and the application of disciplinary rules), and their links to the economic and

political elite, are generally sufficient to neutralize the internal differentiation. In the present crisis, there are no major contradictions between the military hierarchy and the economic and political elite, and
for this reason the external connection between the two elite groups
does not disturb the political role of the armed forces.

The political detente in process is a strategy of limited conservation of power, with the aim of establishing alliances that will result in a
new political design based on the redistribution of regional segments
of government but the preservation of existing controls on the federal
decision-making process. To that extent, it is not the direct result of
bottom-to-top pressures, but an act of political engineering that reflects the rationality of the state, in its bureaucratic–civilian and
bureaucratic–military expressions and in its connections with the political and economic elite.[8]

At this point, however, an explanation is needed of the role of
the middle classes, which constitute an essential point of reference.
The middle classes and their electorates have a pendular ideology,
from a tactical standpoint. Even though they are intrinsically conservative and authoritarian, their behavior may favor democratic guidelines, as depending on their objective conditions of social existence
they meet or repel the demands of dissident elites. Regardless of the
tactical nature of many of their demands for democracy, however, the
Brazilian middle classes have a certain democratic genuineness in
their approval/rejection of the demands of the elite. The deprivation
of freedom, for example, may unleash demands for democracy, even
when their material and specific needs are met. In 1964, for example,
the middle classes supported military intervention because of the
threat implicit in Goulart's reformism. After 1964, deprived of freedom by excessive authoritarianism, the middle classes withdrew their
support for the political system based on the ostensive leadership of
the armed forces, as was evidenced in subsequent electoral confrontations.

The long period of military authoritarianism has corroded the
political authority of the armed forces. The economic crisis and its
social implications have reduced still more their government's basis of
support. Furthermore, the economic development occurring after
1964 increased the size of the middle classes, causing at the same time
more frustration and unhappiness when specific interests and demands for freedom were not met. This situation reached its peak in
1973, a time when the political demands of tactical inspiration and

democratic genuineness came together to exert more pressure on the government than it was able to deal with within the framework of authoritarianism. Thus, today the Brazilian middle classes, in tacit alliance with the elites, value the perception that military intervention in 1964 did not keep the commitment of promoting economic and social development and ensuring democratic stability. Consequently, the assumptions that legitimized ostensive military intervention in the public sector have lost their validity. The entire political history of Brazil does not register even one case of illegitimate military intervention—that is, intervention without the support of the electorates that bring the middle classes and the elite together.

Conventional political analysis shows that, because of their class origin, the officialdom of the armed forces tends to duplicate the ideology of the middle classes. On this argument we would expect military ideology to be democratic at the present time in history. As we have pointed out, however, this conclusion runs into several obstacles. The democratic genuineness that is one of the characteristics of the ideology of the middle classes is not easily adapted to military ideology. The closed nature of the group and its particular set of values separate the military from their class origin. They have a type of ideology of differentiation or substitution based on the fact that many of their interests are met through exclusive demands. Furthermore, at present the military are afraid that democracy may restore the process of criticism of the past, which would be contrary to their immediate interests. On the other hand, however, their essential identity, as with the civilian middle class, is in the field of economic interests and guarantees of self-growth.

What will happen? On the one hand, the ideology of the armed forces makes them appear as a uniformly authoritarian body; on the other, the linkages of class establish a difference between the high hierarchy and intermediate officialdom. The first operates in between its particular ideology and the linkages with the political and economic elite and is therefore more authoritarian. The latter, relatively more influenced by its class origin, is less authoritarian. Thus, there will be some latent opposition between the top and bottom of officialdom of the armed forces with respect to political detente.

How, then, is unity to be achieved? In the first place, through a generous wage policy. Recent increases in military salaries have been higher than increases in civilian salaries. In the second place, through a high turnover of personnel. The new legislation developed by the government of Castelo Branco and still in effect calls for constant staff renewal, making insurrection very difficult. In the third place, through depolitization of the military bases, using the previously mentioned instruments, and applying inflexible disciplinary rules. In the fourth place, through the controlled administration of detente itself, which is gradual and slow, to avoid the criticism of the past. At the end, the top and bottom of the armed forces join in the awareness that unity is essential to their interests, and that these interests will not be preserved if the political and moral assumptions that fostered intervention in 1964 and maintained it for a long time are declared valueless.

So, the armed forces are investing in political detente, but under the strict control of their high hierarchy, hoping that the technocratic bureaucracy of the government will give a new boost to the economy at the end of a time of sacrifices and that the political system will be rearticulated and successfully adapted. In the future, the redistribution of regional segments of government and the effort made to meet the needs of the middle classes will reduce tensions and protect the federal political arena, where the military will continue to act as judges of national affairs, even if they share this task with partisan forces presently operating outside the government.

Economic and Social Tensions and Management of the Political Model

Political action stemming from the worsening of social problems in Brazil is a weapon of the middle classes. At all times in history when the middle classes were upset, there were *coups d'état* or electoral victories of the opposition. Recently, because of the uncontrolled growth of the population in the social periphery, indications of a slow, widespread, disorganized, but real civil war have been detected in Brazil, with increased violence in the large urban centers the most typical symptom.

In 1980, the rules of economic policy adopted by the government forced the transfer of resources from high-income classes to middle classes. This strengthened the middle classes and gave them the capacity to absorb future reductions in living standards. The 1981 wage policy then followed, based on full salary adjustments for low income classes and partial adjustments for middle and high income classes, graduated to transfer income from the middle classes down to the social periphery. Here we have an example of the way in which the state—which in the case of Brazil is also the moderator of social relations—goes against the demands of its main allies in order to save the existing political and economic model.

In Brazil, social peace demands continuously open channels of mobility. Under ideal conditions, the level of mobility should be able to cause population changes from the low middle class to the middle middle class and from this to the upper middle class. Even in the worst of cases, the low middle class should be able to accommodate a continuous share of the upper part of the social periphery. The preservation of this mobility channel between these two parts—from the upper strata of the social periphery to the lower strata of the middle class—is an essential part of the integrity of the social structure of Brazil.

Closing the doors leading to the middle classes would cause frictions that could accelerate the pace of the slowly-advancing civil war unleashed by the periphery of the social system. Up to now, the absorption has taken place with a reasonable degree of success, through processes of vertical social mobility activated by the industrial growth of the past decades. The industrial deceleration imposed by the new economic hardships has reduced the rate of mobility and worsened the pressure of the periphery in relation to the space occupied by the middle classes—a situation that gave origin to the wage policy of 1981. However, since decapitalization of the middle class cannot exceed the limits beyond which it becomes proletarian, the wage policy can only be a stop-gap measure. It will be modified, for the sake of the middle class, without detriment to the low-income classes, either through the use of private resources made available by improved economic performance or through the use of social resources because of higher inflation.[9]

The present time, therefore, may be a period of transition to a situation of better balance—if social mobility is again increased for the sake of the middle class and for the upper strata of the social periphery; or it may lead to even more disturbances and social and political disorganization—if such mobility cannot be restored in a reasonable length of time. In either case, we are at an intermediate point between a high and a low rate of redistribution, and a high and a low rate of democracy. Any pressure exerted at a time of transition, regardless of intensity, is bound to affect the balance of the economic, social, and political sectors. The relative military restraint, in the terms previously explained, will only be maintained, for instance, through a proper balance of economic redistribution and political democracy—a balance that demands readoption of social mobility in the terms just described.

These are, in general, the circumstances leading the government to ambivalence in a process of political detente that has patterns of authoritarian behavior. In the same way that the strict application of discriminatory rules reduces political actions of the young officialdom, the implementation of the National Security Act limits the space for unionized leadership, inhibits strikes, and limits the opposition parties. Other measures increase the efficiency of the national security system, such as the processes of "secret persuasion" used to inhibit personal actions by members of congress and/or political parties. At this time of critical confrontation for the regime, the legal arsenal inherited from authoritarianism still serves to overvalue the governmental majority in congress, especially through a mechanism of passage of laws by expiration of term, frequently utilized to block liberalizing reforms or to activate legislation aimed at reinforcing the system of control. The entrepreneurial system which includes the mass media is limited by economic policy controls, mainly fiscal and monetary, which are very effective in the Brazilian economy, characterized by a high level of dependence on the government. The Catholic Church alone is relatively immune from government control, because it has been structured outside the government. In this case, the government trusts that the deep values of the Church will moderate its impulses of opposition, although it does encourage religious syncretism in the hope of curtailing the action of Catholicism in social action by widening the contradictions in matters of faith. The Church is certainly interested in weakening the government in order to encourage a more just social agreement, but it would not participate in any revolutionary plans.

ALTERNATIVES FOR THE FUTURE

Internal Policy

The arguments I have made in this chapter lead me to conclude that any major setback to political detente is inherently improbable. This implies, in turn, some redistribution of political power by regional segments of government and inclusion of new forces in the federal government. Military arbitration of the political system will be maintained, but liberalized to a moderate degree.

In such a critical economic and social situation—plagued by inflation, unemployment, and high payments of the foreign debt—the plan of the new government can be expected to be based on improving the position of the national middle class, adjusting military nationalism to the expansion of national private capitalism concentrated in the former Popular Party. The widespread military nationalism in Brazil, which is more anti-American than anti-Western European, would allow different combinations. If the present model takes the improbable shape of a "tripod"—national private enterprise is fragile in the eyes of foreign investors and the state—the future model would be designed to strengthen it by increasing the domestic market of goods and services. This does not necessarily imply economic self-sufficiency, but it does demand reduction of dependence on other countries abroad, although on a graduated scale to avoid compromising the foreign capital invested in the country.

The viability of the new model will depend on the freezing of foreign debt service payments or installments for a few years. The resource surplus thus gained would serve to finance the reorganization of the economy in a way strong enough to mobilize the support of the middle class, creating the proper conditions to let it absorb a higher percentage of the low income population without trauma.[10] The temporary freezing of the foreign debt service could be accomplished through Brazilian negotiations with governments of lending countries to sponsor recycling of payments and/or interest through central banks or financial institutions, which often meet under the direction of these governments. Such is the case, for example, with the International Monetary Fund and the World Bank. Brazil could offer, as a counterpart, the assurance of future reactivation of its ability to pay and the availability of reasonable means for operation of foreign capital investments in the new economy based on the new model.

Foreign Policy

Brazil's foreign policy in the near future will depend on a large number of factors, two of which are analyzed here. The first has to do with changes in the Brazilian internal state of affairs in the short and medium terms and their connections with the international situation.

The second refers to results of the economic program and evolution of the foreign policy of the Reagan administration.

It must be emphasized that, in relation to the second factor, the course of U.S. events will affect Brazil's foreign policy not only because of its direct influence on Brazil's behavior, but also because of its impact on the Western system as a whole. Although prediction in this area is fraught with imponderables, it does seem to be clear that the U.S. dream of a restored world is unlikely. The great postwar policies—the organized defense of the North Atlantic (NATO), the Marshall Plan, and the Truman Doctrine, among others—worked exactly because Soviet power had not expanded as much as in modern times, and because U.S. leadership in the Western world was clear and complete. Even without assuming the U.S. intention to restore East–West bipolarity, it is reasonable to conclude that any other type of international coexistence that excludes the basic concept of detente will run into now-powerful regional interests. The best hypothesis seems to be that of a new U.S. foreign policy, which is only a tactical action aimed at indicating, in a moderate way, U.S. conditions for the restoration of detente. In this case, Reagan's policy will alter neither the world order nor Brazil's foreign policy to a significant extent. On the basis of this observation and the arguments discussed in the body of the chapter, I have a prediction for Brazil's foreign policy.

Changes in the political and economic model and their implications for Brazil's national plan will certainly affect Brazil's foreign policy, particularly in light of having to negotiate on the foreign debt service. In the short run, there could be a moderate increase in the degree of dependence of Brazil from lending countries, including some decisions concerning the Brazilian economy imposed from abroad. This would mean an increase in Brazilian subordination to the United States (to a lesser extent) and to Western European countries (to a greater extent). In the medium term, however, Brazil can be expected to recover economically and expand the present model of foreign relations. The strengthening of the middle class can be expected, amidst acute tensions in the international system, as a consequence of the expansion of the domestic market, after economic recovery through the temporary freezing of the foreign debt service—as long as the international negotiations connected with it are made under conditions that do not inhibit the expansion of Brazil's internal market. The economic, political, and social changes derived from this occurrence can then be expected to unleash populist and nationalistic manifestations, anti-American in nature, though moderate, which most certainly will influence foreign policy—probably in the direction of neutral or unimportant political relations between Brazil and the U.S., maintenance of the existing pattern of relations with Western Europe (with the objective of ensuring technological supplies), and expansion of political and commercial relations with the Third World. A foreign policy of this nature could work as one of the factors to legitimize the new internal agreement, which in the absence of immediate political and economic results would turn to the arsenal of populism or nationalism.

A foreign policy with these characteristics would depend, of course, on the restoration and consolidation of East–West detente. The "pendular" policy, which turns changing loyalties into a factor and symbol of independence as well as an instrument of development of the country, is the combined fruit of world detente and internal development. Thus, increasing Brazil's structural diversification of dependence demands a certain degree of pluralism in the world order. The U.S. options may or may not reinforce these trends. The relative ability of Brazil to act independently of U.S. policy reflects, on the one hand, structural changes due to the way Brazil has been able to enter international circles and, on the other, the lack of international tensions strong enough to cause the anti-Communist feelings that are the basis of the Brazilian regime to overwhelm all other considerations. If Reagan's foreign policy leads to a return to the East–West Cold War, which would increase Western political dependence on the United States, anti-Communism among the Brazilian elite, especially the military, would be rekindled. This, in turn, would inhibit further diversification of Brazil's foreign economic development because its foreign policy, which would move toward alignment with the United States, would lose its present flexibility with respect to Europe, Africa, Latin America, and the Socialist world.

It is particularly important to underscore the point that increasing tension between the United States and the Soviet Union would lead the West to reevaluate the strategic position of the South Atlantic—since the Reagan administration has already indicated its intention of doing so by expressing U.S. willingness to strengthen the Pretoria regime. The U.S. opening toward Pretoria and Buenos Aires is being interpreted as a tactical action aimed at increasing U.S. military operations in the South Atlantic. South African and particularly Argentine consent would certainly force Brazil to abstain from adopting a dissenting attitude.

If there were even a moderate increase in the anti-Communist content of Brazil's foreign policy, Brazil's African policy would be greatly affected because its main channels are condemnation of the Pretoria regime and good relations with Socialist-oriented African countries. However, by the same token, the foreseeable Soviet reaction to militarization of the South Atlantic would create and worsen East–West tensions in a geopolitical area of interest to Brazil, justifying even more anti-Communist influence in foreign policy matters.

On a stage of this nature, Brazil's foreign policy would become a factor to restrengthen the conservative aspects of internal policy. Internal political detente would become a problem, and so would the development of a partisan alliance to rule the country with a more democratic base. It is also important to underscore that such a situation could encourage internal conflict between the governing elite and the better-organized sectors of civilian society. The governing elite would adopt conservative positions under the influence of world order, but the better organized sectors of civilian society would try to express their opposition to the increased anti-Communist content of the internal and foreign policies through the exacerbation of anti-American feelings. This civilian reaction would, of course, be radical or moderate depending on the perceived fair or unfair nature of the U.S. position, but this would not be the decisive factor. The direction of the national situation in the medium and long term would in any case become unpredictable.

NOTES

1. Information on the balance of trade, foreign investments and reinvestments, and foreign debt was obtained from Brazil's Central Bank and the Ministries of Finance and Foreign Relations.

2. It should be stressed that Brazilian–American trade declined at rates higher than the rate of increase of Brazil's share in world commerce. This means that there was not only stagnation but a real decline. Conversely, trade between Brazil and the EEC accompanied the increasing participation of Brazil in world trade, which in the last two decades reached the highest rate in the West.

3. Information about the disagreement on nuclear matters between Brazil and the United States at the beginning of the 1950s was obtained from statements— still unpublished—made by Renato Archer, former president of the Foreign Relations Committee, Brazilian House of Representatives, before the Center for Research and Documentation on Brazil's Contemporary History (CPDOC/FGV).

4. In declarations made to the Brazilian House of Representatives, Rep. Renato Archer said that during the negotiations the U.S. government delivered four

secret verbal communications to Brazil. Communication number four said that if Brazil continued to insist on importing the German ultracentrifuges, the United States could consider this action as a threat to its security and that of the hemisphere and take any retaliatory measures deemed convenient. Communication number three referred to the hostile position adopted by Admiral Alvaro Alberto da Mota e Silva, president of the National Security Council, and recommended the establishment of another agency, the National Nuclear Energy Commission, which would be headed by a Brazilian national friendly to the United States and would be given the authority conferred to the National Research Council. Communication number two reaffirmed the U.S. position under the MacMahon Act in relation to the impossibility of transferring U.S. equipment to Brazil for utilization in nuclear research. Communication number one proposed the development of a U.S. research program on radioactive minerals within Brazil—a joint U.S.-Brazil Committee. The recommendations of the four communications were observed. Later, when the Allies granted autonomy to Germany, the German physicists who had received the order to manufacture the equipment tried to send it to Brazil. Under the "new guidelines" existing in Brazil, the transfer was not requested and the matter was closed.

5. In an interview given to the Brazilian television network "Rede Globo" in April 1981, Jânio Quadros declared again that the relations of his government with the Castro regime had been based on Brazil's commercial interests.

6. See Góes (1977) for my views at the time on the basic rationale behind events taking place and trends they represented.

7. During a personal interview in April 1981, Ronaldo Mota Sardemberg, Senior Advisor to the Minister of Foreign Relations of Brazil, offered me a concise explanation of Brazil's foreign policy.

8. Observations made on the nature of Brazil's political opening are based on the classification recently proposed by Guillermo O'Donnel, who compares opening processes originating from the government apparatus and opening processes initiated by pressure from civilian society.

9. The experimental and temporary nature of the wage policy aimed at incorporating the lower strata and the pressure created among the middle classes was confirmed by Dr. Murilo Macedo (1981).

10. The rhetoric would be reformist nationalism or moderate populism.

REFERENCES

Batista Jr., Paul O. Nogueira. "Participação Brasileira no Mercado Financeiro Internacional: Custo e Perfil da Dívida Externa (1968–79)." International Center for Monetary and Economic Studies, Brazilian Economic Institute, Getúlio Vargas Foundation, Rio de Janeiro, March 1981.

Góes, Walder de. "A América Desconhecida de Carter." *Jornal do Brasil* (Rio de Janeiro), 6 March 1977.

———. "Aí vem Helmut Schmidt." *Jornal do Brasil* (Rio de Janeiro), 1 April 1979.

Grabendorff, Wolf. "La Política Exterior del Brasil. Entre el Primer y Tercer Mundo." *Nueva Sociedad* (Caracas), 4 (March/April 1979): 108–19.

Hirst, Mônica. "Impasses e Descaminhos da Política de não-Proliferação Nuclear." Paper presented at Fourth National Annual Meeting of the National Association for Graduate Social Science Studies, Rio de Janeiro, September 1980.

Lima, Maria Regina Soares de, and Mônica Hirst. "Carter e a América Latina: Um Balanço de Fim de Mandato." Paper presented at Seminar on New Adaptations of International Relations in Latin America, Rio de Janeiro, September 1980.

Macedo, Murilo. Interview, *Jornal do Brasil*, 12 April 1981.

6

BRAZIL AND
WESTERN EUROPE IN
A GLOBAL CONTEXT

Carlos Perez Llana

The basic thesis I pursue in this chapter is that the European perception of Brazil (and indeed that of the industrialized world in general) is based on an outdated view of reality. The objective of my contribution is to update this perception.

From the Latin American point of view, Europe would still seem to be seeing Brazil through the eyes of the 1970s, without duly weighing the problems stemming from the energy crisis and internal political events, which will undoubtedly condition the future of Brazil's foreign policy. Consequently, Brazil is important in European eyes because of the size of its economy (among the first ten of the nonsocialist world); the geographical extent of its territory; the importance of its human and material resources; its status as the most important developing country, and one with Western roots; the real and potential size of the Brazilian market; its favorable prospects for investment; and the presumed stability of the Brazilian political system. In addition, Brazil is on Europe's horizon because it is assigned a future status in international relations. Since these perceptions were formed, there has been a major metamorphosis in Brazilian foreign and internal policy. Each will be discussed in turn.

BRAZILIAN DIPLOMACY FROM CASTELO BRANCO TO FIGUEIREDO

Events connected with the succession of the government of General Castelo Branco are generally well known, as are the crises stemming from differences among the armed forces themselves, which had to be faced by the first government of the revolution. What is of interest here, however, are the changes that have taken place within the military institution itself. This subject becomes especially relevant because the force of events could lead to further changes, as I will later argue.

The Original Post-Revolutionary Paradigm[1]

The political paradigm of the Castelo Branco cycle was built around a central idea: the eternal struggle between the West and the Socialist world. In the service of this struggle, a series of ideas was brought to bear: the importance of internal security; the need to count on a strong and efficient democratic system; the advantages of a more liberal economy; the need for foreign investment and technology; the disadvantages of verbal nationalism; and, finally, the need for Brazil's clear alignment with the West—the United States in particular—in the struggle against international Communism. Consequently, during Castelo Branco's term of office, Brazil's foreign policy was built on an optimization of the principal interests of Brazil in the local and international fields, given these ideas, and bearing in mind the means available vis-à-vis the internal and foreign conditions.[2]

In this paradigm, the European continent played a secondary part. In the struggle against international Communism there was no room for doubt, and the alignment with the United States was based on the simple fact of the relationship between the existing forces of the West and the Socialist world. Only with clear leadership on the part of the United States was it possible to face the Soviet challenge. Furthermore, the military experience of soldiers of the Castelo Branco cycle in the European theater during World War II had convinced them of the superiority of the American system. Nor can it be ignored that there was, among these soldiers, a perception that was heavily conditioned by the fact of the European defeat by the Axis and by the role of savior that fell to the United States.[3] Also, curiously enough, Castelo Branco's pro-Americanism was, in the tradition of Rio Branco, favorable to a special relationship with the United States, to the detriment of the time-honored European connection of traditional Brazilian diplomacy.

Finally, in the economic field, Castelo Branco's paradigm was functional in steering the economy toward greater internationalism—the increase in interdependencies that should allow Brazil greater and better access to the streams of capital and trade from abroad—and was the only means for overcoming the structural economic impasse to which Brazil had come after decades of protectionism. In regard to internal affairs, an endeavor was made to reduce the role of the state in economic activity and to put an end to the economic nationalism of "crusades," such as that set up around the subject of foreign capital in the Brazilian economy.

The Freezing of World Power

The assumption of office by Costa e Silva marked the end of the founding paradigm of the revolutionary movement of 1964. As is well pointed out by Stepan (1972), it was military nationalism that pushed the candidacy of Costa e Silva. This nationalism was in the majority in the army, hence Castelo Branco's failure to assure himself of the succession.

Concern about the growing internationalization of the Brazilian economy (brought about by Roberto Campos) was among the causes of the rebirth of Brazilian economic nationalism. Not only did the military groups that followed these ideas fail to share the paradigm based on the East–West confrontation, they also lacked the experience (basic for the Castelo Branco group) of World War II and, generally speaking, were much less sophisticated intellectually than their predecessors. There is no doubt that the "political fire" of this generation stemmed from the famous debate of the early 1950s about petroleum policy—and Petrobras (the Brazilian state-owned oil company) in particular.

National security, conceived in universal and regional terms, began to lose ground to demands oriented toward overcoming the technological strangulation of Brazilian industry and toward increasing its role. Nobody could ignore the fact that the final recipient of this criticism was the United States (in the dearest tradition of economic nationalism). But the return to the style and practice of nationalism was slow until Castelo Branco's paradigm was emptied, the allusions to Cuba diminished (it will be remembered that, during the first military government, Brazil took part in the Dominican Operation with troops), and the accentuation of the economic problems of development became the most important factor in Brazil's foreign policy.

With hindsight we can see that the events connected with the problem of instant coffee in June 1966 were a portent of future events, in that they were a preannouncement of future political-economic differences between the United States and Brazil. From that date on, the subject of the entry of Brazilian manufactured products into the American market would increasingly strain relations between the two countries. The same date saw the beginnings of an increased European presence in Brazil's trade policy and political position, and the start of a clear policy of commercial rapprochement with the Socialist bloc. Finally, the government of Costa e Silva modified the Brazilian position in such important fields as the idea of an Interamerican Defense Force and nuclear nonproliferation in Latin America.

Two names must be associated with the elaboration of Brazil's new foreign policy: Araujo Castro, Goulart's former Foreign Minister and Ambassador in Washington, and President Garrastazu Médici's Foreign Minister, Gibson Barboza. To the former fell the role of ideologue, to the latter that of being the first to implement the new Brazilian foreign policy of identifying with the developing world.

Araujo Castro's thesis centered on criticism of the policy of mutual accommodation (détente), which the United States and the Soviet Union were endeavoring to exercise and which, supposedly, would "freeze" world power for their own benefit and to the detriment of the regional powers (Europe) and the emerging powers (Brazil). The logic of mutual accommodation was based on the mutual perception of a common interest in preventing the rise of autonomous contesting power. According to this thesis, the Soviet Union had ceased to be a revolutionary country and was behaving more like a power that had arrived late for its date with history. Obviously Araujo Castro's thesis implies, for a country like Brazil, a paradigm based on the existence of a North-South situation in which emerging countries like Brazil must strengthen ties with developing countries—as proposed by the concept of collective security in the economic field—and with all the countries hurt by the mutual accommodation policy, especially Western Europe.

Gibson Barboza brought about a singular diplomatic change that placed Brazil in the complex bloc of developing countries. For deliberate economic reasons, Brazil put aside the framework of "anticipatory diplomacy" which had kept her in a rather ambiguous situation vis-à-vis the countries of the OECD (Organization for Economic Cooperation and Development) and the countries of the South. Thus, the idea of a Brazil assuming the position of mediator between North and South was abandoned in favor of one in which

Brazil perceived itself as an interested party, together with the rest of the developing countries.

As proof of this new diplomacy tied to the problems of the developing world, Gibson systematically pursued relations with Africa. It should be pointed out that these ties were developed rudimentarily during the period of the "independent foreign policy" (governments of Quadros and Goulart). In 1972 the Foreign Minister visited nine African countries, giving conspicuous priority to the topics of the black continent. In consequence, Brazilian exports to Africa recorded a spectacular rise—from U.S. $81 million in 1972, to U.S. $186 million in 1973, to U.S. $417 million in 1974.[4]

Although under Médici-Gibson Brazil postponed the idea of joining the "Club of the Big Ones," it was not thrown out. It was rather a case of circumstances forcing Brazil to redefine its tactics—while still holding to its basic long-term strategy—in order to obtain the benefits deriving from its status as an undeveloped country—concession credits, a better access to the markets of the North, etc. This image was also useful in gaining easier access to the markets of developing countries.

Gaullist[5] Diplomacy

The third paradigm—under President Ernesto Geisel and his Foreign Minister Azeredo Silveira—was shaped in a major way by the petroleum crisis and its aftermath, which eroded one of the central components of the post-1964 development process: economic growth. The primary focus of foreign policy since Geisel took over, therefore, has been to try to relieve the petroleum crisis for an economy in need of petroleum, foreign exchange, and markets.

The foreign economic requirements stemming from the combination of Brazil's dependence on energy and the developmental demands of the nationalist sector of the armed forces brought with it conflicting goals and produced the so-called "Gaullist" phase of Brazilian foreign policy, which inevitably lacked coherence and internal consistency. One result of this was to widen the differences with the United States (trade problems, discrepancies regarding the Law of the Sea, American opposition to the German–Brazilian Nuclear Agreement, etc.)—an estrangement for which the theoretical concepts of "responsible pragmatism" and "automatic nonalignment" were thought up to provide a rationale.

During 1975, Brazil made some significant foreign policy decisions that showed the new orientation of the Foreign Ministry. The old concept of "concentric circles" that placed Brazil permanently with the West[6] was abandoned in that year when the MPLA (Popular Movement for the Liberation of Angola), which had the support of the Soviet Union and Cuba, was recognized—in opposition to the policy of the United States to support other nationalist groups which were against the MPLA Marxists. In that year Brazil also voted in favor of United Nations Resolution 3379, defining Zionism as racism. This "Palestine twist," of which Brazil's approval of observer status for the PLO (Palestine Liberation Organization) was another example, epitomized the lack of cohesion and the price of a diplomacy defined by economic needs, to the detriment of political needs. As a culmination of this pro-Arab turn on the part of *Brasília*, the vice-president of Iraq (currently wielding supreme power in Baghdad) visited Brazil in May 1978, thus opening up an area of important, but uncertain, possibilities for Brazilian diplomacy in the areas of both economics and politics.

THE PERCEPTION OF EUROPE IN BRAZIL

The theoretical break with the work of Araujo Castro after 1972 and the implementation of the new Brazilian foreign policy was not confined to Third World rhetoric. The foreign policy makers in Brazil clearly perceived the qualitative change in the international system as a consequence of detente. Opposition to detente was precisely what pushed Brazil into seeking new horizons for its foreign policy—one clear component of which was to reassess the "European connection."

With respect to the political arena, Brazil perceived that Europe was in a similar position vis-à-vis the dangers implicit in the so-called "freezing of world power," and that it was clearly in Europe's interest to widen its international political sphere through a more independent European policy vis-à-vis the Socialist and the developing countries. With respect to the economic arena, the situation was even clearer. The spectacular dynamism of European economies during the 1960s enabled a country like Brazil to count on new economic and technological alternatives. The signing of the Nuclear Agreement with the Federal Republic of Germany in 1975 reflected the scope that could be achieved by Euro–Brazilian technological ties. In the financial field, the Eurodollar market gave Brazil rapid and easy access to the European capital market. In the spirit of Rio Branco, Brazil was seeking a special relationship with the rising power.

As already noted, this did not mean that Brazil abandoned its intention to become an emerging power. Calling on the theory of the Third World in multinational diplomacy, it obtained markets and political credit in both South and North, looking for recognition as a privileged actor in Europe's international system. The visits of President Geisel to Great Britain in 1975 and to France in 1976 were both in the service of this policy, and on both occasions Brazil obtained preferential status through setting up a system of Anglo–Brazilian consultations and creation of a Grand Committee for Franco–Brazilian Coordination.

Finally, there was a convergence of interests between Brazil and Europe stemming from their mutual dependence on petroleum and from a shared vision of the so-called North–South dialogue. There are close ties between petroleum and the subject of North–South relations to the extent that the developing countries and the OPEC have consistently endeavored to tie the supply of energy to the exigencies of a new international economic order that gives special weight to the interests of the South. The forced redefinition of their foreign policies in light of the international circumstances that followed the petroleum crisis of 1974 meant the search for a special relationship with the OPEC countries and the support of claims of the majority of the developing countries (as condensed into the Charter of Economic Duties and Rights of States, and approved by the United Nations General Assembly in 1974).[7]

There were also similarities between Brazil and Europe regarding their position in the Middle East conflict and the OPEC countries generally. Let us remember that as late as 1972 Foreign Minister Gibson Barboza condemned the PLO for "tolerating terrorism." The aforementioned Palestine twist in 1974 permitted Brazil, as it did Europe, to penetrate these important markets with greater ease, not only with respect to exports but also with respect to new technological opportunities.[8]

REALITIES OF BRAZILIAN FOREIGN POLICY

Thus, Brazil's current foreign policy is basically governed by economic factors. As in many countries, both developed and developing, the priorities are set by resource needs, hence the growing (and not too well-studied) importance of the Ministries of Finance and other economic offices in the handling of foreign policy.[9]

As has been aptly pointed out (Roett 1981), Brazil's diplomatic efforts in the 1980s will have to center on the supply of petroleum, the search for export markets, and the obtaining of financial resources. How compatible these objectives are among themselves and how well Brazil's foreign policy can maintain both coherence and independence remains to be seen.

Brazilian diplomacy at times gives the foreign observer the impression of being the prisoner of a multitude of ambiguities and contradictions, somewhat similar to a "diplomacy between two worlds." For example, while seeking a relationship with some of the OPEC countries, Brazil has rejected the creation of other raw material cartels,[10] and, although a fervent partisan of proposals regarding a new international economic order, Brazil (to favor its powerful merchant navy) tries to lean away from the formula supported by the majority of the "Group of 77" in marine transportation matters.[11]

Ambiguities also exist in the financial field. While many countries of the "Group of 77" demand that the developed countries find overall solutions to the international debt problem, Brazil—like other intermediate countries—endeavors to retain its privileged access to the international capital market.

Finally, we cannot ignore the theoretical aspects. From the beginning of the 1970s to date, Brazil has operated internationally on the basis of the paradigm of detente—with the understanding that the East–West rivalry had been displaced by the North–South conflict, which places Brazil provisionally within the developing world. In the first half of the 1980s, everything points to a resurgence of East–West confrontation and the possibility of conflict stemming from an imbalance of force between the West and the Socialist countries, to the benefit of the latter. Consequently, Brazil, like many other countries that made the same bet, must rapidly reassess the theoretical assumptions underlying their foreign policies if they are not to risk the tragic end that comes to those ships which, steering no course, never encounter favorable winds.

INTERNAL POLITICAL ASPECTS AND THEIR INFLUENCE ON FOREIGN POLICY

In the economic area, Brazil has been unable to overcome some of the structural problems of its economy. In spite of the economy's real growth, reflected in the evolution of the gross domestic product, the balance on current account is in bad shape and inflation is high. In the political sphere, the important issue is the continuing feasibility of the transition process started under Figueiredo. Presidential elections are envisaged for 1985 which, if they take place under the conditions now planned, will end the rule of the military in Brazil. The difficult economic situation inevitably raises questions about the feasibility of restoring democracy under adverse conditions.[12] However, the process seems irreversible given the slow deterioration, during fifteen uninterrupted years in power, that has taken place in the system of alliances on which the revolution was built and the erosion of the legitimacy that stemmed from growth as the economic crisis worsens.[13]

EUROPE AND THE FUTURE OF BRAZIL

As we have seen, Brazil is going through difficult times and special circumstances, and, in view of the size of the country and of the economic and political interests at stake, the West—Europe in particular—will have to find ways to accommodate its current reality. This should be defined systematically, within the overall framework of Europe-Third World interdependencies. Otherwise, there is the very real risk of a policy that wanders from one crisis to another without any consistent direction.

Brazil is a typical medium-level country, and will be one for at least a decade. It is a country that has not relinquished the idea of becoming "great" in the next century, but is now in the throes of entering the era of postindustrial society (at least in some areas) before it has quite finished its industrial revolution.

Curiously, Brazil does not accept this identification of itself; at the most it tolerates being characterized as a nontypical country, in a category of its own. Convinced of its possibilities for the future, Brazil has chosen to "dilute" its presence within the developing world, knowing that, in view of its importance, it cannot fail to be recognized for it. The idea of the possibility of a "jump," both qualitative and quantitative, to "rich country" status is permanently in the minds of a large sector of the Brazilian elite.

A wager in favor of the feasibility of such a jump is extremely dangerous, however; it is guaranteed neither by continued economic growth nor by the internal political stability. In addition, it is probable that the arrival of a government elected by popular suffrage would complicate even more the handling of the Brazilian economy, because such a government would be faced with the need to satisfy the legitimate claims of large sectors of the population that have remained outside the benefits of the so-called "economic miracle."

Europe can, and should, develop a policy that enables it to give to Brazil and other medium-level countries (Argentina, Mexico, Venezuela) the kind of economic and technological assistance they need to enable them to handle the economic and political transitions they are going through. The agreements signed in 1981 between Brazil and France represent a good example of this kind of cooperation because they are based on shared interests and the possibility of mutual advantage. Europe can, and should, also make available to these medium-level countries an institutional network that will recognize them as a special category of intermediate countries, entitled to special rights and duties vis-à-vis third parties. The challenge implied by the recognition of a special status for the medium countries calls for a prompt answer. Bad situations have already occurred because of a failure to recognize and adapt to the new international reality.

NOTES

1. Paradigm refers to the analytic framework within which an institution can be systematically examined (Kuhn 1962).

2. It was a question of a foreign policy without contradictions and without casual improvisations (the negative characteristics peculiar to a misinterpretation of pragmatism).

3. Exaggerating the frame of reference, we could place the paradigm of Castelo Branco (and of his circle) as "pro-Atlantic" vis-à-vis the Gaullist "pro-Europe" of the later 1960s.

4. Export figures are given at their FOB value and are from the Banco do Brasil, Foreign Trade Portfolio.

5. See chapter 3 for a discussion of Gaullism.

6. See President Castelo Branco's speech at the Brazilian Foreign Ministry in Brasília, 31 July 1964.

7. The unfortunate Paris Conference on Economic Cooperation in 1975 was the climax of the European (basically French) endeavor to reach a minimum agreement between the interests of the countries of the North and those of the South. Brazil not only went along with this policy but also applauded the intention of Europe to act independently of the United States at a time when Washington was favoring a policy of facing up to OPEC through the International Energy Agency.

8. The similarities between Brazil and some European countries (notably France) are highlighted by the fact that, today, military equipment of Brazilian origin is being used in the wars waged in the Middle East (Iraq versus Iran, Libya versus Chad).

9. The political ministries lose ground, which could perhaps explain the increased rigidity of much diplomacy.

10. See "Geisel Guarantees that Brazil Will Not Cultivate Antagonisms," *Jornal do Brasil*, 19 September 1976.

11. The reasons behind the ambiguity are no secret to the observer of Brazil's foreign policy. While its economy is conditioned by petroleum for price reasons, to guarantee supplies, Brazil is forced to consider certain demands of a political nature (e.g., recognition of the PLO). Likewise, the excessive dependence on supplies (e.g., Iraq petroleum) necessitates accepting the costs of an automatic alignment (a thesis opposed to former Foreign Minister Azevedo Silveira's notion of "nonautomatic alignment"), e.g., support for Iraq in its conflict with Iran.

12. The experience of Spain points up the possible difficulties of efforts to consolidate democratic politics in a time of economic crisis.

13. The possibility of a resurgence in the nonimmediate future of nationalist and authoritarian currents within the army itself should not be completely discounted. The reason for this is the possibility of social unrest, stemming from the fact that a large proportion of the population (estimated at over 50 percent) are outside the economic and political mainstream. The army cannot be expected to completely ignore a major increase in the rate of social risk inherent in this situation.

REFERENCES

Kuhn, Thomas. *The Structure of Scientific Revolutions*. Chicago: University of Chicago Press, 1962.

Roett, Riordan. "Brazilian Foreign Policy: Options for the 1980s." In Thomas C. Bruneau and Philippe Faucher (eds.), *Authoritarian Capitalism: The Contemporary Economic and Political Development of Brazil*. Boulder, Co.: Westview Press, 1981.

Stepan, Alfred. *The Military in Politics: Changing Patterns in Brazil*. Princeton, NJ: Princeton University Press, 1972.

7

BILATERAL AND MULTILATERAL ASPECTS OF BRAZILIAN FOREIGN POLICY

Roberto Fendt Jr.

As Anthony Lake (1981) has reminded us, a successful foreign policy can come only from a correct balance among self-interest, idealism, and power. The consequence of incompatible economic, political, and military goals is posturing rather than policy; the consequence of pursuing national ideals not rooted in the national interest is confusion and suspicion; the consequence of expediency is lack of character, strength, and appeal.

These remarks come to mind as Brazilian foreign policy appears to be undergoing a phase of transition. This transition is manifested in both bilateral relations with the United States, and the new role Brazil is playing in the sphere of multilateral institutions such as the General Agreement on Tariffs and Trade (GATT) and the International Monetary Fund (IMF). In addition, important domestic political events have and will continue to have an effect on Brazilian foreign policy in the near future.

THE CURRENT STATE OF TRANSITION

Bilateral relations with the United States are in the process of change. This was highlighted by the visit of President Reagan to Brazil in November 1982 and other Latin American countries, which occurred after the historical speech of President Figueiredo at the United Nations, deemphasizing the "Third-Worldism" aspects of Brazilian foreign policy, and emphasizing the more general claims for a reconstructed new world economic order. This speech is particularly important to the extent that Figueiredo, while maintaining the notion that Brazil belongs to the group of developing nations—sharing their aspirations for development and sharing their anguish with the current disarray in world economic affairs—went beyond the standard exhortations for a more comprehensive North–South dialogue, to concentrate on more general aspects of Brazil's foreign policy. This is in line with the relative importance of Brazil in world affairs; but one cannot deny that it departs from a deep-rooted tradition.

Brazilian relations with multilateral institutions are reflecting Brazil's new view of itself in world affairs, as exemplified by its attitudes with respect to GATT and the IMF. With respect to the former, Brazil voted to favor the consensus declaration issued at the end of the ministerial-level meeting of GATT member governments on November 29, 1982. This embodied a significant departure from Brazil's previous stance, particularly with respect to trade in services. By supporting the declaration to examine trade in services and to "consider whether any multilateral action in these matters is appropriate and desirable"[1] over the next two years—with a view to including trade in services in the multilateral negotiations at the 1984 GATT meeting— Brazil showed flexibility without abdicating established principles. With respect to the latter, Brazil has applied for IMF unconditional and conditional help to finance a balance-of-payments structural adjustment program. This application, of course, is a direct consequence of the events in the international financial market and the right of a founding member (as when Great Britain and Italy made similar application). What is new is the act of political courage to apply for the funds, given the Brazilian domestic repudiation of the "orthodox" economic policies embodied in granting such applications by the Fund—a repudiation that dates back to the breaking down of negotiations for a similar application during the Kubitscheck administration.

This new attitude toward multilateral institutions has contributed to strengthening the bilateral relations with the United States. Of particular importance in this connection has been the generous support of the Reagan administration in helping fill Brazil's short-term financial needs while these negotiations with the IMF take place; a dramatic change in U.S. views concerning the role of the IMF and the World Bank as international bankers of last resort; and the agreement between Brazil and the United States to extend for two more years the legal acceptance of Brazilian export incentives granted to its exports to the U.S. market.

All these changes in policy, in both Brazil and the United States, raise several important questions about the future of bilateral relations between the two and the nature of Brazilian foreign policy in the coming years. How will these new attitudes toward multilateral institutions relate to changes in the world economic environment? How will they affect Brazil's revived interest in Western Europe and its expanded interest in the Pacific Basin and the nations of the southern hemisphere?

It is the main message of this chapter that Brazilian foreign policy has always been based on a clear understanding that the national interest required representative democracy as a basic option in the international political sphere, and a pragmatic application of the notion of continental interdependence in the economic sphere. These two basic postulates have characterized Brazil's foreign policy at many junctures—during the prevalence of bilateralism in the pre-1959 period, during the Arinos–Quadros "independent" foreign policy, and during the prevalence of the Castelo Branco Doctrine (to cite just a few instances). What has changed over time has been the particular emphasis applied to bilateral relations with the United States.

U.S.–BRAZILIAN BILATERAL RELATIONS

The foreign policies of Latin American countries have always been dominated by the overwhelming importance of inter-American relations, particularly bilateral relations with the United States. Brazilian foreign policy has been no exception. As Roberto Campos (1963) has cogently pointed out, inter-American relations were at the heart of some of the key concepts that have forged them: first, the Monroe Doctrine and the Polk and Roosevelt Corollaries; then, the Good Neighbor Policy and the principle of nonintervention; finally, the Pan-American Operation, the Alliance for Progress, and, more recently, the Caribbean Plan.

The Monroe Doctrine itself, and the Polk and Roosevelt Corollaries of the Doctrine, were more posturing than policy, since the United States at the time did not have the power to impose them. Nonetheless, as Campos has noted (1963, 145), this posturing of U.S. foreign policy was:

accepted without hesitation by the Latin American countries. Colombia and Mexico acclaimed the new Doctrine enthusiastically, and Brazil, although never resorting to the protection of the Monroe Doctrine, tried repeatedly, since the Fourth Interamerican Conference in Buenos Aires in 1910, to transform the Doctrine from a unilateral and nationalistic U.S. posture into a continental partnership.

The post-World War II period marks the heyday of this enlargement of the Doctrine and its assumption as a hemispheric endeavor. It also marks the peak of bilateral relations between the United States and countries of the southern continent. The Doctrine was formally institutionalized with its adoption in the Chapultepec Act of 1945 and the Rio de Janeiro Treaty of 1947. The purely economic aspects of these close bilateral relations with the United States materialized in the Pan-American Operation, launched by Kubitscheck in 1958, and the Alliance for Progress shortly thereafter.

It has been observed that U.S.-Brazilian bilateral relations, although at a peak in purely political terms at the end of World War II, had already embodied all the elements of the increasing detachment to be observed in the coming years. Paramount was the role of unfulfilled expectations, with respect to both the commitment to development in the immediate postwar period and the subsequent failures of the several bilateral economic endeavors to promote the required capital transfer for the development process. Several U.S. economic missions visited Brazil from 1941 on, but their observable results were meager, at least compared with the expectations they raised. Thus, the first of these missions, headed by Alex Taub, concluded that a ten-year program was required to promote a total investment of four billion United States dollars, mainly in infrastructure (Gudin 1945). The Morris Cooke mission (1942) also emphasized the need for infrastructure to promote industrialization, mostly with a view to supporting the war effort (Cooke 1944). The Abbink mission (1948) began a new era of economic relationships between the United States and Brazil. Its recommendations departed from the purely war effort aspects of the previous missions to emphasize the permanent nature of U.S.-Brazilian economic relations. Of particular importance was its stress on the role of *private* capital as the main channel through which support for development financing should flow. From the United States point of view, in other words, the dialogue should be between the Brazilian authorities and the International Bank for Reconstruction and Development, not the government-to-government dialogue wanted by the Brazilians. It was clear that the Marshall Plan developed for Europe—which was now the center of U.S. defense concerns—would not be duplicated in Latin America.

The Korean War appeared at first to change this picture. In December 1950, as a result of both approval by the U.S. Congress of the Act of International Development and domestic political events in Brazil, the Joint Commission for Economic Development was created. The commission started with quite different assumptions from those underlying previous U.S. missions to Brazil—namely, that private domestic investment would only be effective in promoting Brazilian development to the extent that the infrastructural bottlenecks of the economy were eliminated, and that it was the role of public capital flows to eliminate them.

This change was short-lived, however. The foreign exchange crisis in 1951–53 paralyzed all previous intentions of the commission. Although there were several positive results (especially the creation of the National Development Bank), consequences for bilateral relations between the two countries were not positive. All of Latin America perceived the picture as one of massive U.S. support for reconstruction in Europe and Japan, a progressive trade and payments liberalization—which culminated with the return to convertibility of the major European currencies in 1959—and the emergence of the Eurocurrencies market; but within the southern continent, U.S. support for the idea of development was almost entirely rhetoric.

As time proceeded, the distance between posturing and practical realities with respect to the U.S.-Brazilian bilateral relationship increased.[2] Indeed, rhetoric aside, the bilateral relations never had any degree of exclusiveness, such as was true of U.S. relations with the NATO partners or under the Marshall Plan. This distance between facts and rhetoric became clearly apparent in the very modest scale of actual U.S. direct (private and public) investment in the financing of Brazilian development.

Brazil's bilateral relations with the United States in the first years after the 1964 Revolution also provide a mistaken image of a change from established trends. The congruence of common interests in terms of a common defense against the expansion of Castroism in Latin America, and the support of the stabilization program in 1964–66, created the false notion that something special was being *built into* the bilateral relationship.

In reality, there was nothing new. The 1964 period was special in the same sense as the 1950–51 period. In both cases what was at stake was a question of principle, both for Brazil and for the United States. Brazilian foreign policy, like U.S. policy, has always centered on the principle of preserving representative democracy. Expansion of Castroism in the 1960s was similar in all respects to the expansion of Marxism (Chinese-inspired version) in the early 1950s. Thus, the congruence in each case was the natural result of foreign policies based on the same principle. The view that something special existed in the 1960s, but not before, confuses this congruence of principle with a mistaken perception of Brazil's view with respect to the bipolarization of international affairs, as well as the very nature of the "independent" foreign policy doctrine of Arinos–Quadros. The global view prevalent in Brazil in the immediate post-1964 period, that of a bipolar division of the world between two superpowers, is similar in almost all respects to the view prevalent in the 1950s: defense was considered a matter of collective and interdependent intrabloc decisions; but foreign trade and international financial transactions were to take place among economically interdependent regions. Under Castelo Branco, as mentioned, the basic tenets of our foreign policy were reemphasized: strong support to representative democracy, rejection of Marxism, and the notion of political and economic interdependence—an interdependence, however, that should be interpreted on a case-by-case analysis, as indicated by the long-run national interest.[3] Very few recall today, for example, that by 1967, just after the export drive had been inaugurated with the support of the U.S. Agency for International Development—in the climate of what some identified too hastily as a special relationship—the first cases of countervailing duties against Brazilian instant coffee exports to U.S. markets were already occurring.

The following years mark a decisive step in the process of affirming a separate Brazilian identity in the world scenario—a process that developed along two complementary paths. First, the development of the Eurocurrencies market made official flows of capital to supplement domestic savings in the process of Brazilian development financing an obsolete practice. Second, an aggressive trade policy, based on expanding world markets but supported by a broad scheme of export promotion incentives, magnified this access to the private international banking community.[4]

These two circumstances exacerbated U.S.-Brazilian disagreement on the specifics of their bilateral relationship over time. Besides, the spectacular drive to development observed in the 1960s and 1970s magnified some other sources of attrition. In the pre-Revolution

years Brazil and the United States were strictly complementary economies, with respect to both trade and capital flows. Over the 1960s and
1970s Brazilian dependence was reduced with respect to the latter,
while the two economies became competitors with respect to the
former.

From reduced dependency to antagonism, and from antagonism
to conflict on trade matters, was just a step. The conflict emerged in
the form of increasing trade disputes concerning Brazilian export incentives. Between 1974 and 1978, countervailing duty cases against
Brazilian exports to the U.S. market were imposed against shoes
(1974), handbags, soybean oil, and castor oil (1975), scissors and cotton (1976), and textiles and apparel (1978).

These disputes led eventually to recognition of the problem as a
general one, and to negotiations. As a result, Brazil subscribed to several of the codes resulting from the Tokyo round of GATT negotiations. Of particular importance for bilateral relations with the United
States was Brazil's recognition of the subsidies code. Agreement was
reached to phase out Brazil's export incentive program progressively
over five years starting in January 1979.

If the problem of trade disputes was being understood and resolved by negotiation, the same cannot be said of other aspects of the
U.S.-Brazilian relationship. Of particular importance were the
American decision not to abide by previous commitments to supply
processed nuclear fuel for the nuclear power station then under construction by a U.S. firm, and subsequent interference by the Carter
administration in purely domestic political events in Brazil (Fishlow
1982). The fact that the United States was making both restricted access to nuclear fuels and human rights general international policy
issues, did nothing to rectify relations already strained by years of
trade disputes. Brazil was still unwilling to let bilateral relations with
the United States be simply subsumed under the general category of
U.S. foreign relations. From these disagreements it was a small step to
the Nuclear Agreement with the Federal Republic of Germany in 1975
and the denouncing of the Military Agreement between the United
States and Brazil.

STRUCTURAL CHANGES IN THE INTERNATIONAL SCENE

It is important to recognize that throughout this period of deteriorating bilateral relations, basic structural changes were also taking
place, especially with respect to trade and financial flows. As already

mentioned, capital flows were very much influenced by the emergence of the Eurocurrencies market and the multilateralization of the sources of development financing, now supranational. Brazilian trade flows also changed, in response both to market phenomena and to active domestic policy.

Just after World War II, the United States was the destination of almost half of all Brazilian exports, and the originator of about the same percentage of Brazilian imports—a situation that continued unchanged until Brazil's export drive. From 1967 on, the picture changed rapidly. The steady depreciation of the U.S. dollar vis-à-vis the European currencies—notably the Deutschemark—and the yen made Brazilian exports more competitive in those markets, since the cruzeiro exchange rate took the U.S. dollar as the currency of reference. This fact alone explains most of the spectacular diversification in the destination of Brazilian exports. Thus, whereas in 1957–59 41 percent of all Brazilian exports were destined for the United States, compared to slightly more than 26 percent to Western Europe, by 1974 the shares of the United States and Western Europe had changed, respectively, to 21.8 and 35.2 percent. A similar change took place in the geographical distribution of the originators of Brazilian imports, helped by the emerging importance of Middle Eastern suppliers of oil, which required the opening of new markets—outside the United States, Japan, and Western Europe—to help cover huge deficits with the OPEC countries (whence, by 1979–82, originated more than 50 percent of Brazilian imports).

The geographical origin of foreign direct investment also changed markedly in this period. Thus, whereas in the early 1960s still more than one-half of the total foreign investment in Brazil originated in the U.S., by the mid-1970s that percentage had declined to less than one-third (with Western European capital accounting for some 40 percent of the total and Japanese capital for some 12 percent).

Clearly, Brazilian capital and trade flows had changed profoundly in the course of two decades. Brazil was, by the mid-1970s, a large purchaser of Middle Eastern oil, a large seller of manufactured goods to southern hemisphere countries, and a large debtor of the international banking system. The multinationals also contributed in a significant way to allow this diversification, since the Brazilian domestic market (unlike that of smaller countries) was large enough to allow the simultaneous presence of multinationals originating in several different countries. The internationalization of the world economy became effective in the internal Brazilian market as well.

These economic phenomena inevitably became reflected in Brazil's foreign policy. In the closed and bipolar world of the 1950s, it was natural for Brazil to express its foreign policy mostly in terms of our bilateral relations with the United States. Detente rendered the bipolar world out of fashion. If the Americans could supply the Soviet Union with wheat and corn, Brazilians could see no reason why they should not do the same with other kinds of exports and to other countries. This *realpolitik*, for example, led to Brazil's recognition of the independence of Angola, while the United States was still supporting one of the factions fighting Agostinho Neto. It also led to a rapprochement with several of the neighboring countries in Latin America, which had now become major trading partners. Finally, the much-needed equilibrium in Brazil's balance of trade with the Islamic Middle East countries led to trade and political ties much stronger than those observed in the past.

At the same time, it is hard to stress enough how much the long downswing in economic activity in the industrialized nations has hit countries like Brazil. This downswing was the direct result of a fundamental change in policy making in the industrialized world, with direct consequences for the stability of the system as a whole. Probably the most significant feature of the economic scenario of the late 1960s and early 1970s was the progressive abandonment by the industrialized nations of the basic economic principles that had produced the longest upswing in economic activity in the post-World War II period. Thus, the system of fixed exchange rates was formally rejected in August 1971 and, with the generalized floating of major currencies, actually abandoned in March 1973. Major changes in relative prices occurred as a consequence of the two violent increases in oil prices. Finally, the decision of the major industrialized countries—notably the United States and Japan—to pursue completely independent domestic policies had far-reaching consequences for world trade and capital markets.

By mid-1980 the U.S. Federal Reserve had decided to pursue a course of action to fight domestic inflation, which implied a sudden deceleration of the rate of growth of the U.S. money supply, coupled with the decision, on the expenditure side, to produce the largest domestic deficit in American history. An opposite set of decisions was being made in Japan, where the main concern was the maintenance of export markets as a way to sustain domestic activity and employment. To do this, the Japanese maintained a policy of a progressively over-valued yen and negative real rates of interest—precisely the opposite to what was being done in the United States.

The combination of such blatantly inconsistent policy sets in the two nations contributed to make the 1980s a period of the most severe lack of coordination of domestic economic policies since the 1930s. This lack of coordination has been reflected in both trade and financial matters. With respect to trade, it is because the industrialized nations—with the sole exception of Japan—have consistently resisted the much-delayed reindustrialization indicated by new patterns of comparative advantage. With respect to financial matters, it is because the violent variability in domestic interest rates has led to real interest rates comparable to those of the depression years, while the variability of exchange rates has almost completely disorganized capital flows. At the basis of these conflicting national policies is the notion—which is only now starting to fade—that under floating exchange rates the industrialized nations are free to produce domestic economic policies which attend to their immediate concerns, be they domestic inflation (as in the United States from 1980 to mid-1982) or employment (as in Japan over the same period).

Of course, in an interdependent world such inconsistent domestic policies inevitably produce either real rates of interest much higher than the marginal profitability of capital or pressures for a new protectionism to preserve jobs. Thus, the current discussion in the United States Congress on the application of the concept of reciprocity in trade relations effectively turns the multilateral principles created by GATT in 1947 into bilateral rules. By the same token, independent domestic policies with respect to floating exchange rate regimes contradict the basis of the Bretton Woods world, in which fixed rates were supposed to impose the required interdependency in financial and foreign exchange policies.

CONCLUSION

The general feeling today is one of a prevalent turn away from interdependency in economic relations and a prevalent return to bilateralism in trade and capital flow matters. It would scarcely surprise anyone if these developments were not to reflect on foreign policies as well.

What to expect for the future? Concerning Brazilian foreign policy one should distinguish principle from the changing external environment and its own domestic-specific policy actions. As far as the basic principle of Brazilian foreign policy is conccrncd, this chapter has argued that it has remained the same throughout the Republican period: a firm commitment to the view that a representative democratic regime is the basis of foreign policy. Changes in the external environment, however, are outside the ability of Brazil, or any single country, to control. Given the basic interdependence of the world economy in terms of the international division of labor, trade, and capital flows—not to mention advances in communications and technology that require action on a world scale—no single country will be able to affect significantly the new and required return to world order. It is now clear that the current international disarray must be transformed into new forms of multilateral economic relationships that reflect the stage of economic development reached by the world economy. Finally, since there are symptoms that some progress is under way—explicitly, the recognition by the American administration of the need to increase the banker-of-last-resort ability of the IMF through increased quotas, and the GATT agreement to freeze the new signs of protectionism at their current levels—one can expect from Brazilian foreign policy its proven flexibility under new circumstances, together with its rigid adherence to the principle that has provided the basis for our international relationships.

NOTES

1. General Agreement on Tariffs and Trade (GATT), "Ministerial Declaration," Genève, Switzerland, 29 November 1982.

2. That industrialization as a synonym for development was never clearly understood on the U.S. side, although it was always the mainstream of economic reasoning in Brazil. Thus, as early as 1962, Marcílio Marques Moreira pointed out that one of the basic tenets of nationalism in Brazil was this identification of industrialization and development. That industrialization was conceived as primarily aimed at the domestic market is a reminder of the grandeur raised by the size of the country and the inability to participate in the industrial export markets which, until 1959, had not yet established a payments mechanism. On the identification between industrialization and development, and their relation to nationalism, see Moreira (1962).

3. This was precisely the same as the San Tiago Dantas doctrine, which had nothing to do with the neutralism practiced by some at the time. On the contrary, San Tiago Dantas reaffirmed, on several occasions, Brazil's commitment to the basic

principle of our foreign policy (as explicitly expressed, for example, in the Punta del Este Conference in 1961). See Campos (1968).

4. An important side effect of this aggressive export policy was the increasing dislocation of other suppliers to the newly-conquered market for Brazilian exports, particularly in the southern hemisphere, among U.S. firms.

REFERENCES

Campos, Roberto de Oliveira. "A Doutrina e o Jeito." *O Globo* (Rio de Janeiro), 28 October 1968.

———. "Relações Estados Unidos-América Latina." In Roberto de Oliveira Campos, *Ensaios de História Econômica e Sociologica.* Rio de Janeiro: APEC, 1963.

Cooke, Morris. *Brazil on the March.* New York: McGraw-Hill, 1944.

Fishlow, Albert. "The United States and Brazil: The Case of the Missing Relationship." *Foreign Affairs*, 60:4 (Spring 1982): 904–23.

General Agreement on Tariffs and Trade (GATT). "Ministerial Declaration." Geneva, 29 November 1982.

Gudin, Eugênio. *Rumos de Política Econômica.* Rio de Janeiro: 1945.

Lake, Anthony. "Defining the National Interest." In Richard M. Pious (ed.), *The Power to Govern. Assessing Reform in the United States.* New York: Academy of Political Science, 1981 (Proceedings 34:2), 202–13.

Moreira, Marcílio Marques. "Some Socio-Political Preconditions of Economic Growth." M.A. thesis, Georgetown University, April 1962.

8

INTERNATIONAL BANKS, FOREIGN DEBT, AND THE THIRD WORLD QUEST FOR A NEW ORDER

Rosario Green

It is a fact that world affairs have become increasingly complicated in the last few decades. From the days when the international arena was dominated by a "club" composed of very few nations (sharing an economic, political, cultural, and even religious tradition) to the present, there have been many major changes. The decolonization process has brought new actors to the scene, and better knowledge among countries of Africa, Asia, and Latin America has given rise to new and important movements to establish more equitable international relations. Relations between the two world powers, at first cold, became warmer only to become cold again, while Europe and later Japan began to question the total control of the capitalist world by the United States.

It also seems to be a fact that as the world became more complicated the possibilities for coordinated action increased, and it was on this assumption that Third World countries began to look for support in their efforts to participate in the reshaping of a new world. This search for support was widespread: from the socialist countries to Europe, from China and Japan to the United States. Countries varied in their response. Socialist countries expressed their willingness to help as did some European countries (in particular Scandinavia). As far as the United States, Japan, and the most powerful European countries were concerned, however, the situation often was one of jeopardizing change, and even opposing the rights of the Third World to improve and share the benefits of progress and to improve the equity of world order. At the level of private actors, mainly businesses and banks, the reaction was even worse. Believers of the *laissez-faire, laissez-passer* philosophy were against any change that was not the result of market forces. For this reason, any effort to seek new forms of cooperation between rich and poor countries, between capitalist and socialist countries, among poor countries themselves, with governments or even with private actors, must analyze thoroughly the reality of the past as well as the present, before embarking on any prescriptions, predictions, or hopes. This chapter pursues just such an analysis for the particular case of foreign debt of Third World countries—a clear case of international capital, international politics, and lack of cooperation.

My argument is based on the premise that one of the most serious obstacles to the development of the so-called North-South dialogue is in the realm of international finance. In other words, the divergence existing between the rules of the game in the international economy (in this case the current predominance of banks and their logic, in the context of international economic relations) and the demands of the Third World (in this case those specifically urging increased flows of official assistance for development and better conditions for external private financing) is one of the most important factors inhibiting the implementation of a new international order. Lack of congruence between interests of private bankers operating at an international level and needs of the Third World to obtain financial resources under favorable conditions makes agreement unattainable. Consequently, the so-called North–South dialogue, at least in this field, has become a dialogue of the deaf.

My chapter is divided into three parts. In the first, the efforts of underdeveloped countries to set up a new order in the field of external finance are sketched briefly. In the second, the process of transnational banking control of the world economy, particularly in the 1970s, is outlined, along with its consequences, one being the accelerated growth of the Third World's foreign debt. In the third, this debt is analyzed. The chapter closes with some general conclusions that seek to offer, if not alternatives, at least certain guidelines for drawing up possible Third World strategies—with Latin America playing an important role—to confront the powerful position of their main creditors, the big transnational banks.

IN SEARCH OF A NEW INTERNATIONAL ORDER IN THE FIELD OF EXTERNAL FINANCE

Transfer of financial resources from the developed to the underdeveloped countries has always been present in Third World ideas. It has figured in the inter-American agenda practically since the beginnings of the Hispanoamerican movement at the end of the last century. It is a recurrent theme in the Conferences of Afroasiatic Cooperation. It is a central issue in the movement of nonaligned nations, as well as a mainstay in the position of the Group of 77 and motive for constant confrontation in the North–South dialogue.

Although this question was formally included in the Charter of the United Nations, where it forms part of the principle of international cooperation, the widespread organization of efforts to make it an obligation of rich and powerful countries with respect to weak and poor ones really only dates back to the 1960s and, in particular, to its inscription at the heart of the United Nations Conference on Trade and Development (UNCTAD) and its permanent commissions.[1]

When the first UNCTAD was held in Geneva in 1964, the underdeveloped countries, already organized around what would be termed from then on the Group of 77, expressed their concern with respect to the transfer of resources. They pointed out—as did the United Nations First Decade for Development, which established goals of international cooperation to be reached by the world community in the 1960s—that the finance the rich countries were to channel to the poor ones should equal at least 1 percent of the national income of donor countries, and that an important part of it would have to be granted under interest rates no greater than 3 percent per year, good amortization terms, and even the possibility of being partially reimbursed in the debtor's national currency.

Years later, as part of the preparatory work for the second UNCTAD to be held in New Delhi in 1968, the Group of 77 issued a statement known as the Algiers Charter, which insisted on the need for developed countries to recognize the imperative nature of their participation in the efforts of the underdeveloped world to become industrialized, contributing to this end an adequate and just percentage of their national incomes. The charter reiterated that such aid should be made multilateral so as to avoid credits being tied or conditioned; that it be granted under favorable conditions so as to have the smallest possible impact on the already-restricted payment capacity of many debtor countries; and that it be directed to financing programs of a longer-term nature than the projects traditionally preferred by the creditors.

At a later date and based on these proposals, the International Development Strategy in the context of the United Nations Second Decade for Development, specified as the goal for the 1970s that the industrialized countries should channel 0.71 percent of their gross national product (GNP) to the underdeveloped countries in the form of official assistance for development. Nevertheless, when the decade came to an end, rich countries as a whole had hardly offered an average 0.36 percent of their GNP. Although a few countries surpassed the International Strategy goal—Sweden, for example, offered 0.86 percent of its GNP to the Third World in a concessional form—many others failed to reach even the average. The United States, for example, by the first half of the decade had offered hardly 0.26 percent of its GNP.

From the third UNCTAD, held in Santiago (Chile) in 1972, came the famous Resolution 45, which stressed the carrying out of a world community effort to draft a Charter of Economic Rights and Duties of States. This charter was finally passed by a majority of 120 votes (with 6 against and 10 abstentions) during the United Nations General Assembly meetings in 1974. In reference to the question of transfer of resources (in its article 22), the charter again insisted on the need for these resources to reach the underdeveloped countries in appropriate quantities, under favorable conditions, and without any ties.

In 1974, in the Sixth Extraordinary Period of Sessions of the United Nations General Assembly, an important resolution was passed: the Declaration and the Program of Action for the Establishment of a New International Economic Order, which put forward as an indispensable requisite "the creation of favorable conditions for the transfer of financial resources to the developing countries."

In the same spirit of protest the fourth UNCTAD, held in Nairobi in 1976, went even further. It defined questions as delicate and as pressing as the improvement of multilateral mechanisms of finance, the need in the negotiations to encompass not only private debt but also official debt—a demand that motivated countries like Sweden to again convert the official development assistance they had offered the poorest countries into donations. This conference also proposed the need to establish mechanisms to foresee debt crises well in advance in order to avoid the necessity of adopting emergency measures, which are not always constructive.

Between 1976 and 1977, the Conference on International Economic Cooperation was held in Paris. Born under the oil sign, it included in its agenda the real transfer of resources from the rich to the poor countries. Proceedings of the conference, however, made it clear that the intent was not general resource transfer but rather a strategy of the industrialized countries to secure their own energy supply in the wake of the 1973 crisis.

The developed countries see the accelerated growth in foreign debt of the underdeveloped countries as due neither to insufficient transfer of official resources from rich to poor countries, nor to conditions under which this transfer has taken place. In their opinion it is due to the balance of payments of the developing countries for which they are not responsible, aggravated by the poor administration and corruption accompanying underdevelopment. The underdeveloped countries, for their part, place the problem within the context of countries midway through their phase of economic development and the framework of international financial cooperation. To them, the causes are lack of available resources, inflexibility of the conditions to which they are subjected, and the fact that the setting of a just and fair world order is a *sine qua non* for the resolution of their debt and other important questions.

As a consequence of the maintenance of these two opposing points of view, the Paris conference made little or no progress, either at the system level or at the level of individual components. In the field of finance specifically, the only achievement was the "program of special action," granting one billion U.S. dollars to the system's poorest countries with a view to alleviating their balance of payments situation. The industrialized countries thus proposed an isolated and partial solution—isolated because it was not considered within the overall framework of the problems of development, partial because it considered only a subgroup of the developing countries, thus seeking to exploit differences among them. Finally, the solution was insufficient in the face of a total Third World debt at that time of around U.S. $250 billion and a deficit on current account for the Third World already estimated at over U.S. $100 billion per year for the 1980s.[2]

The fifth UNCTAD, held in Manila in 1979, and later economic negotiations carried out in the United Nations really came to nothing, as did the continuation of the North–South dialogue in Cancún (Mexico) at the end of 1981, even though it was convened at the highest possible level, namely heads of state.

TRANSNATIONAL BANKING CONTROL OF THE WORLD ECONOMY

The process of gradual dominance and control by transnational banks and the logic of their international relations were clearly visible in the 1970s and closely linked with the crisis of "stagflation." Origins of the process, however, were much older.[3]

At the beginning of the century, as noted in chapter 2, England was the world economy's hegemonic power and its leading exporter of capital. Approximately half of the foreign investment of the big powers came from England. By 1930, the United States rivaled England in the volume of exported capital, and by 1960, 60 percent of foreign investment by the big powers came from the United States (Caputo and Pizarro 1975). The bulk of this investment, it should be noted, went to developed countries, and the part that did go to under-developed areas was concentrated in the more relatively developed ones—channeled at the beginning to extractive industries and concentrated today in manufacturing. It should also be noted that most of it was private and sought to maximize its return by avoiding the falling profit rates of the countries of origin, evading national controls, and fixing monopoly prices. Moreover, the small percentage that could be considered public (the Marshall Plan for Europe; the Alliance for Progress in Latin America; the contributions to multilateral financial organizations such as the World Bank, the Interamerican Development Bank, etc.) was channeled mainly to projects that in some way or other stimulate and intensify private national and foreign investment.

Direct North American investment abroad has always been one of the main deficit items in the U.S. balance of payments—the more so as it has gradually expanded, due mainly to the installation of subsidiaries and branch offices of the big monopoly enterprises. As the American economy grew after World War II and into the 1950s, stimulated by the Korean War among other events, its balance of payments felt the consequences and the United States was obliged to impose controls on foreign expenditure. Nevertheless, the period 1958–1963 registered the biggest expansion in North American direct foreign investment in the postwar period. Since credit abroad also grew rapidly, the country's balance of payments once again felt the consequences, and for 1963 and 1965 new controls became necessary (Kolko 1975).

The Kennedy and Johnson administrations, like the Nixon administration later on, were faced with the problem of dollars leaving the country in order to evade all kinds of national controls (as well as the devaluation) and to maximize their profits. The Kennedy government taxed loans to abroad; Johnson imposed controls on the outflows of production and banking capital. Nixon prolonged those controls with certain modifications until 1974. The impact of these measures on the U.S. balance of payments was insignificant in the short term, but in the long term it was devastating. Far from being reduced, capital exports increased considerably from 1964 to 1974 with the massive exit abroad of North American banks. As a consequence of the controls imposed from 1963 and 1965, and the policy trend to maintain them, the corporations requiring credit had to find it outside the United States, while the banks, so as to continue their operations with their leading clients (the transnationals), had to obtain and lend capital outside their country of origin. Banking, as productive capital before it, was transnationalized, thus ensuring its rate of profit. Consequences of this for the world economy and particularly for Third World countries were, and still are, of great importance.

The U.S. balance of payments crisis of the 1960s can be explained by the amounts of capital exported by the North American transnationals and the cost of the Vietnam War, aggravated by the falling demand in Western Europe and Japan for North American products. Controls imposed by Washington on the exit of dollars abroad encouraged North American banks to evade these controls and expand their activities in other countries, with a view to continuing to finance the transnational corporations. In addition, restrictive economic policy in the United States produced a reduction in domestic credit demand, which led to a new excess of dollars in the domestic markets as well as in Europe.

The resulting financial surplus or excessive liquidity in international capital markets in the 1970s provoked a wave of strong credit directed to the public sectors of underdeveloped countries. This increased their external debts and strengthened at the same time the power of the big transnational banks responsible for channeling of resources. Other factors that contributed to this double phenomenon of transnational banking control of the international economy and expansion of Third World debt are related to effects of the crisis in the capitalist system itself, characterized by a mixture of stagnation and inflation and the recycling of the so-called petrodollars after the crisis of 1973.

The link between the renewed power of transnational bankers and the crisis of the international financial system has two main slants. On the one hand, it is clear that as recession hit production levels in the developed countries, the capitalist, seeking to secure his profit at all cost, shifted his efforts to the banking sphere, thus producing a shift from productive assets to specifically financial assets. On the other hand, inflation put transnational enterprises, traditionally self-financing, in a weak position, forcing them to incur debt to maintain operations.

With respect to the link between liquidity expansion, the power of transnational banks, and recycling of petrodollars, the result is just as evident. The increase in energy prices generated a surplus which, when not invested locally, had to be recycled in a way that earned it a return. The recent expansion in the market of eurocurrencies, the principal mechanism through which oil surpluses have been recycled, is not an event in isolation. The market has grown from U.S. $14 billion in 1964, to 155 billion in 1973, to 485 billion in 1978, and to 855 billion by September 1981.[4,5]

GROWTH OF THIRD WORLD FOREIGN DEBT

Expansion during the 1970s of the Third World's foreign debt, and the increasing transnational banking control of the world economy described in the previous section, are two closely-linked phenomena. In concrete terms, this close relationship can clearly be observed in the flourishing market for eurodollars, eurocurrencies, or foreign exchange, and its "appropriation" by Third World countries.

Origins of the eurocurrencies market date back to the 1940s, in the large quantity of dollars that arrived in Western Europe as a result, initially, of the Soviet Union's decision to transfer dollars previously deposited in the United States to Europe, fearing the U.S. government might freeze them. These Soviet dollars were redeposited in British banks, which used them to grant loans with favorable returns. These operations increased with the dollar activities of other North American and European banks in the old world, as they sought for bigger and better business transactions. In this way a market was formed, initially named the eurodollar market, later the eurocurrency market, and now the international or transnational foreign exchange market. Right from its initiation, the transnational foreign exchange market registered high and sustained growth rates, until it is now the second largest world financial market.

The accelerated transnationalization of North American banking was a stimulating influence on the eurocurrency market, which served the double purpose (as already noted) of providing liquidity in moments of relative scarcity to the head offices of North American banks whose subsidiaries operated in Europe, and of profitably placing dollars accumulated in these head offices in times of relative abundance. For example, from 1966 to 1969 foreign branches of North American banks loaned around a quarter of their deposits to their head offices for internal credit (demands of the head offices evidently also contributed to establishment of branches overseas). In 1969 alone the remittance of eurodollars to the United States reached U.S. $14 billion.

In 1970 the demand for dollars from head offices of banks operating in the eurodollar market decreased. This forced their foreign branches to look for new customers in public sectors of either those countries with a continuous flow of capital (such as Italy and England), or those underdeveloped countries that suffered from a chronic balance of payments deficit. Furthermore, faced with the possibility of a devaluation of the dollar, Europe established exchange controls, which reduced the possibility of increasing bank loans to transnational companies and improved the image of Third World countries as ideal receivers of this financial surplus.

OPEC's decision to quadruple the price of oil in 1973 marked a critical point for the international private banking system, in that the increase in oil prices gave the banks the opportunity to make very profitable transactions: the total amount of overseas loans from the main international banks in the eurocurrency market is calculated to have more than quadrupled from the end of 1973 to the end of 1980.

Until 1969, the main users of eurocurrencies (the dollar being the predominant currency) were U.S. banks overseas and large U.S. companies. When this type of credit went into decline, credit directed toward public and private sectors in industrialized countries began to gain importance, and underdeveloped countries began to appear as important borrowers. Their emergence in this context was due to the impossibility of satisfying their demands for external finance from exclusively official sources with proven slow growth, combined with the accelerated build-up of excessive liquidity in the eurocurrency market and pressures exerted by international bankers on governments of developing countries in order that they might place their surplus where it would yield better income.

The importance of developing countries as borrowers was highlighted by the world energy crisis in 1973, since countries that were not oil exporters had to face a huge shortage of financial resources in order to cover new energy prices. Paradoxically, as has already been pointed out, it was precisely because of recycling of petrodollars in recent years that some developing countries (oil exporters) also operate in the eurocurrency market as net suppliers of resources.

By 1975, underdeveloped countries were already absorbing 56.5 percent of the world eurocurrency debt and, although it is true that this percentage fell slightly in the three following years as the demand for funds from developed countries also increased slightly, it still represented more than half, and reached a record 57.5 percent in 1979.[6] In 1980, however, it dropped by more than 10 percent, and by the end of 1981 it had reached less than 40 percent (Morgan Guaranty Trust 1980, 1982).

Several important issues come to mind when considering the Third World public foreign debt. First, there is the question we have already raised of its accelerated expansion from the 1970s onward. Second, there is the question of its increasing concentration among a handful of debtors, which can be seen clearly throughout the eurodollar market. Although practically all underdeveloped countries have some kind of connection with it, by the end of 1979 seven borrowers (Mexico, Brazil, South Korea, Argentina, Venezuela, Algiers, and the Philippines) were absorbing more than 60 percent of the developing world's debt with this market. Five countries accounted for an additional 15 percent (Iran, Indonesia, Chile, Morocco, and the United Arab Emirates), and three (Malaysia, Taiwan, and Peru) accounted for an additional 5 percent (The World Bank 1981). Furthermore, in every year since 1975, a Latin American country has been the highest single debtor, making it appropriate to talk about the "Latin Americanization" of the eurocurrency debt.[7]

Third, for a good many Third World countries, the public foreign debt has taken on a private nature—this will sometimes be referred to as "privatization" of the debt—as a result of both the inflexibility of external bilateral and multilateral official assistance that the world has come to know in recent years, and the creation of a surplus supply of loan capital on private international capital markets which reflects, among other things, recession in the principal industrialized countries and recycling of petrodollars. In 1967 private lenders represented only 28 percent of the Third World foreign debt, in 1978 the proportion was already more than 50 percent, and in 1980 more than 63 percent (and in countries like Brazil and Mexico around 80 percent of the entire foreign debt or more) (The World Bank 1979, 1981).[8]

As was to be expected, in those countries that suffered the "privatization" of their debts, financial conditions have become harder, with inevitable repercussions on the burden of their debt service. However, paradoxically, due to the presence of other important variables such as income in foreign exchange for exports, national and per capita income levels, etc., the situation is less distressing for these countries than for those that have low incomes and no access to the private capital market.

Fourth, we have growing transnational banking control over the private component of the Third World foreign debt. Credits from large financial institutions have finally overtaken in importance the previously important loans from suppliers. In 1969, credits from suppliers represented 49.6 percent of total private credit. In 1978 they represented less than 20 percent at the same time as credit from private banking and financial institutions represented around 70 percent. By 1980, supplier credits represented less than 10 percent, while loans by financial institutions approached 90 percent (The World Bank 1979, 1981).

The fifth issue is the continuation of "bilateralization" of the officially-originated debt, in spite of slight modifications over recent years and multiple requests from the developing world for expansion of multilateral credit to balance out and eventually reverse this tendency. In 1969, for example, bilateral credit represented 76.6 percent of the total official lending figure. By 1978, even though this figure had fallen slightly, it continued to account for most of the total (71 percent), reflecting both the slowness with which resources of institutions like the World Bank increase and the power of government agencies that grant loans to Third World countries, many of which tie their credits to conditions that are highly political and of important commercial advantage to the creditor.

The sixth point is the enormously worrying prospect for the developing world's foreign debt in the near and distant future, in times of world recession accompanied by inflation and deterioration of terms of trade in developing countries that have no oil. It is also worrying that, although interest rates continue to be high, there is an increased need for financial resources that will be difficult to meet— endangering both paying of accumulated debts and financing of projects for social demands that would be difficult to satisfy in the domestic political arena.

Seventh, like direct loans from foreign banks, eurocredit has hardened the structure of the Third World foreign debt basically by shortening the time limits, rather than insisting on higher interest rates. It is estimated that by the end of the 1980s more than half of these non-oil exporting countries' new debt with the eurocurrency market will have been used for refinancing bank debts that will have already fallen due. There is increasing concern about Third World countries' ability to pay, since the demands posed by servicing the debt have multiplied so enormously—the "vicious circle of indebtedness." It means that the indebted countries continue getting into more and more debt in order to keep up payments on their accumulated debts. It also means that the contribution of this indebtedness to growth of a good many countries that have found themselves in this vicious circle situation for years must be questioned, if not reconsidered. These countries must now face dangers such as bankruptcy or even adoption of measures that creditors perceive with great hostility—such as massive renegotiations, suspensions, moratoria, and unilateral remittances.[9]

Finally, there is the question of relative "de-North-Americanization" of Third World foreign debt and the new aggressive attitude of European bankers (to say nothing about the even greater strength of Japanese bankers). Even though North American bankers are still the leaders (individually considered) in the eurocurrency market, they have lost an important part of their share in recent years. Such a relative retreat of North American banks vis-à-vis the Third World has created more elbow room for Japanese and European bankers—particularly for the latter, since Japanese bankers are known for their instability in the market, following as they do very tight guidelines put forward by their government (see "U.S. Banks Are Losing" 1980).

There is an important difference between North American and European banks that could be used by the latter to increase their expansion in the Third World in general and in Latin America in particular: the fact that North American banks are more "profit-oriented" and follow higher interest rates, whereas European banks are more "relation-oriented" and are willing to diminish slightly their profit rates in the short term in order to secure markets for the products of their countries of origin, as well as supplies of strategic natural resources (U.N. Center for Transnational Studies 1980).[10] Even though detailed country studies are needed to prove this as a general point, in the case of Mexico it is very clear. There, American bankers shifted their portfolio completely for alleged "profit reasons," changing from providing more than 60 percent of all foreign loans to the Mexican public sector in 1977 to providing less than 30 percent in 1981.

Japanese as well as European banks did not seem to be too bothered that the Mexican government was paying smaller spreads than other public sectors of the world (and even the Mexican private sector), and increased their level of activity. "Profit reasons" also led American banks deeper into the Mexican private sector and, as a consequence, the present financial crisis of the country hit them harder, since their dealings with such a sector have become more tense.

In spite of all these problems and others that are not considered here because of limited space, forecasts seem to indicate that Third World indebtedness will increase and continue to exist as one of the most important variables to be considered in the near future. Forecasts also indicate that external financing could come from three possible sources: official sources, which include bilateral and multilateral assistance; foreign direct investment; and loans from private sources, especially banks. The slow growth of official financing and opposition of certain governments to speeding up that growth mean that its projected participation for 1985 will not surpass a third of what is needed, leaving most of the rest to private financing, mainly from banks (since direct foreign investment is not expected to amount to more than 10 percent).

This decline of official capital in financing developing countries' debt is not desirable. Although it is true that it implies more interference and even more ideological motivations (better and more "untied" mechanisms for official foreign financing can be thought of), the short-term limits of private loans (which are, in any case, now not so "neutral") disqualify them from many kinds of investment. Moreover, as has already been pointed out, private loans harden the structure of the debt and increase the burden of its service. In addition, direct investment and particularly private loans are sources of unpredictable and potentially volatile financing, an uncertainty that adds to the greater financial cost involved in using these kinds of resources. The fact that it is not certain that the international private banks will be able to provide the resources required by developing countries only adds to the uncertainty.

Doubts concerning creditors' capacity for expansion, but especially concerning the ability of the debtors to service their financial commitments abroad, as well as the cases of Poland, Argentina, Mexico, etc., have focused the attention of international organizations and governments of industrialized countries not only on "productive" utilization of foreign credit, but also on analysis of policies for administering the foreign debt in underdeveloped countries. This can be observed in actions of both the International Monetary Fund and the World Bank in these countries: annual consultations, stabilization programs, establishment of plausible goals relating to the structure of the debt, and even occasionally, supervision and control of policies to be implemented. The International Monetary Fund has often acted as a guarantor for investments made by international banking in the Third World, where it directs almost half of all its overseas operations. The World Bank has also often acted as a guide for public policies by favoring with its credit those sectors capable of making more functional the integration of peripheral and underdeveloped economies into the system's central economies.

CONCLUSIONS

What is to be done? We are faced, as this chapter has demonstrated, with a Third World public foreign debt that not only is expanding but is also, in some cases, being increasingly rapidly privatized, and is now predominantly held by transnational banking. The objective of this section is to provide some general guidelines for pursuing a solution.

The first fundamental point to remember is that, though all underdeveloped countries have some kind of public foreign debt, it does not always have the same characteristics. For a small number of countries, the most important part of the entire foreign debt of the Third World is concentrated in the hands of large international private banks, which have become the main creditors. In one way or another, these countries are "captive debtors" of these banks and a large part of their new indebtedness with these institutions is for servicing the debt they have already incurred. These are countries that have been forced by the vicious circle of indebtedness to allocate almost all the nominal increase in their foreign debt to servicing the previous one. However, there are also, at the other extreme, cases of foreign banks whose loans to certain countries are so large that they have become "captive creditors," having to lend to them (always at higher interest rates and shorter amortization terms, of course) in order to be able to carry on charging their interest. This becomes even clearer if one remembers the figures recently published by the Federal Reserve System of the United States. For example, by the end of 1981 the nine largest banks in the United States with financial assets on the order of U.S. $26 billion had over U.S. $57 billion in loans to Third World countries—or more than double their capital, of which a substantial proportion was in Mexico and Brazil alone (Rowen 1982).

Such high exposure to Third World loans has damaged the banks themselves, and leads to my first guideline for action: creation of a negotiating group with the most important debtors to large international banks, led by countries that (like Brazil) have reached the point at which the bulk of their debt with these banks is used in paying them back. As noted, in 1979 seven countries represented almost 65 percent of the total Third World debt incurred with foreign banks. Four of these countries were Latin American (Mexico, Brazil, Venezuela, and Argentina), which by the end of 1980 represented 55.2 percent of such debt. The other three were South Korea, Algeria, and the Philippines. Assuming that at least Algeria would join with the Latin American countries, the five would represent almost 60 percent of the total debt—giving them a good chance of gaining some control over their lenders if they were willing to act as a group.

Such a proposal seeks not so much confrontation and conflict, simply joint negotiation from similar positions. Such a group could be useful in providing and exchanging information to help its members to get better loan terms and conditions. It would also constitute a source of experience that can be useful in terms of concentrated action. Further, it could provide technical assistance to other countries with less bargaining experience. At the same time, it could be useful in attracting the attention of bankers and taking them to the negotiating table—where the main argument would be to negotiate not nonpayment, but payment under better conditions as well as better terms for new loans. Without more financial resources to repay old debts and build new projects to generate foreign exchange, without better financial conditions for those resources, and without greater flexibility from lenders, the borrowers may collapse and the entire international financial community with them.

My second guideline addresses the needs of those countries whose debt is basically of official origin, contracted with bilateral and multilateral financing organizations, but whose burden in terms of foreign exchange needed to service the debt is even more serious because of their weak international trade position. We can, of course, begin by suggesting that they must continue to insist, in all international economic negotiations, on increased net flows of real resources with favorable conditions. We can also make the case, once again, for the need to democratize, reorient, and revitalize international financing organizations such as the World Bank and the regional banks, and we can list some devastating criticisms of their current stance. It is a fact that they are not providing resources in necessary quantities or under appropriate conditions. It is a fact, too, that some of them are detaching themselves more and more from the development spirit or philosophy on which they were established (this is particularly true of the World Bank). It is also a fact that they attempt to determine with their credits the pattern of industrialization in receiver countries, and to accelerate and increase internationalization of the economies of those countries. It is equally true that their decisions are so linked with politics that they refuse resources to countries that follow paths which the powerful countries within these institutions do not consider ideal (as was proven in the case of Chile during the government of President Allende). More commitment should be demanded from the countries in the North to development of countries in the South (for historic, structural, and even ideological reasons this is important), and further cooperation should be sought between socialist countries and the Third World (as a demonstration of better East–West understanding). But when all this has been said, the most urgent issue is greater coresponsibility among the countries of the South. We have already discussed the paradox that while one group of underdeveloped countries is the main debtor in the eurocurrency market, another group is an important creditor; and that a large part of the oil surplus of these countries is the cause of deterioration of the balance of payments and increased foreign indebtedness of other Third World countries.

It is evident, then, that one must propose the creation of new mechanisms for financial cooperation among the Third World countries and restructuring and reorientation of mechanisms that already exist, in order to increase their pool of resources and put them in an untied way at the disposal of the poorest countries—in the same way as the transfer of resources from North to South should take place.

A few last words concerning the possibility of a new role for Europe in what has been discussed, with respect to the developing world in general, and to Latin America in particular. Up to now Latin America has not been of any real importance for Europe or vice versa. Important and even "special" relations have existed between specific countries in Latin America and Europe; the relationship between Brazil and Germany could be a good example. However, the overwhelming influence of the United States in the Latin American region has, by and large, inhibited European penetration. True (for the Third World in general), a relative retreat of North American banks has meant a relative advance of European banks (but most of all of Japanese banks), particularly in the field of loans, but this is insufficient evidence to support speculation on "a new presence of Europe in Latin America." So far, the North American presence has been only part of the story. There has also been lack of interest and enthusiasm on the part of Europeans vis-à-vis Latin America; and, even more important, there has been no meaningful difference between the way Europeans in general deal with Latin America and the way North Americans do. Therefore, Latin American expectations as to the feasibility of Europe as a real inspiration to diversify dependence on the United States have not gone beyond pious hopes. Maybe now, with a socialist government in France (and the hope that this may positively influence voters in other European countries) as well as in Spain, Latin America can expect a greater and more productive (and more humane) approach from Europe.

NOTES

1. A more extensive and more structured treatment of the "third world strategy" in political as well as economic terms can be found in Green and Heller (1980).
2. A more complete treatment of the obstacles faced by the third world countries in their search for a new order in the field of international financing—as well as in other fields such as those of international trade, money, technology, etc.—can be found in Laszlo et al. (1980). See also Lozoya and Bhattacharya (1980).
3. A more complete and detailed study can be found in Green (1981).
4. Esteves and Green (1980). The 1981 data are from The Morgan Guaranty Trust Co., *World Financial Markets* (1982), 15.
5. Moreover, the process of internationalizing these financial flows has led to the appearance of autonomous generators of additional liquidity, mainly in the eurocurrency markets. Specifically, these are banking multipliers, whose secondary money-creating effects are increased by virtue of the lack of control exercised by national and supranational authorities on those markets, authorities incapable of establishing reserve norms, bases of expansion, and contraction of the multiplier impact. For a detailed discussion of this question see Raphael, in Lozoya and Bhattacharya (1980), 175–79.
6. See United Nations Conference on Trade and Development (1978), and OECD (1980).
7. This process can be explained in part by the behavior of moneylenders. First, bankers operating in the eurocurrency market (whether one is talking about

North American, European, or Japanese banks) who make loans to developing countries prefer the "oil producers." Second, they favor the relatively larger countries with "high incomes." Third, they prefer those countries with "stable" political regimes, growing economies, and a wide mineral resource base (not only oil), which maintain permanent solid contacts with the international banking community and which, in the case of countries that have recently become independent, maintain a good political relationship with their mother countries.

As far as the issue of what the funds obtained by developing countries on the eurocurrency market are to be used for is concerned, moneylenders do not appear to be demanding or even interested—an apparently nonideological attitude which is open to question (as discussed later in the chapter).

Public sectors of developing countries, and not the private, have been principally benefited from eurocurrency credit; in particular, public enterprises connected to the extractive and transformation spheres, as well as others that are even less attractive to official financing (with the exception of the IMF), to support the balance of payments. For example, from 1971 to 1973, 90 percent of the credit obtained by developing countries on the eurocurrency market was absorbed by governments (36 percent) and public sectors (54 percent) of the borrowers, and only 8 percent was channeled into the private sector. Recently this proportion has been altered in countries like Mexico and Brazil which have flourishing private sectors, although in both cases the public sector foreign debt continues to be greater than that of the private sector.

8. This tendency to privatize the debt does not apply in all cases. For example, there are countries like India and Pakistan where the official lenders represent an extremely high percentage—more than 90 percent—of the debt which, moreover, was contracted with a high proportion in concessional terms. This does not mean that they are countries without debt problems. Quite the contrary, they have very serious problems, but the solutions, as will be seen, must be different.

9. As far as the Third World's payment capacity is concerned, as in the case of other issues discussed here, the intensity of the solution is a function of the intensity of the problem. Even though countries with high incomes face complications of a growing "privatization" of their foreign debt, the very dynamics of their economic process make the burden of service of their debt relatively less costly than for countries with low incomes, often characterized by possessing a foreign sector that is simultaneously undynamic and excessively dependent. Therefore, this last group of countries, in spite of owing mainly to official agencies and benefiting from concessions, has seen its foreign exchange service/income ratio increase (meaning that more money is used to repay debts and less to buy imports) between 1977, when such ratio stood at 12.5 percent, and 1976, when the figure registered was 23.3 percent; this points not only to an expansion of their foreign debt but also to a deterioration of their ability to pay it. This situation does not leave high-income countries without problems, as has been recently shown in the case of Argentina, Brazil, and Mexico. The case is quite different for oil-exporting countries. While it is true that they also saw their service foreign exchange income ratio increase from 2.6 percent in 1967 to 6.7 percent in 1976, the increase turned out to be less serious for them in the context of their economies than for low-income countries. As for countries with average incomes, their situation improved as their service foreign exchange income ratio fell

from 10.4 percent in 1967 to 9.7 percent in 1976, with periods of even further relief registered in between (in 1974 and 1975 this relationship was at only 8.5 percent).

10. A more detailed study on differences of bank strategies according to geographic origin can be found in United Nations Center for Transnational Studies (1980).

REFERENCES

Caputo, Orlando and Francisco Pizarro. *Imperialismo, dependencia y relaciones internacionales.* Buenos Aires: Amorrortu, 1975.

Caso Raphael, Agustin. "Changing Patterns in International Liquidity and Eurocurrency Multipliers." In Jorge A. Lozoya and A. K. Bhattacharya (eds.), *The Financial Issues of the New International Economic Order.* New York: Pergamon Press, 1980.

Esteves, Jaime and Rosario Green. "El resurgimiento del capital financiero en los setentas: contribución a su analisis." *Economia de America Latina* (March 1980).

Green, Rosario. *Estado y banca transnacional en México.* México: CEESTEM-Nueva Imagen, 1981.

Green, Rosario and Claude Heller. "Surgimiento y Proyección del Tercer Mundo: de Bandung a los ochenta." *Foro Internacional,* 21:2 (October/December 1980):161–93.

Kolko, Joyce. *Los Estados Unidos y la crisis del capitalismo mundial.* Espana: Avance, 1975.

Laszlo, Ervin, Jorge A. Lozoya, A. K. Bhattacharya, Jaime Estevez, Rosario Green, and Venkata Raman. *The Obstacles to the New International Economic Order.* New York: Pergamon Press, 1980.

Lozoya, Jorge A. and A. K. Bhattacharya (eds.). *The Financial Issues of the New International Economic Order.* New York: Pergamon Press, 1980.

Morgan Guaranty Trust. *World Financial Markets* (monthly). September 1979, December 1980, March 1982.

OECD. "Access by Developing Countries to International Financial Markets." *Financial Market Trends,* 13 (1980).

Rowen, Hobart. "Nine Major Banks Highly Exposed on Third World Loans." *The Washington Post,* 24 October 1982.

UN Center for Transnational Studies. *Transnational Banks: Operations and Strategies and Their Effects on Developing Countries.* New York: The United Nations, 1980 (mimeo).

UN Conference on Trade and Development. *The Flow of Financial Resources.* TD/B.C.3.150, September 1978.

"U.S. Banks Are Losing Their Share of the Market." *Euromoney* (February 1980).

The World Bank. *Borrowing in International Capital Markets.* Washington, DC: The World Bank, 1981.

———. *World Debt Tables.* Washington, DC: The World Bank, 1979 and 1981.

9

DEFENSE AND SECURITY ISSUES: IMPLICATIONS FOR THE "NEW ATLANTIC TRIANGLE"

Alexandre de Souza Costa Barros

The Atlantic Triangle is a collective term[1] used to refer to the system of trilateral contacts among the United States, Western Europe, and Latin America. My thesis, in brief, is that although such contacts are increasing, and will continue to increase for the foreseeable future, triangle is not necessarily a useful concept to apply to them. It seems to imply that the relationship as a whole is more than the sum of its parts—in other words, that the three parties are willing to adapt important aspects of the triangular relationship in order to preserve it. I regard this implication as untenable, especially in the areas of defense and security. In my view, both centrifugal and centripetal forces operate on the partners of the relationship. These work against each other to different degrees at different times. But both types are strong enough that total atomization is as unlikely to occur as is an alliance system tight enough to imply a resignation of individual freedom of action. I shall refer to the implications of these counterbalancing forces as "distributive" implications.

DISTRIBUTIVE IMPLICATIONS OF THE TRIPARTITE RELATIONSHIP TO DATE

Since the late 1930s, when the United States emerged as a world power, it has, qua nation state, established a privileged position in international affairs which was tailored to serve its national interest. Recently, however, as noted in many chapters in this volume, the international position of the United States is being severely questioned. In this context, particularly with respect to defense, several competing theories have been put forward whose *raison d'être* seems to be to preserve the status quo and, thus, the historically dominant position of the United States, although such doctrines are assumed to preserve and enhance the interests of other international partners as well (Child 1978).

One of these doctrines, dating back to the late 1950s and early 1960s, is that of the Atlantic Triangle. The concept is a triangle comprising Brazil, the United States, and Western Europe, formed to defend more effectively than the three acting separately, the interests of the Western world. This notion was, in effect, merely a more systematic articulation of the pragmatic defense arrangements of World War II, developed in the late 1930s to serve the specific Allied goal of setting up bases on the northeast promontory of Brazil, in order to defend the South Atlantic. In the context of World War II, such arrangements made eminent sense for the United States and its European allies, although Brazil remained somewhat less enthusiastic.[2] After World War II, the military bases were deactivated and new arrangements were set up more in line with U.S. needs of the time. The so-called triangle was placed in abeyance, as the United States sought to implement its interests by means of NATO on the one hand, and the military arms of the OAS (the Inter-American Reciprocal Defense Treaty, the Inter-American Defense Board, the Inter-American Defense College, and related institutions), on the other. The keystone of U.S. foreign policy in the immediate postwar era was the political problem of containing communist expansion. The important implication of these post-World War II arrangements with respect to Latin America was that, from the defense point of view, contacts between Latin American and European countries were reduced to a lower level than the one that prevailed prior to World War II. The European military missions that had trained Latin American armies were replaced by United States counterparts, the hardware that had previously come from Europe started to flow from the United States,[3] and the doctrines that guided the Latin American military after World War II became those of the United States.

Although the basic doctrines underlying the tripartite relationships continued to be the same in the 1960s as those prevailing in the immediate aftermath of World War II, the 1960s brought changes that rendered them increasingly outdated. Latin American countries were locked in a dependent relationship with the United States that demanded that they make a greater and greater effort to end up selling less and less to the United States. But European markets were beginning to open up for Latin America. And although U.S. influence continued to be pervasive, contacts among European and Latin American countries began to increase.[4]

These increased contacts, in turn, encouraged several countries in South America to start their own "national security diplomacy." Ironically, this kind of diplomacy became possible in part as a result of the military governments that took over the seats of power in Latin American countries—either under the sponsorship of the United States, or with its open or disguised support—facilitated in many instances by the development of higher war colleges, also under the inspiration of the United States.[5] One of the most important implications of this new diplomatic style, from the military point of view, was that the lines of supply of military materiél connecting Western Europe and Latin America, virtually severed after World War II, were gradually but steadily rebuilt. From the point of view of Latin American military elites, the advantage of these new relationships was that their countries were free to acquire the most sophisticated hardware their money could buy, rather than merely what the supplying countries wanted to sell for their own political ends—as was the case with respect to the United States. U.S. policy in this area was based on the premise that poor countries should not invest "development" money in expensive and sophisticated equipment which brought more prestige, but was not strictly necessary for their defense.[6] European suppliers were under no such constraints.

Interestingly, the situation was not perceived as a threat by the United States because the Western European–Latin American–U.S. relationship was not seen as involving the interdependence of nation states. Europeans were supplying Latin America with weaponry and with doctrines that implied a potential diminution of U.S. influence over Latin America. However, as long as the keystone of U.S. foreign policy continued to be fulfilled—the containment of the communist advance in the Americas—there was no cause for concern. The only Latin American incidents that worried the United States during the 1960s and early 1970s were the Russian support to Cuba and to Salvador Allende.

Under the Carter administration, however, the same cannot be said of Latin American perceptions of U.S. actions. Its policy of linking violations of human rights (and, ultimately, what were perceived as the U.S. national interests) more directly with arms sales (and, ultimately, U.S. profits) pushed the linkage between the two to a point where both elites and counterelites in countries under authoritarian rule started to fear the next move of the U.S. president.[7] Coupled with the development achieved by some Latin American countries, and their renewed contacts with Western Europe, the Carter policy was suicidal from the U.S. point of view. European competition entering Latin American markets showed a remarkable aggressiveness. In addition, two countries in Latin America had made substantial progress in producing weapons for themselves and for export: Brazil and Argentina.[8] The end result was greater independence on the part of many Latin American countries vis-à-vis the United States (some would prefer to call it diversification of dependence) and stronger contacts with their Latin American neighbors (as well as with Western Europe).

A NEW ATLANTIC TRIANGLE?

Revival of the idea of the Atlantic Triangle, from the defense point of view, may be considered as an attempt to lock the interests linking Western Europe and Latin America with those linking Western Europe with the United States into a system under which U.S. interests are not impaired (see Hayes 1980). The recent loss of U.S. military power in the world[9] makes the idea of such a triangle attractive from the U.S. point of view. This is so because the new Atlantic Triangle, in a sense, revives the status quo "ante-decadence," i.e., it restores primacy to the interests of the United States. The idea of the triangle, then, either tries to revive or to restore North American control over relations among Latin Americans and Western Europeans. As was mentioned earlier, the fact that this is a convenient arrangement from the point of view of the United States, however, does not mean that it is a plausible conceptualization of the wider reality. The basic flaw in the reasoning on which it is based is that it tends to equate the interests of the United States with the interests of capitalism generally. The set of relationships is, in fact, more complex than the one which simplistically considers "the State as executive committee of the bourgeoisie." Except in a situation of major East–West crisis, sectoralized capitalist interests in neither Western Europe nor the United States coincide necessarily with the interests of the United States as a nation state.[10]

The first important point to be stressed is that the three vertices of the so-called triangle are highly uneven, a fact that makes it hard to define shared common defense interests. The second point is that one of the vertices (the United States) is a single country, whereas the other two are each occupied by several countries that, although located in the same geographical region, may—and do—have diverse interests in relation to the countries located in the other two vertices. The third point (and here I am using the geometrical analogy more strictly) is that the actual drawing of a defense-oriented triangle, considering the characteristics of the vertices, necessitates an obtuse angle for the United States, implying angles for Europe and Latin America that are together smaller than $90°$. Such an imbalance in the triangle would be tolerable only if all parties involved perceived that their interests were sufficiently threatened for them to accept involvement in such a limiting relationship. This is not the case, and it does not look likely in the future.

The counterargument is that the limitations are not due to the triangle but to wider systems—that both NATO and the Inter-American Military System imply limitations on the freedom of the "junior" partners. However, this is not adequate refutation. If we consider NATO, the limitation can be explained by the fact that the perception of the threat posed by the Soviet Union justifies the restraint, which the Europeans imposed on *themselves*, and the consequent posture of relative submission to the United States. The Inter-American Military System is a similar situation. The threat of communist subversion as perceived by civilian and military sectors of the elites of South American countries *themselves*, was sufficient to justify and rationalize their interlocking in the system. The existence of these two systems of alliances,[11] thus, finds justification in the *perception of threats* which are operative *for specific theaters*. The idea of a triangle involving Western Europe, South America, and the United States implies a more complex, more general, and more difficult to rationalize arrangement. It implies a "socialization of danger"—that is, the transfer and acceptance of threats that may be present (and credible) locally, but that are not interchangeable and not real outside the specific theaters in which they originated.

Defense interests of the United States below the equator have been analyzed by Hayes (1980). A sizable portion of these interests is related to the protection of the oil routes of the South Atlantic which, as of 1980, accounted for about 25 percent of U.S. imports, and for approximately 60 percent of Western European supplies. In this area, it is possible to define common interests of the United States and Western Europe. Latin America, however, does not perceive itself as *equally* threatened.[12] Furthermore, although the proportion of European oil transported by the South Atlantic is larger than that of U.S. oil, Western Europe seems to perceive the Soviet threat in the South Atlantic as less serious than does the United States. This is because competition between the United States and the Soviet Union is related to world hegemony (ergo, any threat is a major threat), whereas the problems between Western Europe and the Soviet Union are much more confined to the European theater.

We also have to take into consideration the fact that the foreign policy interests of the same country may differ over time, and may also differ with respect to different parts of the world.[13] For these reasons it is even difficult to define common interests shared *within* Western Europe toward Latin America. This is not due to any diminution of the perception of the magnitude of the Soviet threat in the European context. It simply means that, outside the European context, Western European countries may have foreign policy interests that are not consonant (they may even seem, at first sight, somewhat contradictory) with those they have within the European environment. In many cases, it is possible to sort out the dissonance by separating defense interests into those that are limited to Europe, those related specifically to South America, and those related specifically to Africa. Any relatively tight alliance involving the United States and any third geographic area would certainly clash with this sorting out of different interests and dealing with them piecemeal. Such an option is not likely to interest Western European countries because it would impose a limitation on their freedom which brings with it neither protection against a serious threat nor new advantages.

As noted, the United States and the Soviet Union, in contrast, are competing for global hegemony, so any threat is a serious threat. For instance, the presence of Cuban troops in Angola is perceived by the United States as a major danger, as much as it is perceived by the Soviet Union as an important step toward victory. This is not so from the point of view of either Western European or South American governments, even though many of these are conservative and staunchly anti-communist.

Despite the strong anti-communist postures of the Brazilian government, for example, not only on the internal front but also in the inter-American context, the presence of Cuban troops in Angola does not appear to bother Brazilian policymakers: Brazil supports the Angolan government and seems to be extending its influence in Angola as much as it can. The same is becoming true of Brazilian relations with other black African countries. Argentina, through different channels, appears to have a similar posture. Although it participated in a recent crisis in the South Atlantic, and is publicly identified as one of the major advocates of some sort of South Atlantic defense alliance, Argentina has reaped profits by trading with the Soviet Union at the expense of the United States grain embargo. Indeed, in early 1980, there were fears that Argentina might be tempted to develop closer ties with the Soviet Union (which made U.S. policymakers shiver, and increased the traffic of higher-echelon U.S. diplomatic and military personnel between Washington and Buenos Aires). The fact that Argentina—or sectors of the Argentinian elite—has been advocating some sort of common defense arrangement for the South Atlantic, including South Africa, does not seem to be perceived by the Argentinians as necessarily clashing with their relations with the Soviet Union.[14]

Defense of the South Atlantic does not affect other South American countries as *directly*, with the possible exception of Chile, which is a peculiar case. Although Chile's interests are not affected by the hypothetical threat to the South Atlantic, it does have a major interest in participating in anything related to the Atlantic, in the hope of enhancing its position in the Beagle dispute. Participation in *any* Atlantic arrangement, in other words, strengthens Chile's claim over the channel islands.

The conclusion is clear. Defense of the South Atlantic, which seems to be the most relevant strategic issue involving the United States, Western Europe, and South America, does not seem able to attract enough consensus to justify or rationalize any tightly-defined triangular relationship.

Examining the issue of where exactly the southern vertex of the triangle should fall simply strengthens this conclusion. The Reagan administration would seem to want this vertex to fall around the fiftieth parallel—that is, involving Argentina. Such a location would probably face opposition from several Western European governments that would rather see Argentina out of such an arrangement, given the heavy political cost of having any more defense relations with Argentina than absolutely necessary in view of the recurrent accusations of violations of human rights in that country. Brazilian displeasure is no less likely. The fact that Argentina and Brazil managed to come to terms over the use of waters of border rivers does not mean that either country would welcome the idea of having important issues related to their national defense defined from the outside if they can avoid it.[15]

The other obvious possibility would be to locate the tip of the triangle somewhere in Brazil. In this case it would, as a matter of necessity, exclude virtually all of the rest of South America, a fact that would imply a retrogression of Brazilian foreign policy—the abandonment of the recent policy of *latinoamericanização*.[16]

From the point of view of Western Europe, this alternative would prove to be equally unacceptable, since it would imply the exclusion of the rest of Latin America from the immediate sphere of interest of Western Europe—including such issues as the sponsorship of democracy in Venezuela and Bolivia as much as the sales of submarines to Chile and nuclear plants to Brazil. From the point of view of the United States, this arrangement would increase anti-American feelings in the rest of Latin America, a favor the United States does not need from the viewpoint of its own interests as a nation state. Furthermore, such alienation would go against the interests of U.S.-based multinational corporations with Latin American subsidiaries.[17]

In conclusion it is worth mentioning two other, more minor points that also argue against the plausibility of a formal tripartite partnership. The first is the imbalance that would be created *internally* among armed forces in individual countries. The navy and airforce would inevitably gain at the expense of the army—tending to introduce destabilizing internal political changes and the triggering of internal arms races. The second is the touchy issue of the definition of "Latin America." Throwing Central and South America explicitly into the same bag equates the importance of countries that *are different,* culturally, geographically, and, most important in this context, from the point of view of national defense and national security. The existence of a formal alliance—such as is implied in the notion of the triangle—would inevitably force the explicit definition of differences which, though widely acknowledged on an implicit level, are best left ambiguous.

NOTES

The data that made this paper possible were partially collected while I was a Rockefeller Foundation Fellow in the Conflict and International Relations Program. I am grateful for comments on an earlier draft by Bernardo Quagliotti de Bellis, Mario Esteban Carranza, Ulrich Albrecht, John Child, and Carlos Portalez, which have been incorporated into the final draft to the extent possible.

1. The use of such collective terms in many instances either does not reflect reality adequately, or reflects it in such a blurred way as to be at best not useful and at worst distorting (see Huntington 1971).

2. About Brazil's position with respect to joining the allies, see Hilton (1975) and Gambini (1977).

3. To get an idea of the magnitude of these programs and of their evolution over time, see *Foreign Military Assistance Facts*, published yearly by the Department of Defense, Data Management Division Controller, Washington, DC.

4. It should be noted also that some countries that had traditionally maintained a more European "face" also fell under the spell of the United States. A discussion of the Argentinian and Brazilian positions vis-à-vis the United States focusing especially on the arena of the Organization of American States, can be found in Ribeiro (1980).

5. A detailed discussion of the bases and origins of national security diplomacy can be found in Barros (1975).

6. At the time there was practically no public discussion of effective versus sophisticated weaponry. Despite this, the problem was already present, especially in the case of less developed countries where the military manpower handling equipment was, on average, much less educated and trained than their counterparts in more developed countries. For a discussion of the issue in the U.S. case, see Fallows (1981).

7. Some implications of the U.S. arms sales policy to Latin America are discussed in Barros (1978).

8. The latter was mostly implemented through a state-owned corporation (Fabricaciones Militares); the former was a *formally* free enterprise policy of stimulating private corporations to produce weapons. The two experiences met with different degrees of success.

9. The question of the loss of U.S. power in the world was discussed in a special issue of *Business Week* (March 12, 1979) and also in Barros (1979).

10. Some people argue that linkages between Latin America and the United States will tend to be reinforced in the near future and that, in any case, the linkages between Latin America and Western Europe are mainly economic. The point I am trying to stress is that this is changing and that, despite efforts of the Reagan administration to rebuild the linkages as they have existed in the past, this is hardly possible because of irreversible changes in the world. In addition, the concentration of U.S. arms production in "high technology" weaponry is making it a less competitive supplier in the Third World where "it is the small arms which have been the instruments of most of the hundred wars since the Second World War from Lebanon to Biafra, from Yemen to Katanga, and which have been the cause of most loss of life. And it is

the trade in rifles, machine guns, or mortars which reveals the cold heart of a business in which diplomacy and wars are translated into orders, balance sheets and profits" (Sampson 1977).

11. The question as to whether the inter-American military system is or is not an alliance is discussed by Child (1978).

12. Although there may be some potential threat perceived in this area by Latin American elites, other interests are considered even more important.

13. For instance, the period following the defeat of Palme and the victories of Thatcher and Reagan produced headlines and analyses that stressed the advent of a "conservative wave about to sweep the world." The recent election of Mitterrand, together with the prospects of socialist administrations in Italy and Holland, have clearly diminished the size, force, and perspective of permanence of the "conservative wave."

14. It is possible to view all this as a need for muscle-flexing in the form of diversification on the part of Argentina and Brazil. As they feel that they develop, there are attempts to widen the horizons of their foreign policies in an effort to increase their own freedom of action.

15. A further point not discussed, but of paramount importance, is that in the event of any South Atlantic defense arrangement there will be need for bases involving, necessarily, the ceding of territory that would almost certainly be requested from Brazil—either in one of the Brazilian Atlantic islands, or in the Brazilian northeast promontory.

16. In other words, it would mean reviving the doctrine of the preferential ally—which may have flattered the egos of the Brazilian elite, but which was in the worst interests of the country. The term *latinoamericanização* is being used to convey the recent orientation of Brazilian foreign policy aimed toward a closer relationship with Latin American countries, especially, as a first stage, South American ones. As has also been pointed out, creation of a South Atlantic military alliance would reintroduce an issue which currently is being overcome—namely, the division of South America into Atlantic South America and Pacific South America, both with their backs facing each other. This would de facto go against the move being made by Brazil to get closer to its Latin American neighbors.

17. The lack of a formal alliance should not, however, rule out the possibility of joint naval operations in specific circumstances which might involve the United States, Latin America, and eventually South Africa if the situation so demands. From the point of view of South American countries, this might be "the best of all worlds" since they would not get involved in restricting alliances, to face hypothetical threats defined by the United States, but they would be available for specific military actions within the scope of their own interests.

REFERENCES

Barros, Alexandre de S. C. "The Diplomacy of National Security: South American International Relations in a Defrosting World." In Ronald Hellman and H. Jon Rosenbaum (eds.), *Latin America: The Search for a New International Order.* Beverly Hills, Ca: Sage/New York: John Wiley & Sons, 1975, 131–50.

------. "Ética e Economia na Venda de Armas." *Jornal da Tarde*, 26 December 1978.

------. "Os Riscos de um Gigante Atordoado." *Jornal da Tarde*, 16 June 1979.

Child, John. "The Inter American Military System." Ph.D. dissertation, American University (Washington, DC), 1978.

Fallows, James. "America's High Tech Weaponry: Why More Money is Buying Less Defense." *The Atlantic*, 247:5 (May 1981): 21–33.

Gambini, Roberto. *O Duplo Jogo de Getúlio Vargas: Influência Alemã e Americana no Estado Nôvo*. São Paulo: Editora Símbolo, 1977.

Hayes, Margaret Daly. "Security to the South: U.S. Interests in Latin America." *International Security*, 5 (Summer 1980): 130–51.

Hilton, Stanley. *Brazil and the Great Powers: The Politics of Trade Rivalry*. Austin: University of Texas Press, 1975.

Huntington, Samuel. "The Change to Change: Modernization, Development and Politics." *Comparative Politics*, 3 (April 1971): 283–322.

Ribeiro, Luciana de Nóbrega. "Dependência Econômica versus Dependência Política: Análise das Posições Brasileira e Argentina face aos E.U.A. na Organização dos Estados Americanos-O.E.A." Masters thesis, Universidade de Brasília, Departamento de Ciências Sociais, 1980.

Sampson, Anthony. *The Arms Bazaar*. New York: The Viking Press, 1977.

10

SECURITY ISSUES AND THE THIRD WORLD: A GERMAN PERSPECTIVE

Ulrich Albrecht

As commentators generally agree, "it is only during the past few years that West Germany has made its true weight felt in international relations" (Northedge 1974, 273).[1] The major reason for the new emergence of West Germany on the international scene is its relative economic strength, which now compares favorably with the foremost economic power, for many years the United States, and which is becoming an increasingly important indicator of a country's relative importance in international relations (Livingston 1976). West Germans are second only to the United States in international trade, exporting U.S. $188 billion in 1980 versus U.S. exports of $253 billion. However, they keep the largest monetary reserves in the world, reaching an all-time record of U.S. $40 billion at the end of 1978 (twice as much as the United States). In addition, they can now afford to be the second biggest spender on the military in the capitalist world—also a well-established yardstick for measuring relative importance in the international system.

THE NEW GERMAN ROLE IN WORLD AFFAIRS

The new economic importance of West Germany has stimulated expectations abroad about a more activist role for the Federal Republic in world affairs. "The United States, in particular, sees Germany as a likely recipient of some U.S. international responsibilities," according to one analyst (Bergsten 1975, 180).[2] The role anticipated for Germany seems to center in three areas: "an explicit bilateralism reflecting the two countries' predominance in the world economy"

(Bergsten 1975); "German political and economic involvement in countries such as Spain, Portugal, Italy, and Turkey, where we [Americans] are handicapped by past policy mistakes or failures" (Livingston 1976); and consultative procedures expanded "beyond Berlin and GDR [German Democratic Republic]–Federal Republic subjects to other political and economic issues" (Livingston 1976). The thrust of the third argument is clearly in the direction of the U.S. role in the southern spheres of the globe. It is no accident that the sources for this new perspective, particularly West German policy toward "the South," are non-German. Such frank wording is found neither in official German statements (which are still preoccupied with fears that a more active role may trigger unpleasant remarks about Germany's search for "Weltmacht"), nor in the texts of the established West German analysts of foreign relations. They may well be aware of the actual strength of the German position in international affairs, but there is a taboo involved, which is traditional with respect to German "preeminence" in world affairs. The few West German writers who have elaborated their views do make strong references to the, at least implicit, effects of the stark international role the Federal Republic is going to acquire, but they also challenge the view that this is an independent decision. Thielen (1973, 1) was the first to articulate such an assessment.

> First, the very existence and structure of the Federal Republic are a product of Western allied, specifically North American, interests and strategies of foreign policies . . . resulting in structurally identical domestic and foreign policy interests as well as power elites. . . . Second, any specific foreign policy goals of this dependent West German power elite . . . can only be converted into a foreign policy strategy if based on the external policies of the NATO Alliance and on those of the various members, according to their respective power potential.

In his widely read textbook on West German foreign policy, Besson (1970, 453) goes so far as to place policies toward the South as only the fifth priority in his system of West German foreign policy. United States–German relations, NATO, policies toward the Soviet Union and the German Democratic Republic are judged by Besson to be more important to and receive more attention from German politicians than the South, because he evaluates Third World countries as mere instruments for the pursuit of other, more high-ranking priorities.

Hence development policies certainly are more than a humanitarian demand. It shall dampen the uprising of the poor, shall channel revolution into the bed of evolution. Similarly as public social policy overcame class struggles in Western European industrialized states in this century, and made a reformist force out of socialist protest, development aid must strive to balance the violent demand of former colonies for emancipation with the requirements of international stability.

In northern Europe, the West German view that Scandinavia forms the "northern flank" of continental defense measures, which implies far-reaching German interests in the region, is usually rebutted. The north is regularly considered as politically and militarily stabilized within itself; West German invitations for cooperation are perceived as disturbing, to say the least. A Finnish analyst goes so far as to recommend to the West Germans that they abstain from any active policy in the Baltic region (Apunen 1977).

In contrast to political designs of the Federal Republic aimed at the North, there is no Third World voice that rejects specifically the acceptability of such notions. The policies of West Germany toward the South are to be assessed in a much more complicated setting. There is a German colonial heritage with respect to some Third World countries, and there are overwhelming West German economic interests in the raw-material-rich countries of the southern half of the globe. The policies of the Federal Republic toward the Third World have long been embedded in the more general framework of external relations as patterns in the East–West confrontation. It is the central hypothesis of this chapter that the emergence of the Federal Republic as a major actor in international affairs is not attributable to sheer economic might. Rather, the international system and its development have set the conditions for West Germany's rise to global status, although there was also always a countervailing trend at work that managed sometimes to challenge the course of developments.

WEST GERMAN FOREIGN POLICY: FROM EAST-WEST TO SOUTH

After World War II, the basic features of the first West German foreign policy moves were dictated by the rise of the Cold War and its aftermath. A complex set of contradictions and specific conflicts, mixed with fears and uncertainties about the next step of the Federal

Republic's principal opponents in the East, but also with suspicions about the reaction on the Western side, led to a high level of tension among West German policymakers. Cold War attitudes on all sides were characterized by little inclination to seek even partial compromises on the issues at stake, and by high levels of military preparedness. With the exception of developments in the second half of the 1960s, the West German government never took an active role in promoting detente. Indeed, lessening tensions came as something of a surprise to the West Germans—something to which they had to react rather than something they had helped engineer. The experience of surprise about global developments with respect both to increased tensions and to detente was indeed the principal setting for West German foreign policy planning, and opened the way for two possible policy orientations. The first alternative was a passive one—to be as close as possible to the leading Western power, the United States, in order to gain maximum insurance against all eventualities as well as maximum information on and interpretation of global currents. The other choice was more active: to strive for gradually increasing leeway in international political actions. The necessary consequence of the latter would be certain rivalries with Western allies, not only in the economic sphere, where German competition was always considered to be tough, but also in the diplomatic sphere.

Both passive and active strands may be identified in the foreign policy of successive West German governments, including those regarding the Third World. The phases of detente, not surprisingly, correlated with the active phases in German global politics, when the domestic debate and decision process perceived more and safer freedom to maneuver. The first move toward the Third World, for example, can be seen in the provision of money for what was later called development assistance. In 1956, the Federal Diet accepted a Social Democratic motion and voted DM 50 million for underdeveloped countries within the budget of the foreign office.[3] In the following phase of increased Cold War tensions after the uprisings in Poland and Hungary, the Germans favored channeling funds budgeted for Third World countries into multilateral efforts. The brief relaxation of Cold War tensions during 1957–1958, combined with the first experience of an economic recession in the brief history of postwar Germany, led to the decision to invest predominantly in heavy industries, providing the breakthrough for the Rourkela Project's steel plant in India.[4]

The 1957–1958 Indian affairs remained an isolated episode for the West German government as well as for foreign relations detente, as the Cold War reached new heights in the following few years. The German government experienced heavy pressure, particularly from the United States, to share the burden for defense of the free world, and to contribute financially to efforts tying the emerging Third World to the free West. From 1957 to 1959, Germans paid more multilateral aid than any other Western government except the United States. The Federal Reserve Bank acquired shares and obligations amounting to DM 1.7 billion from 1957 to 1960 (White 1965). The development fund of the European Common Market received another DM 0.8 billion of multilateral German aid between 1958 and 1962.

In general, political attitudes started to change in late 1962, indicated most clearly by the increasing detente between the major powers, which had direct implications for West German policies toward the Third World. After the beginning of the 1960s, the significance of multilateral aid lessened (Kruse–Rodenacker 1970). West Germans embarked on several initiatives that were felt to have been beyond the reach of Germans in earlier years. A military aid program was conceived and carried out with considerable vigor, involving the government in severe international problems, particularly in the Middle East, but also in Black Africa. Initiatives for the rebuilding of traditional trade relations were launched coinciding with redefined tasks of the German Reconstruction and Development Bank (*Kreditanstalt für Wiederaufbau*), formerly engaged in domestic credit work, and with the establishment of a special ministry for economic cooperation.[5] Because this phase is still continuing with little disturbance since the invasion of Czechoslovakia by the Soviet Union and other Warsaw Pact member states in 1968, its features are worth delineating in some detail.

Military aid is one means for safeguarding economic as well as political interests by noneconomic means, and the German aid program has been no exception in this respect. Economic aid, at least in theory, is aimed at enhancing the economy. Military aid is a supplement to this in the sense that its objective is not only the building of an army, but also the far broader objective of enhancing development of political institutions, whose stability is considered a prerequisite to the effective use of the economic component of the aid. As the incumbent Minister of Defense, von Hassel, stated in 1966:

Without certain means of coercion, those goverments will fail to establish the vital domestic stability in their countries and maintain it. . . . [Military aid] hence supplements economic and technical aid, which cannot be brought to bear without domestic stability. I am of the opinion that civilian development aid and military aid supplement each other. Both are directed towards the same aim [*Afrika Heute* 1966, 93].

A similar view was expressed by a West German government spokesman as early as 1963: "[Those measures] mean technical aid in the military sector for friendly states being in the process of build-up."[6] The West German government rejected claims (particularly from Eastern Europe) that her military aid had the function solely of protecting economic interests. A fair balance of the conflicting views is given by the American writers Holbik and Myers (1968, 125):

As part of their unqualified denunciation of West German foreign aid, Eastern sources also regularly charge that military aid is really part of the West German program, in spite of Bonn's assurances to the contrary. Once again, there is some truth in this allegation: but here, too, it is necessary to look closely at the West German position on this subject. . . . As long as it remains reasonably clear that military aid, let alone an alliance, is not a *prerequisite* [emphasis added] for capital or technical assistance, the Ministry for Economic Cooperation has no objection to a discussion of economic and military aid to the same country.

Recently, however, acceptance of the new role alongside the United States is reflected in statements about military rule in the Third World, which reveal a more "pragmatic" attitude than formerly observed. A notable example is provided by Carl Friedrich von Weizsäcker, advisor to a series of social–liberal cabinets, in an important recent book (1976, 76):

Politically safe areas . . . are those countries in which revolution can be suppressed with some certainty, military dictatorships above all. Military dictatorships correspond to the objective economic interests of international capitalism, and therefore linkage with capitalism corresponds to the objective policy interests of military dictatorships.

Such insights provide background for the recent development of German arms export policies.[7]

GERMAN EXPORT INTERESTS IN THE SOUTH

Inspection of the actual policies pursued by West Germany with respect to the southern half of the globe reveals systematic and persistent patterns. In his first message as head of government, as early as 1949, Konrad Adenauer set the tone with the first phrase that addressed non-East–West problems: "The development and the freedom of international trade is the subject of our special attention."[8] As noted, however, an independent foreign policy, at least in the formal sense of the word, did not start before the mid-1950s when the Federal Republic of Germany became a sovereign state. When it did begin, it took place in a rapidly expanding field of actors. The number of formally independent governments in Africa, Asia, and Latin America rose slowly from 48 in 1949 (when the Federal Republic was founded) to 53 in 1955, to 76 by 1960, and 104 Third World governments by 1970.

The rise of *Ostpolitik* as well as a fresh approach toward the quarrels within the Western Alliance earned the new SPD/FDP Cabinet considerable credit and, for reasons discussed above, could be expected to lead to significant change in the "Third World Politics" of the governments after 1969. The transition was not completely smooth, at least at the beginning, because of confrontation between the established forces—which so overwhelmingly exerted influence in foreign policy-making—and the newcomers of the SPD. The confrontation was particularly sharp with respect to the question of future arms sales to Third World countries.

When the SPD was in opposition, it had asked repeatedly for strict limitations on German arms shipments in the context of NATO countries. In April 1966, for example, the SPD faction introduced the following motion.

> The Federal Government is asked to limit in principle future arms sales and military aid as well as the transfer of excess military weapons to the members of the North Atlantic treaty.[9]

Two months later, the SPD renewed their efforts, this time asking for a law to prohibit the involvement of Germans in the manufacture of arms abroad.

> Germans according to the Basic Law are prohibited from developing in foreign countries arms of war, producing them, contributing to their manufacture, or transferring them.[10]

The then Defense Minister (and later Chancellor) Schmidt decided to engage in a direct exchange with industry.

> With respect to the export of arms and weapons systems, I arrived as a member of parliament, together with friends, at a fundamental position in the 1950s, which has not changed in the 1960s, nor since I became minister of defense. There are no new insights which could have led me to change my views . . . the present defense minister is not willing to act as the substitute of the sales managers of German arms industries.[11]

The last statement in this vein was issued by the secretary of state in the defense ministry, Berkhan, in 1974.

> It would be irresponsible to let the arms industry of the Federal Republic grow into the role of a foreign exchange earning export industry. Not only for good political reasons, but also because of moral judgments, this government has decided that as a matter of principle arms of war may be exported to NATO countries only [Berkhan 1974, 471].

The waves of the 1970s economic depression, and the rise in the price of crude oil in 1973 in particular, led to second thoughts within the ranks of the Social Democratic–liberal Cabinet. There was a general fear that the electorate, despite all the successes of *Ostpolitik*, would blame the Socialists for the slowdown of the economy, which had generally flourished under the Social Democrats. Opposition both from the established power groups and the electorate would be insurmountable for any government. Gradually, as well as secretly, the government stepped away from former major positions—creating tensions with the SPD faction in parliament, annoyed about the repeated requests to defend a government course of action for which at least a minority in the faction felt no enthusiasm whatsoever. Industry did their utmost to push the issue, and brought immense pressure to bear on the arms export question particularly. The Federation of German Aerospace Industry (BDLI) declared:

> The restrictive course of the Federal Government with respect to the export of military planes has cost the aerospace industry sales worth billions of marks in the past. The chances for the export of military goods are extraordinary. With respect to the repeatedly hinted economic shifts on world markets and the pressure to sell

high-technology products in order to maintain the economic position of the Federal Republic on world markets, a review of this restrictive policy is urgently required. In this context it is worth mentioning that France and Britain now are undertaking the greatest effort to export military hardware, without any foreign policy reservation.[12]

Commercial sales of German weapons developed from a meager U.S. $100 million when the Social Democrats took over in 1969, to U.S. $1 billion in 1977.[13] According to figures from the U.S. Arms Control and Disarmament Agency, arms exports destined for Third World countries rose to some U.S. $150 million during the same time period. When the Shah of Iran left his country in early 1979, orders placed with the German armament industry were valued at DM 1 billion—small if compared with the U.S. $20 billion spent on arms deals with the United States, but comparable to French and British figures.[14] Government spokesmen commented lamely on this drastic change of attitude: "As long as the business cycle does not change, one may become more flexible . . . but only to safeguard jobs."[15]

Although redirection of government policies was most dramatic in the field of arms exports, other sectors of production much more relevant for the growth of the German economy quickly followed suit. The experience of the nuclear industry, another prime example of sophisticated technology, provides a good example. The commercial interest involved in the transfer of nuclear power stations is more formidable than in the case of arms sales; at a unit cost of DM 5 billion, each sale creates 6,000 jobs for six years (Hoffmann 1979). The German nuclear industry paid, for 20 years, a fairly high entry cost into this technology because it lacked the huge military orders for nuclear facilities enjoyed by its main competitors. By the mid-1970s however, the nuclear industry seemed to have passed the threshold of profitability.

> In order to use existing capacities economically, under given contract volumes the sale of six power station units per annum is mandatory, KWU export sales manager Hildenbrand recently revealed to a confidential circle of experts [Hoffmann 1979].

After orders from Brazil and Iran, the German industry foresaw orders for eight power stations annually, four of them for export. Experience since, however, has been much bleaker. When environmentalists brought construction work for nearly all nuclear power stations to a halt domestically, and the biggest firm in the business, Kraftwerks-union (KWU), failed to secure a single domestic order for four years, pressures to go into exports mounted sharply. In 1979, with eight nuclear power stations contracted to the Germans (out of a total of 20), the Shah left behind in Iran uncompleted facilities that had cost DM 5 billion. This meant another shock for the German nuclear industry, which was unable to secure other nuclear power station export orders during the late 1970s, even though there was a demand in the Soviet Union, as well as in South Africa. Fighting for survival, the West German nuclear industry is now in no position to weather another storm of international criticism of the kind it had to ride out in the case of the nuclear deal with Brazil. The Social Democrat-liberal coalition also saw no flexibility in this respect—in Bonn, nobody was willing to write off for good the DM 9 billion which the establishment of a nuclear capability had cost the taxpayers in the past 20 years.

This picture could be delineated in nearly as dramatic a fashion for other strongholds of German industrial competence: steel, ship-building, computers, heavy engineering equipment, to name just the few that suffered most from the combined impact of a shrinking home market and the high cost of the mark (which has had to battle dollar prices on increasingly disadvantageous terms). For foreign economic policies, the room for purely political considerations was also dramatically reduced, as diplomats had no real choice but to underwrite the claims of German firms who fought for survival on world markets.

GERMAN POLICY PERSPECTIVES AND PERCEPTIONS

The most far-reaching perspective was offered in 1974 by the then German Minister of Economics, Hans Friderichs. He suggested repeatedly a triangle between the Ruhr area, Brazil, and Iran. On the occasion of a visit to Teheran, for example, he proposed joint Iranian–German ventures in Brazil, with the Federal Republic contributing advanced technology and Iran providing the necessary capital—because he saw a great demand both for capital and technology in Latin America.[16] Industrial relations between Iran and West Germany developed accordingly; from 1970 to 1977, German exports into Iran multiplied eight times (rising to one-quarter of all Iranian imports). Little wonder that there were speculations on how this dynamic could be transferred to Friderichs' third corner of the triangle, Brazil.

When the Shah was deposed, however, the Asiatic corner of this triangular relationship that fitted so marvelously into U.S. world schemes was lost. Brazil could have opted to import her oil from Khomeini's Iran, but the Brazilian side changed, as was carefully noted, to Iran's antagonist Iraq. This change was strongly related to a quite different trade area, weapons, to which I now turn.

Brazilian arms exports and the policies behind them have not gone unnoticed globally. *Newsweek* credits one Brazilian government arms sales director with a statement about the lesser importance of political preferences (compared to go-ahead decisions in the capitals of industrialized countries): "We're looking to the Third World, and we'll sell to the right, the left, and the center." And this is no mere rhetoric. The Stockholm International Peace Research Institute (SIPRI) attributes the lead in Third World arms exports to Brazil (45.6 percent of the Third World total, followed by 21.2 percent for Israel). The booming arms industry in Brazil is characterized by sales of the Engesa Company (reportedly 1,000 armored vehicles a year to 32 countries), Avibras (credited with, among other things, air-to-ground missiles to Iraq), and Embraer (which markets a wide range of aircraft including jet trainers, counterinsurgency aircraft, and transports). The Brazilian arms industry employs some 100,000 people (compared to some 300,000 in West Germany) and over 350 companies are involved directly in the production of military matériel. Brazil has ceased to fit the classic role of a Third World country in this area, equipping its armed forces with imported weapons. SIPRI estimates that 60 percent of the military equipment used by Brazil's armed forces is produced in the country itself.[17]

A feature that has particularly impressed its Western rivals is that Brazil has started to supply arms to other Third World countries, as well as to industrialized countries. The Canadian police force was the first metropolitan customer for Brazilian armored cars (said to have a decisive competitive edge in having exhaust pipes that are proof against Molotov cocktails). The French air force selected, in a strong competitive market, Embraer's Xingu trainer/light transport aircraft, deliveries of which started in 1981.

The notion of Brazil as a rival supplier of weapons is, in the German perspective, even more prominent in the arms-for-oil relationships with OPEC members in the Middle East and Africa. Trade figures suggest to German analysts that Brazil has selected Iraq as a major partner; beyond the above-mentioned Avibras missiles, Brazil is credited with supplying a major share of consumables like artillery shells and bombs to this side in the war between Iran and Iraq. With a view to the prospective sale of German tanks to Saudi Arabia, there is continued haggling over whether Brazil and Germany are each tied to a particular combination of the two growth areas of international transfers, oil and weapons.

The case of arms exports also provides a more general pattern in the world distribution of labor among nations. The long-held assumptions that the future pattern will see the more sophisticated products of industrial activity like weapons, computers, and other advanced hardware being manufactured in the metropolitan centers of the globe, and that multinational corporations are returning with their major growth activities to the North, are now clearly wrong. In terms of economic competition, the relationship between the North and advanced countries like Brazil tends more toward symmetry: for their industrialization needs, such Third World countries compete for the same precious crude oil that the industrialized world needs so desperately; and in order to meet the costly oil bills, arms and other sophisticated hardware (not secondary durable consumer goods, mass steel, or chemicals, as hitherto assumed) will be offered by the newcomers on world markets.

There is a possible alternative to competition: direct cooperation. The German–Brazilian nuclear deal, allegedly the biggest contract ever negotiated between two nations,[18] is still the outstanding example of this approach. The question is whether this scheme could be expanded to include manufacturing of arms. The Brazilian plan to build 150 modern naval vessels for example, is certainly enormously attractive business for the North German shipyards with their perennial problem of excess capacity.

In this context, the French–Brazilian accord of January 1981 made considerable impact on West German politicians. During a state visit to France, President Figueiredo raised the issue of development of French-Brazilian cooperation in military production. Apparently, following the pattern addressed by Friderichs back in 1974, the French are bringing advanced technology *and* capital to Brazil (reflected by a credit for U.S. $2 billion at low interest rates).[19] It is understandable that German industry, remembering the contribution of

German industrialists and engineers to early postwar arms production in Latin America, are anxiously considering how to secure their share in such collaborative activities.

CONCLUSION

The Federal Republic of Germany does not appear particularly prepared to accept any formal role in a new global arrangement (such as a triangular relationship). From past political behavior, however, an invitation to *informal* participation might well meet a more positive reaction. This hesitation on the part of the functional elites to embark on extra-European or non–U.S. relationships has far-reaching roots. The few proposals to move West German foreign politics into a more global position (also in order to bring this issue area more in line with foreign economic politics) remain isolated, despite receiving considerable attention. If the issue of security precautions for safeguarding any transatlantic triangle is raised, West Germany appears even less willing and prepared to accept formal commitments, despite agreements such as the Brazilian–German nuclear accord, or selective arms transfers.

The rise of Latin America in the course of its industrialization, including the arms sector, is reshaping relationships with the continent far beyond trade. This is having strong repercussions in the field of national security, particularly in its commercial aspects, which appear to be stable and likely to persist.

NOTES

The first half of this chapter reflects an earlier paper of the author that received some attention, "The Policy of the Federal Republic of Germany Towards 'The South,' " in Ekkehart Krippendorff/Volker Rittberger (eds.), *The Foreign Policy of West Germany. Formation and Contents,* German Political Studies, Vol. 4 (London and Beverly Hills: Sage, 1980), 171–96.

1. See also Besson (1970).
2. Cf. also Löwenthal's rejoiner to Livingston's (1976) article about "a diplomatic division of labor that would leave judgments on West European internal problems to reliable allies both closer to the scene."

3. It may be characteristic for the West German approach that the *Handelspolitische Grundsatzreferat* section on basic trade policy issues in the foreign office was assigned the task to define ". . . first time whatsoever the principles, methods, and objectives for cooperation with underdeveloped countries" (Kruse–Rodenacker et al. 1970, 96). The authors, closely linked with German development aid policy (Kruse–Rodenacker et al., acting then as the chairman of the board of advisors to the Ministry for Economic Cooperation, Dumke being a civil servant at this department), maintain this has nothing to do with export promotion, and that no political strings were attached. One wonders why they do not ponder the fact that it was the *trade policy* section that was asked to define the purpose of those DM 50 million.

4. India experienced at this time a heavy crisis in her balance of payments, making investment hardly attractive to anyone other than the German latecomers. The Indian government found itself unable to honor debts amounting to DM 1.2 billion; and the financial burden incurred by the Rourkela Project was estimated at DM 2 billion, including local costs. The "go ahead" decision by the Federal Republic in this situation was to offer India credits for refinancing amounting to DM 660 million—a step never taken before by the Germans toward any Third World government. (Two years earlier, the total volume for this kind of refinancing amounted to a mere DM 1 million.)

5. In 1961 the *Kreditanstalt* was given the task of implementing financial aid projects, after the political decision process in the government was more or less completed. Establishment of a special ministry for Third World problems is often explained with reference to Chancellor Adenauer's problems in arriving at a compromise cabinet formula that would accommodate the new coalition with the Liberals after the loss of his one-party majority in the 1961 general elections. The need for coordinated measures as well as the requirements of basic principles for Third World relations appears a more convincing cause.

6. From the minutes of the *Bundespressekonferenz*, July 6, 1963.

7. Past social–liberal cabinets had their difficulties in sticking to restrictive transfer policies when the focus of German politics turned away from the East–West confrontation and concentrated on global issues (even before the Christian Democratic Party took over government in 1982), as has been noted by a number of observers. See Pierre (1982).

8. Erste Regierungserklärung des Bundeskanzlers Dr. Konrad Adenauer vor dem Deutschen Bundestag vom 20. September 1949, quoted from Auswärtiges Amt (1972, 148).

9. *Antrag der Fraktion der SPD*, Deutscher Bundestag, 5. Wahlperiode, Drucksache V/535 v. April 20, 1966, paragraph 1.

10. Antrag der Fraktion der SPD, *Entwurf eines Zweiten Ausführungsgesetzes zu Artikel 26 Abs. 2 des Grundgesetzes*, Deutscher Bundestag, 5. Wahlperiode, Drucksache V/601 v. June 15, 1966, paragraph 1.

11. Interview, quoted from *Bulletin*, 110 (August 19, 1970), 1167.

12. Statement by Drs. Benecke and Baumeister, BDLI, hearing on aerospace, Bonn, Sept. 24, 1975 (quoted from *Wehrdienst*, August 4, 1975). There are numerous parallel statements by other industry spokesmen at this hearing.

13. Figures taken from *Zwischenbericht der Arbeitsgruppe Waffenexport* (of the SPD faction in the Bundestag), Bonn, March 16, 1978, p. 73.

14. Iran figures are discussed in detail in Albrecht (1979).
15. Quoted from *Industriemagazin*, April 1976.
16. Quoted from the *Journal de Teheran*, May 6, 1974.
17. Data in this paragraph are from *World Armaments and Disarmament, SIPRI Yearbook 1982* (London: Taylor and Francis, 1982), 187, 404–06.
18. There is broad debate about the general implications of this deal in the literature in Germany. Two significant evaluations are by Mirow (1980) and Wilker (1978).
19. Cf. "Frankreich und Brasilien wollen gemeinsame Rüstungsproduktion," in *Süddeutsche Zeitung*, Jan. 31/Feb. 1, 1981.

REFERENCES

Afrika heute, 7 (April 1, 1966), 93.
Albrecht, Ulrich. "Der Iran und die Bundesrepublik." In Fred Halliday (ed.), *Iran* (Berlin, 1979), 278–85.
Apunen, Osmo. "Pohjolan Tasapainon teoriat—osa Lännen strategia." In *Ydin* (Helsinki; April 1977), 11–13.
Auswärtiges Amt (ed.). *Die Auswärtige Politik der Bundesrepublik Deutschland*. Cologne: Wissenschaft und Politik, 1972.
Bergsten, C. Fred. "The United States and Germany, The Imperative of Economic Hegemony." In *Towards a New International Economic Order*. Lexington, Ma.: Heath, 1975, 180.
Berkhan, K. W. "Rüstungspolitik: Verpflichtung auf das Gemeinwohl." In *Die Neue Gesellschaft*, 21: 6 (June 1974), 471.
Besson, Waldemar. *Die Außenpolitik der Bundesrepublik. Erfahrungen und Maßstäbe*. München: Piper, 1970.
Hoffman, Wolfgang. "Fehlstart in die Zukunft." In *Die Zeit*, February 2, 1979.
Holbik, Karel and Henry Allen Myers. *West German Foreign Aid 1956–1966. Its Economic and Political Aspect*. Boston: Holmes and Meier, 1968.
Kruse-Rodenacker, A., H. Dumke, and N. von Götz. *Kapitalhilfe*. Berlin: Dinder und Himblot, 1970.
Livingston, Robert Gerald. "Germany Steps Up." In *Foreign Policy*, 22 (Spring 1976), 114.
Mirow, Kurt Rudolf. *Das Atomgeschäft mit Brasilien, Ein Milliardenfiasko*. Frankfurt a.M.: Campus, 1980.
Northedge, F. S. (ed.). *The Foreign Policies of the Powers*. London: Faber and Faber, 1974.
Pierre, Andrew J. *The Global Politics of Arms Sales*. Princeton, NJ: Princeton University Press, 1982.
Thielen, Helmut. *Thesen zur machtpolitischen Stellung der BRD im kapitalistischen Bündnissystem—Rüstung als Machtpotential von Außenpolitik*. Paper for the International Conference, "Arms Race Dynamics and the MICs," Frankfurt a.M., April 5–7, 1973 (mimeo).

von Weizsaecker, Carl Friedrich. *Wege in der Gefahr. Eine Studie ueber Wirtschaft, Gesellschaft und Kriegsverhuetung*. Munich: Carl Hanser, 1976.

White, J. *German Aid*. London: Overseas Development Institute, 1965.

Wilker, Lothar. "Das Brasiliengeschaeft—Ein 'diplomatischer Betriebsunfall'?" In Helga Haftendorn et al. (eds.), *Verwaltete Außenpolitik. Sicherheits- und entspannungspolitische Entscheidungsprozesse in Bonn*. Cologne: Wissenschaft und Politik, 1978.

11

ENERGY DIMENSIONS OF LATIN AMERICAN– U.S.–WESTERN EUROPEAN RELATIONS

Carlos J. Moneta

The initial years of the decade of the 1980s find Latin America confronting a critical economic situation. There are complex domestic and international elements at work, covering a broad spectrum of political, socioeconomic, and strategic factors which range from domestic developmental models and political systems, to the East–West and North–South conflicts. In this context, special importance attaches to the examination of Latin America's relations with the United States and Western Europe. With respect to the United States, this importance is due to its status as a superpower. With respect to Western Europe, this importance is due to its double role, as perceived by Latin America—first, as an actor capable of performing a certain supportive and autonomous function vis-à-vis the United States, and second, as a constituent part of the bloc of industrialized countries dominant in the Western subsystem. This chapter examines the impact of energy (particularly petroleum) on the current relationships among the three regions, pinpointing factors—some making for conflict, some for cooperation—that emerge in the web of interactions among states, and among regional, transnational, and subnational actors.

THE ENERGY CRISIS AND THE PREVAILING INTERNATIONAL ORDER

The "energy crisis" is usually seen as the rapid and accelerating rise in the price of oil (and to a lesser extent of other fuels), its shortage relative to demand, and the progressive reduction in its absolute availability. However, this approach covers only some aspects of a major crisis that is affecting the entire international system at various levels. It seems more appropriate to consider the energy crisis as a composite of interrelated phenomena in the political, social, economic, technological, and strategic fields, linked to the energy aspects of the process of restructuring capitalism (both state and oligopolistic capitalism), in the face of the gradual exhaustion of natural resources as a result of present production and consumption patterns.

Price increases in crude petroleum, whose nominal value in 1973 rose four to five-fold through the action of the Organization of Petroleum Exporting Countries (OPEC), are having repercussions on the process of economic development and affecting employment levels, the cost of industrial and agricultural production, balance of payments situations, and the rules of the international financial and monetary system.

The energy crisis has been repeatedly adduced, in the United States and Western Europe alike, as the prime cause of the steady fall-off in world economic growth. However, this view fails to take due account of the fact that the crisis is occurring within a world economy already in distress because of inflation in the United States and Western Europe, the loss of competitiveness of the North American economy vis-à-vis other industrialized economies, and declines in the rate of investment and growth.

Thus, the energy crisis is not the central causal factor. It is, rather, a crystallization of the deterioration of a model of accumulation, leading to increased costs of exploitation, reduction of accessible raw materials, diminishing levels of earnings and, in short, the need for complete reorganization of the conditions of production and accumulation of the capitalist system as a whole.

Perceptions of the significance of the crisis vary radically, depending on whether it is observed from the standpoint of the industrialized powers that are members of the Organization for Economic Cooperation and Development (OECD), or from that of the Third World. For the former, the oil crisis is a bottleneck caused by basing their developmental models too excessively on one single energy resource: petroleum. For the vast majority of the developing countries, it is one of underconsumption (Iglesias 1982), contrasted with the excessive consumption of the industrialized powers.

The following may be mentioned among the most salient factors contributing, over the 10 years that have elapsed since 1973, to important changes in the world's economic structure and in the distribution of economic and political power in the current international system.

- The East–West conflict has led to an intensification of tensions and friction among the superpowers over the strategic control of the major production sources, especially those of the Persian Gulf.
- North–South conflicts have led to a redistribution of economic and political power, previously concentrated among Western industrialized powers and transnational oil corporations, in favor of petroleum exporting developing countries. This has led to more conflicts and tensions between the industrialized powers and Third World countries over the control, access to, and use of critical energy and mineral resources.
- North–North tensions have led to increased "trade wars" between the United States, Western Europe, and Japan, and keener rivalry for more secure access, on adequate economic terms, to the energy resources and strategic raw materials of the developing countries.
- South–South tensions have led to rising oil prices. This, in turn, has established significant differences between the group of oil exporting developing countries and the nonproducing countries, in terms of possession of sufficient economic resources to promote development and bestow greater political, economic, and strategic influence in the regional and international context. In addition, the number and type of participating actors have changed; bilateral negotiations and trade agreements have increased; OPEC's relative share in the petroleum supply has been reduced; new deposits have been discovered; important technological advances in the exploitation of off-shore oil and of natural gas (e.g., Alaska) have been made; regions potentially rich in hydrocarbons (e.g., Beaufort Sea, Antarctica) are being explored; and advances in the use of new sources of energy are under way.

The world hydrocarbon market is most unstable and susceptible to rapid change in terms of who controls hydrocarbon prices and production. For a period of six to seven years (1973–79), OPEC managed to gain and exercise control over the price and the bulk of oil production at the world level. However, the world economic recession, energy conservation, and development of new sources of energy by the industrialized countries, have now combined to reduce demand. Also, the appearance of new and significant non-OPEC producers has increased supply.

No one really knows what will be the future direction of the energy market. Serious analysts in both the North and the South take drastically divergent positions as to the evolution of the petroleum sector. The majority believe that current surpluses are only temporary and will disappear with the recovery of the world economy.[1] A substantial number, however, take the contrary view.[2] If account is taken of the future needs of the Third World and the socialist and industrialized countries (although economic recovery may be tardy and growth rates low), and given the consensus that it will be impossible to substitute alternative energy sources for petroleum to any significant degree, at least until far into the 1980s, an appreciable rise in oil demand, perhaps in the second half of the decade of the 1980s, seems the more realistic expectation.

GLOBAL NATURE OF THE INTERNATIONAL ECONOMIC CRISIS AND ITS IMPACT ON LATIN AMERICA

The international economy has been in recession in recent years, due to both structural factors and inappropriate economic policies pursued by industrial powers and developing countries alike. Policies designed to curb inflation have contributed to increased unemployment in the developed economies, while financial stabilization strategies—especially in the United States—have spawned extremely high interest rates on the international capital markets and wild fluctuations in the exchange rates of the principal foreign currencies. Added to this has been considerable fluctuation in international oil prices, which are now following a notable downward trend. Contraction of economic growth in the principal industrialized centers and the adjustment and stabilization measures they have adopted have had important repercussions on the monetary and financial system and on international trade, with deleterious effects for developing economies.

Latin America has been particularly hard hit by this process. Its pace of economic growth is at its most sluggish in the past 40 years. Just as other developing regions, it had to face growing protectionism from its principal export markets, acute external and current account imbalances, and an explosive spiraling of the external debt, which reached approximately U.S. $300 billion at the end of 1982, despite the growth of exports (CEPAL 1982).[3]

Latin American petroleum exporting countries have not been immune from the negative features of the international economy.

These countries had surpluses in 1974 (U.S. $6.026 billion) which dissipated rapidly (to only U.S. $523 million in 1976). In spite of the second price increase (1979–80), the oil exporters' current account balance declined (falling from U.S. $5 billion to U.S. $2 billion in 1980). The importing countries, for their part, witnessed a 42 percent increase in their trade deficit between 1973 and 1974, due to the oil price rise. During the period of 1979–80, the current account deficit jumped from U.S. $13 billion to U.S. $22 billion.[4] The case of Brazil furnishes a good example. While its oil imports grew by a mere 160,000 barrels a day between 1973 and 1979, the value of those imports grew from U.S. $600 million to U.S. $7 billion.[5] Added to this were extremely high interest rates accruing to external loans, acute inflation, difficulties in placing certain exports, and the upsurge in the overall value of the debt—which grew by over 500 percent while the debt with the private banking sector increased by 600 percent (Deese 1981).

The whole situation has given rise, in both oil exporting and nonexporting countries, to the need for greater external capital resources to cover their growing current account deficits and to maintain a minimum of economic growth commensurate with their developmental needs.

In this context, payment for petroleum imports by nonproducing countries, reduced oil revenue of exporting countries, collapse of international commodity prices, impediments in the way of access to international markets, and effects of explosive interest-rate increases on huge external debts have combined to place Latin American countries in a critical situation—thereby significantly increasing their dependence on industrialized countries, international private banks, and multilateral funding agencies.

Variations in oil quotations on the world market throughout the last decade represent an important factor in the foreign debt equation. Latin American deficits used to be sustained by a copious influx of funds from international private banks, which were in turn fed by the recycling of OPEC's petrodollars. This situation has now been altered drastically, however, with the abrupt restriction by private international banks of their loans to Latin America—due to alarm over the magnitude of the debt and the difficulties of its repayment, combined with the reduced financial flow from OPEC as a result of falling oil prices.

In the decade of the 1980s, U.S. $240 to 280 billion will be needed to meet the needs of Latin American energy expansion based on the use of the region's vast resources (in other words, from U.S. $22 to U.S. $26 billion annually), of which 60 percent must take the form of foreign exchange. If these enormous foreign exchange requirements cannot be met (and meeting them will certainly not be easy, given the bleak growth prospects of the world economy), Latin America will be compelled to import more hydrocarbons. This is a doubly critical alternative, in view of the region's grave balance of payments problems and the continuing serious distortions in the way Latin America uses its energy resources. Obviously, if the region cannot satisfy its internal energy demand, its possibilities for economic growth will be reduced and its financial dependence increased.

WORLDWIDE AVAILABILITY OF ENERGY RESOURCES AND POTENTIAL GROWTH OF LATIN AMERICAN HYDROCARBONS

A factor of fundamental importance in the strategic assessment of energy resources is the very recognition of their existence. One of these assessments affirms that world reserves of nonrenewable mineral energy resources that can be utilized with present-day technology (or technology soon to come into use) are 1,030 times present coal consumption; 85 times present petroleum and natural gas consumption; and 1,045 times present uranium consumption (in breeders). Altogether, these figures represent 2,160 times current world consumption. However, it should be noted that, as regards petroleum, the total volume of oil reserves is in fact unknown. Assessments of proven and estimated reserves over the last 30 or 40 years have been growing appreciably; as exploitation increases, estimates of total reserves can be expected to continue to increase as well.[6] Renewable energy resources (hydroelectricity, solar, wind, biomass, tidal energy, etc.) could, in principle, provide an annual energy flow equivalent to 272 times present consumption.

With respect to Latin American petroleum reserves, the growth potential is considerable. In 1979, the Latin American Energy Organization (OLADE) (1979) considered that proven reserves of crude petroleum in Latin America surpassed 40 billion barrels and could last until the beginning of the twenty-first century. This figure seems conservative, if account is taken of the new discoveries and estimates of reserves made by Venezuela and Mexico in recent years. In the category of heavy petroleum, for example, Venezuela's "Orinoco Belt" represents reserves of over 700 billion barrels. If world market conditions rendered this economically feasible, as of 1988–89, Venezuela could increase its current production of 2.1 million barrels a day by 200,000 barrels a day from the Belt and, in the year 2000 by one million barrels a day from the same source. Mexico, for its part, at the end of 1982 was producing around 2.8 million barrels of crude daily, 1.5 million of which went to the international market. It occupies third place among exporting countries and fourth place worldwide in terms of proven reserves, with the equivalent of about 72 billion barrels of petroleum. Despite Mexico's intention to measure its production in terms of its development needs and not to exploit its deposits rapidly or intensively, export levels could rise rapidly.

In addition to these deposits, there are others of smaller size in Ecuador, Peru, and Brazil. There are also other potentially favorable areas in many Latin American countries that have not been properly explored (see Tables 11.1, 11.2, and 11.3), and the sedimentary basins in the Argentine submarine platform should be included. These cover a submarine area of almost 400,000 square kilometers along the Argentine Patagonia. In the basins further north of the San Jorge Gulf there has been no success, but drillings made in the former have brought excellent results and suggest an estimated three billion barrel reserve (480 million cubic meters) (Pocovi 1977).

Finally, even though—for technical (difficulties of exploration), policy (an accepted regime for hydrocarbon exploration and exploitation has yet to be found), and economic (high cost) reasons—a reliable determination of its potential has still not been made,[7] the off-shore Antarctic zone offers extremely favorable conditions for hydrocarbon accumulation. Various countries (United States, Soviet Union, England, Argentina, Chile) have already conducted geological studies and exploratory drillings in different areas near the coast and inland (Moneta 1981).

If account is taken of other responsible analyses of reserves, proven and potential, in the Third World (see Table 11.4), the following three factors are clear:

- The geographical distribution of petroleum resources is largely the result of exploration policies pursued by developed countries and large transnational companies, which have up to now concentrated their efforts in the Middle East and the Persian Gulf.

Table 11.1.   Classification of Latin American Countries According to Their Possession of Hydrocarbons (By Percentages)

Developing Country Net Exporters of Petroleum		Developing Country Importers of Petroleum[a] Net Imports of Crude Petroleum as Percent of Energy Demand[b]			
OPEC Members	Non-OPEC Members	0–25%	26–50%	51–75%	76–100%
Algeria	Bolivia	Argentina	Chile	Brazil	BAHAMAS
Gabon	Mexico	Colombia			Barbados
Iran	Peru				COSTA RICA
Iraq	Trinidad and				Cuba
Kuwait	Tobago				DOMINICAN
Libya					REPUBLIC
Qatar					Guatemala
Saudi Arabia					GUYANA
United Arab					JAMAICA
Emirates					EL SALVADOR
Venezuela					GRENADA
Ecuador					HAITI
Indonesia					HONDURAS
Nigeria					NICARAGUA
					PANAMA
					PARAGUAY
					URUGUAY

[a]Countries which in 1978 had a per capita GNP higher than $3,000 are excluded.

[b]1978 imports.

Note: Countries indicated in lower-case letters are producers of petroleum and/or gas.

Source: *Energy in Developing Countries*, World Bank, August 1980, 5.

Table 11.2.   Selected Latin American Countries That Have Current Estimated Recoverable Reserves of Hydrocarbons

Latin America		
Argentina	Costa Rica	Honduras
Brazil	Cuba	Jamaica
Chile	Dominican Republic	Nicaragua
Colombia	El Salvador	Panama
Bahamas	Guatemala	Paraguay
Barbados	Guyana	Suriname
Belize	Haiti	Uruguay

Source: Bureau d'Etudes Industrielles et de Cooperation de l'Institut Francais du Petrole (BEICIP), 1975. World Bank, August 1980, 91.

Table 11.3. Prospective Area of Petroleum Exploration in Latin America (In Square Miles)

Country	Area of Continental Prospecting	Offshore Square Miles
Brazil	1,480.0	240.0
Argentina	590.0	215.0
Mexico	305.0	170.0
Peru	400.0	9.5
Colombia	350.0	26.0
Venezuela	141.0	33.0
Bolivia	254.0	—
Paraguay	78.0	—
Ecuador	60.0	18.0
Chile	58.0	5.0
Nicaragua	25.0	28.0
Honduras	30.0	20.5
Uruguay	31.0	17.0
Guatemala	33.5	4.8
Panama	14.5	22.0

Source: Table 11, U.S. Geological Survey Bulletin No. 1411, cited in *Petroleum and Gas in Non-OPEC Developing Countries: 1976–85*, World Bank Staff Working Papers No. 289, April 1978, Annex I, 1.

Table 11.4. Estimates in Recent Petroleum Resources of the Third World (In Thousands of Millions of Barrels)

Area	View of Private Petroleum Industry[a]	Grossling (USGS)[b]	Ministry of Geology USSR[c]
Latin America	150–230	490–1225	620
Africa	120–170	470–1200	730
South and Southeast Asia	55–80	130–325	660
Totals	325–480	1090–2750	2010

[a]Based on statistics from R. Hehring, *Giant Oil Fields and World Oil Resources* (Santa Monica: Rand, June 1978).

[b]B. F. Grossling (USGS), "In Search of a Probabilistic Model of Petroleum Resources Assessment," *Energy Resources*, Michel Grenon (comp.), 11ASA, 1976.

[c]Visotsky et al., Ministry of Geology, Union of Soviet Socialist Republics, "Petroleum Potential of Sedimentary Basins in the Developing Countries," Michel Grenon (comp.), 11ASA, 1976.

Source: Petroleum Economist, January 1980, quoted in Marcela Serrato, *World Reserves of Crude Petroleum, Notebooks on Energy Perspectives* (College of Mexico, 1980).

- Changes in the energy system occurring during the 1970s led transnational corporations to explore new areas in both developing and developed countries. This gave rise to a series of significant finds. Yet, drilling patterns in the area of developing countries on the one hand, and in Latin America, Southeast Asia, and the Pacific on the other, are still totally asymmetrical. In North American and Middle Eastern territory, for example, oil well density was on the order of 0.96 wells per square mile in the 1970s; the figure for Latin America was only 0.5 percent. In Latin America there are currently 8 or 9 drillings per square meter; in comparable prospective zones in the United States and Canada, there are over 200 drillings per square kilometer.
- Finally, whereas the United States, Canada, the Middle East, and the socialist countries account for 75.6 percent of the cumulative production and for 65.3 percent of projected potential petroleum resources, Latin America and Africa's share of cumulative production is a mere 18.4 percent, though they account for 35.34 percent of the projected potential.

These factors, combined with non-Middle Eastern discoveries of enormous deposits such as those in the North Sea and Mexico, serve to emphasize the likelihood of finding substantial and widespread new oil deposits in Latin America. It should not be forgotten that the region already accounts for over 10 percent of the known world reserves.

PROBLEMS LATIN AMERICA MUST CONFRONT IN LIGHT OF THE WORLD ECONOMIC AND STRATEGIC SITUATION

The international financial and trade situation, the limited technological capacity available for hydrocarbon exploration and exploitation, the interests of transnational corporations involved, and the economic and strategic interests of the United States and other non-Latin American powers all combine to create major problems for Latin America. These problems extend to their internal development and their foreign policies, causing intraregional and international conflict.

The Energy Factor in the Context of Problems of Latin American Development

Latin America exports 77 percent of its fuel production to the United States and the remaining OECD countries, leaving only 23 percent for its internal use. It is thus obliged to import the bulk of its consumption, with deleterious effects on its balance of payments, its external debt, and on resources available for development (OLADE 1979). This situation is exacerbated by oil price fluctuations which, at different times, have adversely affected net importing and exporting countries alike. Thus, for instance, the cost of 800,000 barrels imported by Brazil daily in 1973 was U.S. $600 million; in 1979, the import bill for 960,000 barrels daily was U.S. $7 billion. At current prices (U.S. $34.00 per barrel), Mexico's total exports would be insufficient to cover its annual external debt commitments.

Distortion of the energy profile, in which oil consumption represents 50 percent of overall energy consumption (if gas is included, the figure oscillates between 75 and 80 percent of that consumption),[8] places most of Latin America in a situation of extreme strategic vulnerability. Furthermore, being a developed region, the energy consumption indices are relatively low, amounting to 5 percent of world consumption (10 percent of the consumption of industrialized countries). This means that Latin America is not in a position to restrain its demand, without sacrificing all prospects for economic growth. Different growth scenarios have been painted, with rates fluctuating from 8 to 3.5 percent annually; but even a 3.5 percent growth in Latin America's gross product would necessitate a 60 percent increase in energy consumption. In the decade of the 1980s therefore, assuming this modest growth, the region will need U.S. $240 to 280 billion in order to meet its energy growth requirements. Of this enormous flow of necessary resources, 60 percent must take the form of foreign exchange. Investment of this magnitude would correct the present energy profile distortions and develop the region's vast and as yet untapped energy resources. The prospects for achieving this goal, however, are not encouraging. Failing it, the present pattern of oil import dependence will continue, the problem of lack of resources will arise, and there will be no remedy for the present distortion.

Latin America offers striking contrasts in resource distribution. According to currently available data, 92 percent of its coal resources is concentrated in Mexico, Brazil, and Chile; 89 percent of its oil is to be found in Mexico and Venezuela; and 80 percent of the natural gas is in Mexico, Venezuela, and Argentina. Venezuela and Brazil boast the bulk of nonconventional hydrocarbon deposits; Argentina, Brazil, and Mexico account for 100 percent of the uranium reserves; and finally, 76 percent of the hydroelectric resources are distributed among

Brazil, Colombia, Peru, Argentina, and Venezuela (OLADE 1981; Trenova 1980).

Latin American consumption patterns also vary widely. Brazil and Mexico represent 70 percent of the region's overall energy consumption. A mere five countries (Argentina, Brazil, Mexico, Venezuela, and Cuba) consume over one ton of oil equivalent per capita annually; the analogous figure for the rest is a mere 0.2 to 0.5 tons. A third of the population has access only to firewood, which represents 20 percent of Latin America's total energy consumption.

Impact of the Energy Factor on Foreign Policy

Latin America's hydrocarbon distribution can be seen in the country groupings of net oil exporters and importers shown in Table 11.1. The effects of the energy situation on both groups have been considerable.

With respect to importing countries, both smaller (e.g., Central America and the Caribbean) and larger (e.g., Brazil) alike, increases in the oil bill have contributed to the recessionary picture of the international economy, engendering greater indebtedness on their part. Although for these countries the oil bill is now decreasing again, oil still represents a significant part of their imports. The pressing need for external financing to alleviate debt problems is leading smaller countries to change the direction of their foreign policies in order to satisfy their financial suppliers. Costa Rica, for example, which was on the verge of economic bankruptcy, radically altered its foreign policy with respect to the Central American and Caribbean subregion, adapting it to the guidelines imposed for the "Caribbean Basin" by the Reagan administration (Centro de Estudios Internacionales 1980).

In the case of net exporters such as Mexico and Venezuela, the gigantic growth of their foreign debt—concentrated mainly in private North American bank loans[9] and inputs from European and Japanese banks—requires them to be subject to orthodox financial discipline, based on the criteria of the International Monetary Fund and the private banks of industrialized countries and, in a field that transcends the economic plane, to adjust the central elements of their foreign policy accordingly. This means not only accepting economic terms that could be detrimental to their interests, but also softening their political and strategic stances against their will.

During the years of the oil boom, the situation was different. Given that the United States was the most important net importer of their hydrocarbons, and was also sustaining a growing strategic dependence on those imports, Mexico and Venezuela sought to obtain greater negotiating autonomy and power vis-à-vis the United States, by diversifying their markets and using "supply guarantees" as an instrument of foreign economic policy.

The marked slump in prices and the oil surplus have now changed the situation from one in which the United States needed to attract them and, in its interest, to forge closer links,[10] to one of such dependence that Venezuela and Mexico alike are considering proposing to the United States that it grant them a "preferential hemispheric treatment." This agreement is that:

> Venezuela and Mexico play a fundamental geopolitical role and the United States should be very aware that we are making a considerable effort in Central America and the Caribbean, in the interest of the region's social and political stability. . . . We consider that if a tax is to be levied on crude imports, as is being discussed in the North American Congress, Venezuela and Mexico should receive preferential treatment for geopolitical reasons.[11]

Role of the Energy Factor in Intraregional and International Conflicts

The nations of Latin America are experiencing conflicts and tensions over possession and use of energy resources located in disputed border areas (e.g., exploitation of the oil in the Gulf of Venezuela [Drekonja Kornat 1982]), or in countries with territories potentially rich in hydrocarbons whose status is being debated (e.g., Belize-Guatemala).[12] These conflicts are either partly or fully linked to the present or future exploitation of oil basins (e.g., confrontation between Argentina and Chile over the "Beagle Channel Question"), or of other energy resources (e.g., use of the hydroelectric potential of the Alto Parana which, up to the beginning of this decade, caused serious tensions between Argentina and Brazil).

Such tensions can be confined to Latin America or extend beyond. Examples of the latter would be the situations involving Belize, the Malvinas, and Antarctica. In the case of Antarctica, the highly probable existence of vast off-shore oil and natural gas deposits has rapidly aroused the interest not only of the members of the Antarctic Treaty and of the three countries in dispute over one of the sectors—Argentina, Chile, and England—but of numerous other countries, both developed and developing, that are seeking to associate themselves with the treaty, with a view to sharing benefits that could flow from future hydrocarbon exploitation.

Interests linked with the economic and strategic role of energy resources have also provoked conflicts with the United States and other industrialized Western actors, as well as between the latter and the United States. In addition to the role of hydrocarbons in bilateral policy between the United States and Mexico, Ecuador, and Venezuela, there are German–U.S. tensions over Federal Germany's financial and technological support for Brazil's relatively independent nuclear technological development, and North American concern over growing ties between Argentina and the Soviet Union with respect to furthering development of Argentina's autonomous nuclear capacity.

In the case of both bilateral border and territorial disputes among countries of Latin America, and disputes that involve extraregional powers directly, the existence of conflict makes for the intervention of external national or transnational actors who, in pursuit of their own economic and strategic interests, take advantage of those antagonisms to enhance their negotiating power. Sometimes (as in the case of Belize), such intervention contributes to polarizing the situation.[13]

Attitudes of national actors embroiled in the confrontation between Argentina and Chile over the Beagle, for example, have hampered cooperation between the two national petroleum enterprises, with respect to both developing joint projects and improving their bargaining power vis-à-vis transnational oil corporations. Indeed, the situation has enabled transnational corporations to increase the stringentness of their bargaining conditions with both countries.

Furthermore, the Latin American countries' modes of participation in the international economic system, and the adherence of the dominant subnational groups in several of these nations to the economic philosophy prevailing in most of the industrialized West, have engendered profound changes in the internal socioeconomic, political, ideological, and cultural structure. In some cases, for example, economic groups directly or indirectly dominating the state apparatus opt for the privatization of public-sector enterprises, including state hydrocarbon entities, thereby greatly facilitating access to control over this resource by the private and transnational sector. Argentina provides one example.[14] Ecuador's decision to join OPEC in 1973, despite warnings and pressure from the U.S. government, provides another.[15]

Even countries where state hydrocarbon entities have gained in strength—Brazil, Mexico, and Venezuela—have not been without their problems. In the case of Brazil, the discussion turns on the role to be played by the state body, and the need to resort to the private sector and transnational corporations, after the regime's ideology had influenced the direction of national petroleum policy. In Mexico and Venezuela, the discussion turns on what model and what patterns of capital accumulation and distribution will guide their economic development, given the importance of the growth of the hydrocarbon industry to the economies of those countries.

All three countries demonstrate the growing strength of the highly consumer-oriented development model, which is imitative of Western industrialized powers. The continued strengthening of this model implies a serious obstacle to redefinition of development styles that should be adopted in Latin America if the region is to be equipped to meet the new challenges of the international economic system and, in particular, of the emerging "New Energy Order."

This is not to say that Latin America fails to respond promptly and positively to opportunities for such redefinition when they arise. New organizations and mechanisms (OLADE, ARPEL) have made their appearance, and there are intraregional and bilateral energy cooperation and coordination programs.[16] Nontraditional sources of energy are being developed; and moves are afoot to organize multinational hydrocarbon enterprises (involving linkages between the national enterprises of Brazil, Mexico, and Venezuela). Leading countries in the field of nuclear energy—such as Argentina and Brazil—are also developing vast scientific and technological cooperation programs with other countries of the region, and the two foremost oil exporters—Mexico and Venezuela—have signed an agreement (the San Jose Accord) for the supply of oil to nations of Central America and the Caribbean, on highly favorable terms, to lighten the burden of their oil bills and stimulate their development. The point is that these efforts are still far short of what is needed to meet the region's energy development requirements.

THE ENERGY FACTOR IN THE CONTEXT OF LATIN AMERICAN RELATIONS WITH THE UNITED STATES AND WESTERN EUROPE[17]

If Latin America is to maintain minimally satisfactory progress in economic development, it must undertake a thorough reformulation of its objectives and policies in national, intraregional, and world contexts. Central to the new direction must be the strengthening of regional cooperation and integration (although this alone will not be enough).

Furthermore, the worldwide nature of the economic crisis and its impact on Latin America and other regions of the Third World calls for solutions which involve coordination among developed and developing countries. This, in turn, demands a new conception of Latin America's relations with large industrialized centers, grounded in an ordered, fair, and solid restructuring of the international system.

Latin America's external vulnerability—defined as the inability to avoid or neutralize negative effects of actions originating outside it—is manifest at various levels. In the economic sphere, note should be taken of: (a) dependence on the internal economic policies of industrialized countries, and (b) Latin America's own lack of resources and of political alternatives, which places constraints on its freedom of international action. This vulnerability implies the necessity to organize efforts of Latin American countries in search of collective regional security.

Security is a relative concept, and the extent to which it is necessary depends ultimately on the probability of the threat and harm it could cause to a broad spectrum of values (welfare, status, capacity for independent action, survival, etc.). What is needed is the strengthening of Latin America's economic structure, its capacity for independent development, and its internal political stability. "Security" is thus bound up with development: it is conceived as a reduction of vulnerability, beginning with the nation-state unit, and extending to the region as a whole, in which concepts of "national security" managed by Latin American military dictatorships play no role.

The capacity to achieve set development targets depends on existing internal and international power relationships. The region has already taken the first juridical and institutional steps in its quest for collective regional security in the face of the Malvinas conflict. At its eighth Reunion Ordinaria, held in August 1982 in Caracas, the Latin

American Council of the Latin American Economic System (SELA) adopted a decision providing for the creation of a procedure for consultation, coordination, and action, enabling it "rapidly and effectively, to give concrete expression to its regional solidarity" vis-à-vis coercive economic measures, and "to reduce the external dependence and vulnerability of the Latin American economies." It was also noted that this mechanism must receive tangible support through actions by countries of the region in such fields as trade, external financing, international transport, insurance and reinsurance, technology and food self-reliance by means of "economic complementarity and integration among them."[18] Energy is a key element of this new Latin American strategy, as laid down in the agreement establishing OLADE, as that organization promotes solidarity among its members in the face of any type of external action, sanction, and coercion arising as a result of measures adopted to safeguard and maintain energy resources at the service of national development plans and objectives.[19]

But Latin America still falls far short of satisfying its technological needs, despite the appreciable achievements made through the action of OLADE and, in particular, of the state hydrocarbon enterprises of Mexico, Venezuela, Brazil, and Argentina. Thus, it still needs to resort to the services of transnational corporations for prospecting, extracting, and processing. Further, the insufficiency of research and development efforts will, despite notable exceptions (advances made with alcohol, utilization of the biomass, geothermy), render adaptation of consumption patterns to nonconventional energy resources extremely difficult.

The ability to modify current patterns of participation in international relations, and to intensify and strengthen the process of regional cooperation and integration in each specific sector, will be the key to reducing vulnerability and to enhancing future possibilities for attaining autonomous development. These factors are interdependent, interacting levels of action, and the energy factor plays a pivotal role in each.

The System of Linkages Between Latin America, the United States, and Western Europe—Limitations of the Latin American Approach

Latin America has already wisely made the decision to strengthen its ties with developing countries in other parts of the world. This is not enough, however. It must also strengthen its role in the international system more generally. In fact, the process has already begun. Latin America, despite factors outlined in previous sections of this chapter, has already increased its relative weight in the international system. This is not merely the result of economic factors; it is attributable also to the ability it has shown throughout most of the past decade to play a political role in the international arena. To this must be added a certain capacity for harmonizing efforts, both within the group of Latin American countries and with respect to other developing countries, and increased sophistication in understanding the dynamics of the system.

Latin America has furthered its role in the world system through creation of new subsystems. Thus, Brazil has forged important links with the Arab countries of OPEC and North Africa, due basically to conditions on the world hydrocarbon market of 1973, and also broadened the spectrum of relations with West Africa. Mexico has notably intensified its economic ties with Japan by means of a highly accelerated growth of its oil exports;[20] it has also broadened its economic relations with France and England. Venezuela has taken the same direction in its sales of hydrocarbons to the principal powers in Western Europe; and Brazil has developed close ties with these countries, based on its exports of commodities, foodstuffs, and light manufactures. The Pacific Basin countries of Latin America are striving for increased trade and cultural contacts with Southeast Asia. Similarly, moves were made through the Andean Group in an attempt to intensify trading relations with the EEC. To a lesser degree, this commercial rapprochement was also sought with the socialist countries, with some significant results (e.g., in the case of Argentina).

These developments do not place Latin America in a position to replace entirely the weight previously given to the United States and Western Europe with the newly emerging centers; but it does widen Latin America's room for maneuvering by diversifying its international links.

The Place of Japan

To the United States and Western Europe, Japan must be added as a center of the capitalist system. All adhere to a common system of values and interests. However, the international recession and restricted market access, among other economic factors, have generated growing competition among them. To the enormous deficits posted by the United States and Western Europe in their bilateral trade with Japan, and the deep divisions over the stance to be adopted vis-à-vis the Soviet Union and in East–West affairs more generally, must be added problems in the adoption of common positions with regard to developing countries—due to competing interests and to differing perceptions of what should be the means and strategies used to safeguard the essence of the current North–South structure.

In the field of energy, dependence on oil imports and their concentration in the Persian Gulf (see Table 11.5) place Western Europe and Japan in a vulnerable situation, the extent of which varies with the percentage of energy consumption accounted for by petroleum; the percentage of that consumption that can be covered by domestic production (of oil or through other energy resources); the diversification of its sources of supply; and the degrees of stability and security these offer.

All three regions have reduced their petroleum imports in recent years.[21] Within their common vulnerability, however, there are serious differences of criteria and interests between Japan and Western Europe versus the United States over energy policy, especially with respect to the energy-related aspects of security.[22] Although such differences by no means herald the end of basic agreements among the principal Western powers and Japan, they do open up room for action

Table 11.5. **Western Europe: Petroleum Dependence, 1978**

	Petroleum as Percentage of Total Energy Utilized	Percentage of Petroleum Imported	Percentage of Petroleum Imported from OPEC	Percentage of Petroleum Imported From Persian Gulf
West Germany	54	95	58	31
France	63	99	84	70
England	45	55	67	60
Italy	68	99	80	61
Belgium and Luxemburg	56	100[a]	—	—
Holland	50	98[b]	82	57

[a]Belgium alone.

[b]1977.

Source: CIA (1980); the Committee for Energy Policy Promotion (1980); and British Petroleum Statistics (1978). Cited in David A. Deese and Joseph Nye, *Energy and Security*, 395.

by Latin America in the commercial, financial, and technological fields. This should become more and more feasible in the 1980s, as Western Europe (and to a lesser degree, Japan) gains a fuller perception of the potential role of emerging regions such as Latin America. The criterion generally accepted in Western Europe and Japan until a few years ago—that Latin America was an almost exclusive sphere of influence of the United States—is being gradually debunked (especially by Western Europe), not only at the commercial, but also at the political and strategic levels.

Increasing relations between Latin America and Western Europe and Japan should also be facilitated as the loss of competitiveness suffered by North American industry in some key sectors and the greater European competition for new markets is accompanied by increasing political action—especially by those countries displaying greater economic power (West Germany) or unusual drive due to the political orientation of their government (France). Thus, on the occasion of a visit by Chancellor Schmidt to Latin America in 1979, an influential West German newspaper stated that "a measure of rivalry with the United States should not lead to overcautiousness in South America, as if it were wished to demonstrate to the whole world that Federal Germany is a political dwarf."[23]

In the context of the North–North capitalist competition and North–South relations into which these policies fit, the underlying notion for Western Europe (and also for Japan) is that the links between developed and developing countries should be organized as contractual market arrangements: a mutually convenient international division of labor between national economies acting in freedom and sovereignty. If this equality does not exist as yet, aid policies should be implemented[24] to strengthen and facilitate the growth of the developing economies, creating international structures and mechanisms to cushion and control the effects of "savage capitalism."

This European and Japanese orientation of reformist liberalism, at least in principle, furnishes Latin America with a tactical and strategic basis for establishing agreements with both. Feasibility of such agreements, however, is contingent on the ability of Western Europe and Japan to rise above the internal pressures and contradictions stemming from their short-term interests and requirements. These, if allowed to predominate, in practice rule out—especially in the case of Europe—progress toward economic complementarity and political support that takes Latin American interests into account, even though that goal is clearly perceived as feasible and desirable for all parties over the long run.

Latin American–U.S. Relations

The historical record of interactions between Latin America and the United States has left in its wake certain elements that inevitably influence their current, and probably their future, relations.

At the center is the "inter-American" concept, overridingly based on the supposed identity of interests between the United States and Latin America, with respect to both economic development and strategic security. The first was construed as the adoption by Latin American countries, at both political and economic levels, of liberal values and the Latin American style of development; the second implied a mutual defense commitment—at least from the North American viewpoint—against potential threats from other parts of the world.

This strategic perception, in addition to furnishing the context of relations, also provides the values guiding these relations. For this reason, proposals forthcoming from Latin America, which contain elements of autonomy and demands for more open trading, have been systematically resisted by the United States. Proposals have been advanced to deal with the amount, type, and location of investments, with means for the transfer of technology, and so on. As such, they have affected not only the general ideological perspective, but also specific interests within the overall structure of U.S.–Latin American relations. The result has been deep disappointment and frustration on the part of Latin America, and the downgrading and distortion of Latin America's requirements on the part of successive North American administrations.

Because of this, the scant achievements of Latin America in recent decades have been possible only by means of concerted effort, involving the combined power of Latin American actors. Latin America's proposals have generally been resisted by the United States, which has sought to delay their implementation, modify their objectives, or limit their content and scope. To this end the United States has used its economic (and, therefore, political) power to form "special relationships" with selected Latin American countries, whose resources and political weight could exercise at least a moderating if not a disruptive influence on intraregional coordination efforts.

The extent and depth of U.S.–Latin American differences have become obvious, both in international (e.g., the United Nations Conference on New and Renewable Sources of Energy) and multilateral forums (e.g., the World Bank Energy Program), as well as in economic policy declarations and documents of the Reagan administration and the bilateral energy policy followed with respect to individual countries.

With respect to energy, as a great power with world interests and one involved in constant jockeying for position vis-à-vis the Soviet Union, the United States conceives its dependence on imported petroleum and that of its allies as a serious menace to the security of the Western subsystem which it leads. Significant supply interruptions, as well as volatile fluctuations in price, would gravely harm their economies and jeopardize their capacity for military action. For this reason, the present North American administration is placing particular emphasis on energy, in terms of both the strategic aspects of the East–West conflict and the impact of energy on the U.S. economic recovery.[25]

It should be noted, however, that in this they are not breaking with the continuity of strategic thinking of previous governments, which has also been based on the following fundamental objectives.[26]

- To achieve and consolidate more military capacity in oil areas of crucial importance, and to obtain the support of allies in reaching this goal.
- To strengthen the overall operation of the financial, monetary, and economic system, reducing and controlling the impact of oil on the world economy, and strengthening the North American balance of payments.
- To reduce North American vulnerability (and that of its allies) as regards energy hydrocarbons.
- To control the Soviet presence and its possible expansion in the crucially important oil zones (Persian Gulf and other areas of the developing world, sea lanes, and strategic straits, etc.).
- To cultivate special relations with selected producing countries.

Within the framework of strategies designed to bring about "energy autonomy" (conservation, substitution of petroleum with alternative sources of energy, accumulation of reserves, etc.) and to regain control over prices, the United States favors primarily increased production in countries considered politically reliable or at least "neutral" and which, if possible, can be the object of economic sanctions or rewards. Enough additional production could be brought about in this way to affect OPEC's percentage share of crude supplies on the world market, thus reducing OPEC's power to control the market and indirectly increasing that of the principal consumers. In pursuit of this goal—given the extreme instability of the Persian Gulf—the United States would like to move the centers of oil production to more secure and reliable areas.

This does not mean—at least for a considerable period of time—that the centers chosen will be able to replace the major part of the gulf petroleum supply.[27] Nevertheless, it would give the United States (a) the ability, in the short run, to cope with sudden temporary interruptions in supply, whether for political reasons or extraneous circumstances; and (b) the chance to organize, over the longer run, a system for providing the United States with essential hydrocarbon imports in the case of major conflicts which could disrupt supplies from the Middle East more permanently.

These objectives have extremely important implications for the petroleum exporting countries of Latin America. As Neff (in Deese and Nye 1981, 41) put it:

> The most desirable way to increase the supply would be the creation of additional production in stable and politically neutral areas . . . the consumers could try to convince Mexico, Norway, England and other producers to create a greater supply capacity for times of crisis.

There is, therefore, the potential for severe external pressures on producing countries to change their energy policy to meet the needs of other actors. Mexico, Venezuela, and Ecuador are all potentially at risk.

In the short and probably in the medium term, the United States will not have to resort to such measures, since the present situation places the principal Latin American exporters in a position of extreme dependence on the markets and the sources of financing that come directly or indirectly from the superpower. The same is true of countries with untapped hydrocarbons and of countries that are net importers. Nevertheless, since this model does not coincide with objectives of Latin American "regional energy security," it is not optimal from Latin America's perspective. Even though "guaranteed access" to the United States energy market would be a temporary relief for the problems of the oil exporting countries, the conditions likely to accompany the guarantee (unless there are profound changes in the present American administration's position) will impede efforts of Latin America to achieve an integrated energy development policy tailored to their own needs.

The critical problems and the profound frustration that marks the present stage of Latin America's relations with the United States favor a serious and carefully thought out effort to reorder and revalue links with other industrialized countries. Western Europe and Japan stand out as particularly worthy of consideration.

Japan, as already noted, has so far been relegated to a subsidiary position with respect to Latin America's efforts to diversify its economic interests. Western Europe, however, has a long history of cultural, political, and economic relationships with Latin American countries. This makes it all the more regrettable that over the period since the founding of the European Economic Community (EEC), the relative importance of Latin America in the EEC patterns of trade has diminished.

Imports to EEC countries (principally France and Spain) from Mexico have been growing rapidly, thanks to the purchase of petroleum products, which increased from U.S. $2 million in 1979 to U.S. $620 million in 1980, and accounted for 42 percent of total EEC imports from that country. Imports from Venezuela have also consisted, in large measure, of petroleum products, which covered 86 percent of its total exports to the EEC in 1979, increasing to 98 percent in 1980. Ecuador also increased its sales of petroleum products to the EEC, from U.S. $0.7 million in 1979 to U.S. $42 million the following year.

Considering overall economic interactions with the EEC since its creation, however, Latin America has felt increasingly frustrated over the contradiction between the apparent importance Europe assigns it from the political, economic, and strategic point of view as a potential "partner" and the reality of commercial relations which are in open decline.

Some countries of the EEC (e.g., Italy, France, West Germany) are currently promoting a rapprochement with Latin America. Latin America, in turn, is studying the possibilities of renewing contacts with a view to establishing more and closer economic links. However, one does not see many significant changes in the priorities and forms of linkage specified by the EEC itself for its relations with other countries. Its priorities, in descending order of commitment, involve: countries that are candidates for accession to the EEC (e.g., Spain, Portugal); members of the European Free Trade Association (EFTA); the United States, Japan, and Canada; Turkey, Cyprus, and Malta; ACP countries (Africa, the Caribbean, the Pacific); Mediterranean countries (including Yugoslavia); beneficiary countries of the generalized system of preferences of the EEC (particularly the economic cooperation agreement signed with ASEAN in 1980); and Latin America.[28]

Thus, the EEC is maintaining its traditional position on commercial relations with more advanced developing countries, emphasizing the protectionist orientation of its commercial policy. This represents a serious problem for the furthering of economic relations with the EEC on the part of the bigger countries of Latin America that do not have bilateral cooperation agreements. Naturally, the possibility of their future negotiation is not excluded where there are defined and concrete interests on both sides, but this means special relationships with individual countries, not with the region as a whole.

It is precisely the field of energy (and mining) that will hold the most promise for existing bilateral cooperation arrangements, or for the beginning of new accords that develop the abundant sources of energy which Latin America possesses, and which favor its development in the nuclear field.

Naturally, Latin America has opposed the policies of the EEC that signify nonrecognition of its identity as a region and indirectly favor "balkanization," generating ruptures in the adoption and implementation of concerted policies by the region. Nonetheless, the path of bilateral accords based on objectives, criteria, and principles decided previously by common agreement with Latin America, could gradually contribute to breaking the current deadlock and lead to establishment of an institutional mechanism that allows for regular dialogue and serves as a forum for mutual consultation and negotiation between the EEC and Latin America. To this can also be added the possibilities of "extra-community relations" with EEC member countries.

In any case, experience shows that to be able to negotiate adequately with the EEC, Latin America needs greater political and economic resources to strengthen its negotiating potential. These elements could come both from its internal resources (e.g., Latin

American "purchasing power"), and from the region's capacity to utilize adequately the current international situation and the diverse—and, in part, contradictory—interests of the principal developed countries.

NOTES

1. Of the analyses predicting increased short-term demand, mention should be made of those done by British Petroleum, Cambridge Econometrics, the United States Department of Energy (IEA), and OPEC. These analyses differ significantly as to the volumes of petroleum that will be required, the levels of savings resulting from conservation measures implemented in the industrialized countries, the percentages that could be covered by other energy sources, etc. Naturally, the results of these analyses are very sensitive to growth rates assumed for the different countries.

2. See, for example, Wionczek and Serrato (1981). Although divergencies persist, the two positions come closer together as the analyses approach the year 2000.

3. The debt was largely due to the need to meet obligations arising from international monetary and exchange instability, from inflation and the factors mentioned which made greater external indebtedness obligatory in order to maintain adequate product growth rates (5 percent during the 1970 decade).

4. *Estudio Economico de America Latina, 1974* (New York: United Nations, CEPAL), 204; *Estudio Economico de America Latina, 1976* (Santiago: CEPAL), 14, Table 10, cited by Mata (1982).

5. *The Economist*, May 17, 1980, 21–32.

6. At the World Energy Congress (1977) and the World Oil Congress (Bucharest, 1979), the traditional figure for total petroleum (300×10^9 mt) was drastically altered, rising to 950×10^9 mt.

7. There are widely varying estimates as to the hydrocarbon wealth of Antarctica, oscillating between 15 and 50 billion barrels of petroleum (Wright and Williams 1975; Tinker and Holdgate 1979).

8. World Bank figures raise this amount to 80.8 percent for 1985. See *Petroleum and Gas Non-OPEC Developing Countries; 1976-1985*, World Bank Staff Working Paper No. 289 (Washington, DC: World Bank, April 1978), Annex I, 1.

9. According to data furnished by U.S. Secretary of State Schultz, the debt with North American banks is as follows: Mexico, of an overall U.S. $64.4 billion debt, 24.3 billion are owed to U.S. banks; Venezuela, of a total debt of U.S. $27.2 billion, 11,000 million are owed to U.S. banks. UPI cable, Washington, DC, 24 February 1983, cited in "Deuda: Bomba del Tercer Mundo," *El Nacional*, Caracas, February 25, 1983.

10. For the North American position, see for example, "Relations between Venezuela and the United States: Democracy, Petroleum and Commerce," speech by the Ambassador of the United States in Venezuela, William H. Luers (New York: Center for Inter-American Relations, 19 November 1980), esp. 12–14. The position of the Venezuelan government can be found in "A Speech by the President of Venezu-

ela, H. E. Luis Herrera Campins" (Vienna: OPEC Secretariat, 14 February 1980), *OPEC Bulletin*, 11:12/13, esp. x–xii. On the energy factor in Mexico–United States relations, see Fernandez (1980).

11. "Calderon Berti: el Petroleo y la Perspectiva Internacional," reports to the Minister of Energy and Mines of Venezuela, *El Nacional*, 29 March 1983, A–8.

12. The Belize Basin in the eastern extension of the southern Peten Basin of Guatemala, for example, holds sufficient quantities of petroleum to encourage its commercial exploitation.

13. See *The Times*, January 28, 1982; and Paz Salinas (1979).

14. The economic policy imposed by Minister Martinez de Hoz and his successor Roberto Alemann, on Yacimientos Petroliferos Fiscales (YPF) of Argentina under the administration of the military regime that assumed power in 1976, is an example of these processes. Argentina has a distorted profile, based on a 70 percent share of petroleum in overall consumption (while the proportion of proven existing resources is 65 percent gas and only 35 percent petroluem). YPF, the state enterprise, is compelled to sell this petroleum to refineries at a price five times lower than that of the international market. The major part of the receipts then goes to the state in the form of taxes, rendering adequate economic management impossible. To be able to survive financially, the enterprise was forced by the Minister of the Economy, Martinez de Hoz, to contract dollar loans abroad. The YPF's foreign debt reached U.S. $4.1 billion in 1981. It was then charged that the YPF had demonstrated its inability to perform its specific duties and that many of its activities shpuld pass to the private sector. The ministerial conduct of YPF policy led to a lawsuit against Martinez de Hoz. Several military men were arrested for opposing privatization.

15. The attempt to increase the Ecuadorian State Petroleum Corporation's share in Texaco Gulf from 25 to 51 percent led in 1974 to the replacement of the Natural Resources Minister (who had organized Ecuador's entry into OPEC). To counter the nationalist moves by the government, transnational companies working in the country organized a crude production and export boycott, producing losses for the state of over U.S. $200 million between the last and first quarters of 1974 and 1975, respectively. In the face of a government attempt to fix a minimum production quota, the companies responded by paralyzing production during the following months. See "Ecuador. El Golpe de Estado y el Factor Petrolero," *Comercio Exterior* (Mexico), February 1976.

16. For a more detailed treatment of the vast action of OLADE, see the different documents issued by this organization and its magazine, *Boletin Energetico*. For consideration of the activities of bilateral, subregional, and regional cooperation being undertaken by Latin American countries, see Moneta (1981).

17. This section is based on my paper "America Latina en la decada del ochenta. Vulnerabilidad economica y vinculaciones con los centros. Posibilidades de cooperacion con Japon" presented to the symposium on *Las relaciones Mexico-Japon de la posquerra en los años ochenta* (Mexico: El Colegio de Mexico, 16–18 March 1983).

18. Decision No. 113, "Seguridad Economica Regional," VIII Reunion Ordinaria del Consejo Latinoamericano (Caracas: SELA, 16–25 August 1982).

19. See "Objectivos," *Convenio Constitutivo de la OLADE* (Convenio de Lima), 2 November 1973.

20. The total volume of trade between Mexico and Japan grew 19.8 times between 1960 and 1980, with a significant percentage expansion between 1980 and 1983 (from U.S. $139 million to U.S. $2757 million), due to Mexican oil imports. Crude imports in 1981 were worth U.S. $923 million, or 64.2 percent of Japanese imports from that country.

21. Between 1979 and 1980 the United States reduced its petroleum imports by 1.2 million barrels a day; Japan by 0.48 million; France by 0.3 million; Federal Germany by 0.2 million; and Great Britain by 0.25 million.

22. On this subject, see Haig (1980); Evans (1979); Conant (1982); *Japan's Energy Strategy. Toward the Twenty-First Century* (1979); Deese and Nye (1981).

23. *Frankfurter Allegemeine Zeitung*, 4 April 1978, cited in Evers (1982, 87).

24. Hence the "humanism" approach to the policy of Mitterrand and of German Social Democracy and, to a differing extent, of Japan. Regarding the position of social democracy, see Evers (1982). For the French position, see Cot (1982). The Japanese perspective emerges from the "White Paper on International Trade" (Tokyo: MITI, 1982).

25. See "Energy and Security," address by Robert D. Hormats, Assistant Secretary for Economic and Business Affairs before the Japan–American Energy Forum (Washington, DC: U.S. Department of State, 22 June 1981), 1–3.

26. See "Policy Objectives of the Federal Government" (esp. 136 and 160) of the summary of "An Evaluation of the Options of the U.S. Government in the Relationship to U.S. Firms in International Petroleum Affairs," in "Multinational Oil Companies and OPEC: Implications for U.S. Policy," *Hearings before the Subcommittee on Energy of the Joint Economic Committee*, 94th Congress, 2nd Session, June 2, 3, 8, 1976 (Washington, DC: Government Printing Office, 1977); Conant (1982).

27. A representative analysis of this line of thought is that by Henry R. Nau, member of the National Security Council of the United States, "Securing Energy," *The Washington Quarterly*, 4:3 (summer 1981), 107–20.

28. The Latin American view of relations with the EEC may be gleaned from several documents prepared by SELA. See, for example, *The External Relations of the European Communities and Latin America*, SP/CL/VIII.O/Di No. 1 (Caracas: SELA, 4 August 1982).

REFERENCES

Centro de Estudios Internacionales. *Centroamerica en Crisis*. Mexico City: El Colegio de México, 1980.

CEPAL. "La Evolución economica de América Latina en 1981." *Notas sobre la Economia y el Desarrollo de América Latina*, 355/356 (January 1982).

Conant, Malvin A. *The Oil Factor in U.S. Foreign Policy, 1980–1990*. Lexington: Lexington Press, 1982.

Cot, Jean-Pierre. "Winning East–West in North–South." *Foreign Policy*, 46 (Spring 1982): 3–18.

Deese, David A. "The Oil Importing Developing Countries." In Deese and Nye (eds.), 1981.

Deese, David A. and Joseph Nye (eds.). *Energy and Security: A Report of Harvard's Energy and Security Project.* Cambridge: Ballinger, 1981.

Drekonja Kornat, Gerhard. *Colombia, Política Exterior.* Bogotá: Universidad de las Andes-Fescol, 1982.

Evans, Douglas. *Western Energy Policy. The Case for Competition.* New York: St. Martin's Press, 1979.

Evers, Tilman. "European Social Democracy in Latin America: The Case of West Germany." In Jenny Pearce (ed.), *The European Challenge: Europe's New Role in Latin America.* London: Latin American Bureau, 1982, 80-129.

Fernandez, John Saxe. *Petroleo y Estrategia. México y Estados Unidos en el Contexto de la Política Global.* Mexico City: Siglo XXI, 1980.

Haig, Alexander M. (ed.). *Oil Diplomacy of the Atlantic Nations in the Oil Crisis of 1978-1979.* Philadelphia: Foreign Policy Research Institute, 1980.

Iglesias, Enrique. "Exploding the Myths." *South* (February 1982).

Japan's Energy Strategy. Toward the Twenty-First Century. Tokyo: Ministry of International Trade and Industry, 1979.

Mata, Hector Malave. "La Crisis Petrolera internacional y su incidencia en América Latina." *Comercio Exterior,* 32:8 (August 1982).

Moneta, Carlos J. "Antarctic, Latin America and the International System in the 1980s. Toward a New Antarctic Order?" *Journal of Interamerican Studies and World Affairs,* 23:1 (February 1981).

OLADE. *Boletín Energetico,* 13 (October-December 1979).

———. *Place.* Quito: OLADE, 1981.

Paz Salinas, Maria E. *Belize. El Despertar de Una Nación.* Mexico City: Siglo XXI, 1979.

Pocovi, Antonio Sebastian. "Hidrocarburos bajo el Mar Argentino." *Estrategia,* 49-50 (November-December 1977 and January-Feburary 1978).

Tinker, J. and M. Holdgate. *Oil and Minerals in the Antarctic. The Bellagio Report.* London: Scott Research Polar Institute, 1979.

Trenova, Jorge. "El Desarrollo del Sector Energetico de América Latina entre 1950 y 1976." In H. Munoz (ed.), *Desarrollo Energetico en América Latina y la Economia Mundial.* Santiago: University of Chile Press, 1980.

Wionczek, Miguel and Marcela Serrato. "Las Perspectivas del mercado mundial del petroleo en los ochenta." *Comercio Exterior,* 37:1 (November 1981), 1214-66.

Wright, N. and P. L. Williams. "Mineral Resources of Antarctic," *U.S. Geological Survey Circular* 705. Washington, DC: Government Printing Office, 1975.

12

DOES THE UNITED STATES HAVE A FUTURE IN LATIN AMERICA?

Riordan Roett

The "future" of the United States in Latin America will be determined by the ability of decisionmakers to come to grips with a startling and, at times, unsettling "new" Latin America. Perceptions change slowly. Institutional mechanisms for dealing with new realities emerge even more slowly. The United States finds itself in a period of transition from being a dominant economic and political force in the hemisphere to something else—*that* is the "future." How will Washington respond to the new and more vigorous assertion of Latin American regimes to determine their own economic, political—and geopolitical—futures? The United States will have a significant role in the decades ahead only if it understands the inexorable movement toward autonomous action by Latin American states, and the growing irrelevance of old North American policies.

It is my assertion that the ties of history, for better or worse, will necessitate a "negotiated settlement" between the United States and Latin America some time in the future. The nature of that settlement—amicable or hostile—will require great willingness on the part of the United States to discard favored, but outmoded, interpretations of the international conduct of Latin states that were relevant in the immediate postwar period. On the part of Latin America, there will be a need to assess the new future of the United States seriously and realistically, without the rhetoric that has blinded much of the writing about U.S.–Latin American relations in the last decade.

THE EVOLVING POSITION OF THE UNITED STATES

The evolving international position of the United States is a crucial element in assessing that country's future in Latin America. The relative decline in America's economic power, confirmed by the rise in oil prices in 1973–1974, was a process (as discussed in other chapters) that grew out of the rapid growth of Japan and Western Europe in the 1960s and 1970s. It complemented America's weak balance of payments situation specifically, and a growing concern generally, about America's capacity to compete and to continue to provide economic stewardship for the West that accompanied its position as *primus inter pares*. Its most recent manifestation is the current debate about "reindustrialization" in the United States. The diminished economic authority of the United States has highlighted the growing interdependence that has come to characterize the international system. That reduction in economic power occurred at a time in which the political authority of the United States in the world, and in the hemisphere specifically, faltered. The weakened position of the United States was as much a result of actions taken—or not taken—by Washington as it was part of an expanding and complex process of "coming of age" politically and economically by the more developed Latin American states, and the advanced political deterioration and disintegration of the most backward of Latin American states. The United States found itself in a position in which the resources once available to deal with Latin America and to maintain its primacy were not only not available but, even if they had been available, would not have been usable in the same way as they had been in preceding decades. With the leveling off and decline in an American presence economically and politically—in the more developed states, at least—nonhemispheric actors became increasingly involved in Latin America, politically and economically.

The situation has become, and will remain, complex. Although the United States has not and will not come to collapse, it will never regain the position of power it held in the Cold War period. Although the process of change under way in Latin America is slow and tendentious, it is permanent. Further, although the presence of Japan, Western Europe, and other actors is only now emerging as relevant to Latin America's future, it will become increasingly relevant and, therefore, increasingly a determinant in the future of the United

States in Latin America. There is no Monroe Doctrine for the 1990s, nor is there a real possibility of reasserting the "big stick" or reinventing a Roosevelt Corollary for the Americas. Current United States policy in the Caribbean Basin, particularly with reference to Cuba's actions in Central America, indicates a resurgence of the thinking prevalent in the 1950s. Defining international relations in essentially strategic, East–West terms, the Reagan administration sees Central America as an area in which American interests must be clearly and forcefully implemented. In the zealous efforts of the United States to maintain the status quo in the region, they run the risk of permanently damaging their overall links with Latin America and the Caribbean.

If Central America provides one significant dimension in the changing relations between Latin America and the United States, the war between Argentina and Great Britain in April 1982 graphically illustrates another. The bloody battle over possession of the Malvinas (Falkland) Islands forced the United States to "take sides" and, following a brief effort at mediation, to oppose Argentine action on the grounds that the United States "could not and would not condone the unlawful use of force to resolve disputes." Subsequently, the United States ordered limited economic and military measures affecting Argentina, and stated that the administration would respond positively to requests for materiel support for British forces, but without any direct U.S. military involvement. Among the states of the hemisphere, the United States found itself in a distinct minority. At a meeting of the Rio Treaty Organ of Consultation on April 26, 1982, attended by the foreign ministers of the organization, the United States abstained on a resolution that urged an immediate truce, recognition of the "rights of sovereignty of the Republic of Argentina over the Malvinas (Falkland) Islands and the interests of the islanders," and called for "negotiation aimed at a peaceful settlement of the conflict" ("The South Atlantic Crisis" 1982).

The emotional response of a number of countries has receded; but the essential message remains clear. The sense of "betrayal" by the United States, and its opting for a traditional ally, Great Britain, confirmed the belief by many Latin American leaders that U.S. interest in Latin America will always yield to the abiding ties between Western Europe and the United States. The historical, cultural, and political linkages between the United States and Great Britain, and by extension to the developed Western world, stood the test and strain of the

South Atlantic conflict, but in a way that Washington never imagined. Choosing to support Great Britain on grounds of nonaggression was either ignored or misunderstood. The clear message received in the capitals of Latin America was that the United States, when forced to choose, chose badly.

The crisis in the South Atlantic merely exacerbated and hastened a process under way for some years. It served as both an emotional outlet for Latin America and a clear indication of where and how the United States stands in time of crisis. No matter that the United States has repeatedly stated that it takes no position on the matter of sovereignty. By "hiding" behind international law, which favored Great Britain, the "betrayal" was viewed by many Latin Americans as even more disreputable. The aftermath of the Falklands War has confirmed the continued, slow but steady, deterioration of U.S. influence in the hemisphere and an even greater assertiveness on the part of the major Latin American states to seek policies that represent primarily Latin American interests. Whether or not those interests coincide with the interests of the United States has become far less important.

It is interesting to note that the momentarily-strained relations between the European Common Market, which voted sanctions against Argentina, and the Latin American states, are once again normal (with the exception of Great Britain). The burden of guilt weighs most heavily on the United States, given the long and intricate linkages between the northern and southern hemispheres.

CHANGE IN LATIN AMERICA

The development initiative under way in the more advanced Latin American states has led to an intricate set of international linkages that is both economic and political in nature. The search for markets, for technology, for access to capital markets and related imperatives, has resulted in stronger ties with the OECD countries as well as with the Eastern bloc and the Third World. The economic imperative itself is not surprising, given the difficult domestic agenda each country faces at home. Two related facets of Latin America's linkage with the international system, however, are surprising. First is the growing ideological pluralism of Latin America's global contacts, second is the dynamic and autonomous thrust of Latin America's foreign policy, in part economic but more generally geopolitical and strategic.

In the postwar period, ideological conformity was *de rigueur* for the foreign policy of the countries in the hemisphere. Deviation brought retribution. Guatemala is the classic and tragic example of that period. Castro's triumph in Cuba, and corresponding changes in the United States view of the Third World in the 1960s, resulted in a greater superficial tolerance for diversity, but, as the Dominican Republic in 1965 and Chile in the early 1970s demonstrated, it was shallow indeed.

The late 1970s and early 1980s have brought a surge of independence in the external relations of advanced countries. Authoritarian governments have chosen to ignore ideology in their search for trade and investment opportunities. The Soviet Union is now Argentina's most important trading partner. Brazil recognizes the MPLA government in Angola and has taken a contrary position from that of the United States on Namibia, Cuban troops, and South Africa. No one will argue that either country is "soft on communism." Both seized opportunities for an expansion of state sovereignty that has become the hallmark of the foreign policies of the most influential of Latin American countries. The most notable example, of course, is the Mexican position with regard to Cuba and Nicaragua. Contrary to the belief of some observers, the transition from the Lopez Portillo to the de la Madrid government in December 1982 did not introduce a qualitative change in Mexican foreign policy in the region. In spite of the severe financial crisis that Mexico confronts, thereby reducing the amount of economic aid at its disposal for regional purposes, de la Madrid has made it clear that his government will continue with its independent foreign policy and traditional Mexican support for recognition of political and ideological diversity in Latin America.

The thrust outward has brought both the "friends and the enemies" of the United States into the hemisphere. Whereas Japanese investment in Brazil and European Common Market ties with Argentina and Mexico are today viewed as legitimate, the extension of Soviet Union ties with the region would have been viewed, just a few years ago, as highly alarming. They may be *viewed* as alarming today, but there is little that the United States can—or will—do to stop Soviet penetration. Moreover, the Latin American states no longer view Soviet economic presence as necessarily a direct threat. As Robert Leiken (1981) has written:

> Soviet credit to the region, excluding Cuba, grew from 2 percent of total Soviet credits to developing countries in the 1960s to 25

percent by the mid-1970s . . . By the late 1970s the Soviets were helping build 20 large-scale hydroelectric and thermoelectric power plants in Latin America.

The Soviets are assisting Mexico in nuclear reactor technology and radiation testing and have offered to supply Argentina and Brazil with enriched uranium. Brazilian and Soviet officials are also discussing technical cooperation in metallurgy, including a project that would unite Brazilian titanium and vacuum metallurgy with the highly advanced Soviet metallic titanium technology. Metallic titanium is an important material used in the aerospace and submarine industries.

Although economic and technical assistance from the Soviets is considered acceptable, even by authoritarian governments of the right, it is clear that ideological subversion by Marxist groups will continue to be opposed. It is the new combination of pragmatism in economic and technological ties, a disregard for U.S. feelings or concerns about the ties, *along with* the maintenance of a formal ban on communist party activity, that puzzles many current observers.

A second aspect of note is the growing linkages among countries of the region, particularly but not exclusively on the continent of South America. Brazil has dramatically reoriented its traditional foreign policy, which once relied heavily on the bilateral relationship with the United States. Brazil's search for markets for its exports, to deal with a serious balance of payments burden due to oil prices, has led to increasingly stronger ties with Africa and the Middle East, although the former will always play a greater role than the latter. Its trade and investment ties with the OECD countries are also substantial today. Although the United States remains the largest investor in Brazil in absolute terms, as documented in other chapters, its relative position has declined. Brazil and Argentina have undertaken a rapprochement that offers immediate returns in trade and natural resource areas, and may well have significant implications for development of the continent—economically and politically. Brazil's new emphasis on the Spanish-speaking states of South America has resulted in an exchange of presidential visits and signing of a wide range of agreements on trade, energy, nuclear cooperation, natural resources, and Amazon Basin development. The old shibboleth that Brazil would never collaborate with its neighbors may not be dead, but surely it is dying. Mexico's increasingly important regional role in the Caribbean Basin is related to its economic influence, to an analysis of its linkage to events in Guatemala and other Central American states, and to a growing belief that there may well be a touch of destiny in Mexico's becoming a more active and dominant regional influence.

Venezuela and Mexico have taken a new and assertive posture with regard to the Caribbean Basin. Both countries joined in offering an oil concessionary facility for the countries of the Caribbean Basin that is estimated to be of far greater value than the total U.S. bilateral aid to the area. Presidents Lopez Portillo and Herrera Campins have undertaken a number of peace initiatives in the Central American region. In April 1981, the two heads of state met in Mexico City to harmonize their policies "to prevent the Caribbean Basin from becoming a focus of East–West tensions." In September 1982, both presidents appealed to the United States, Honduras, and Nicaragua to reduce tension in Central America. In a letter sent to heads of state of the three states, the presidents pointedly referred to the continuing clashes on the border between Honduras and Nicaragua.

During the visit of President Ronald Reagan to Latin America in December 1982, both the presidents of Brazil and Colombia criticized existing United States policy in Central America. Newly-elected Colombian head of state Belisario Betancur did so publicly. In January 1983, the foreign ministers of Mexico, Venezuela, Colombia, and Panama met in Panama to discuss possible new regional initiatives to promote peace in Central America. The meeting was particularly significant in that the presence of the new foreign ministers of Colombia and Mexico indicated the desire of those countries to maintain a high profile in regional politics.

While the future of the Inter-American System is being widely discussed, slow but deliberate efforts by the Latin American states to build a parallel or complementary set of institutions proceeds apace. SELA (Latin American Economic System) and ALADI (the recently-organized Latin American Integration Association, which replaces LAFTA) demonstrate the ongoing search for appropriate mechanisms among the Latin American states for economic development goals. The Andean Common Market, although less influential economically than originally imagined, has begun to assume a political role that is more forceful than once conceived. Participation of the Market foreign ministers in the negotiations over the outcome of the Nicaraguan conflict was positive. Individual units of the Inter-American System, such as the Inter-American Human Rights Commission, play a substantial and salutary role in the Americas. With the exception of the last, these initiatives have been undertaken without the participation of the United States.

THE EUROPEAN OPTION

The European Option is attractive in both economic and political terms. Economically, it links Latin America to an alternative source of finance capital and investment as well as new markets and sources of technology. For Europeans, it offers the possibility of access to the hemisphere's natural resources and the opening of a new region for public and private investment. Politically, it suggests a set of institutional relationships both state–state and state–private, which are attractive to Latin America. Strategically, European states are not viewed with suspicion. Long banished from the hemisphere by American decision, they have escaped the conflict-laden heritage of the United States in the nineteenth and twentieth centuries.

Although Europe has not been involved in the traditional sorts of conflict encountered by the United States in Latin America, it has recently become an important adjunct to Latin American preparations for conflict. Inexorably, the percentage share of United States arms sales to Latin American states has declined. By the end of 1980, just under one-half of all the arms sold to South America came from Western Europe (United Kingdom, France, Italy, and West Germany). The U.S. share of the market fell to 21 percent. In Central America, the United Kingdom's share of sales has risen to 21 percent, while U.S. sales represent but 8 percent of the market (Barrow 1982).

It is becoming clear to many observers that the North American political model is increasingly marginal to Latin America. The Westminsterian dream of democratic societies harmoniously coexisting in the hemisphere is not now and will not, in the foreseeable future, be the reality of Latin America. The European Option, in political terms, provides for the first time in this century a breakthrough in the search for usable institutional alternatives to the U.S. model. Again, this need not result in conflict if the United States understands the importance of this trend and accepts and indeed nurtures it.

The essence of the alternative is to be found in the profoundly different role of the state in Western Europe and in Latin America— and not in the United States. Linkages that are growing between Latin

America and Western Europe are not based on a model of social harmony and political tranquility. Neither are they transfixed by balances of power among equal branches of government. Montesquieu and Locke are interesting, but not determining, lines of political thought. The strong European state influence over private initiatives and the very different nexus between the state and society in Europe may have profound implications for Latin America.

The intricate interrelationship among the state and trade union organizations, and the growing importance of transnational links within the Roman Catholic Church, are part of the new reality in Latin America. Transnationalism is no longer limited to the conduct of multinational corporations. It extends well beyond formal state-to-state ties. It encompasses a vital set of church-to-church, labor-union-to-labor-union, and political-party-to-political-party ties that are little understood in the United States and are increasingly the future in Latin America.

The U.S. political party model offers little to Latin America, given the role of the state, the legitimacy of interest group politics, and the role of the Congress in the United States. Latin America has never provided a similar role for Congress, parties, or pressure groups. The Latin American state has become, and will remain, a principal—perhaps *the* principal—arbiter of power. In so doing, the state recognizes and accepts a set of transnational and international institutional linkages that are foreign to, and avoided by, the United States and its political process.

THE UNITED STATES AS POLITICAL MODEL

In conceptual terms, Latin America and the United States have been like the two proverbial ships "passing in the night." They may occupy the same ocean, but the two vessels fly very different flags. A statist and corporatist Latin America has never had much in common with an assertively pro-private enterprise and democratic United States. The absorption of America's democratic values by postwar political leaders in Latin America led to the illusion that the U.S. model was viable. Actually, it flew in the face of the realities of Latin American societies. Again, the issue is not that Latin Americans were incapable of becoming American or that they cunningly were avoiding the inevitable. It is merely that Latin American societies, through no fault of their own, given the dependent path they were forced to follow, conformed to a growth and development path (or model) that is state-centered. It is more given to state initiative and interpenetration with social and political institutions and organizations. Such a realization does not at all necessarily "condemn" or relegate Latin American societies to military governments or authoritarian regimes. It merely emphasizes that the European alternative may well be in greater harmony with Latin America's social and political needs in the late twentieth and early twenty-first centuries than the American option so long held dear by the U.S. policy-making elite.

An unpleasant fact of life in the hemisphere is that armed conflict at times, and class differences most of the time, will dominate the agenda of change in the least-developed countries of Central America and the Caribbean—as well as in the Andean countries—for the foreseeable future. The U.S. fixation with "democratic elections" is a reflection of its own political and social modernization, and not of Latin America's, as many will argue. First must come the social and economic changes on which some form of politically participatory society can be constructed. The historical moment has passed in which U.S. pressure on dominant oligarchies might have produced gradual change. Convulsions in Central America will not respond to "democratic elections" generally—although if they do, all the better. Mexican, Venezuelan, and West European support for radical change is neither aimed at undermining the United States in the hemisphere, nor at supporting "communism" in the Americas. It is their view, which needs to be carefully considered and respected, that it is preferable to have revolutionary change without "democratic elections," than to continue to subject the mass of people to unbearable levels of violence and repression.

For those who accept this position, U.S. policy is bemusing. Debates in Congress whether to grant small amounts of economic aid to Nicaragua unless "democratic elections" and other Westminsterian reforms are implemented are ludicrous. The threat of covert action is not. But the U.S. view that it is preferable, in all cases, to undermine or postpone indefinitely more radical social and political institutions in the backward countries of the hemisphere is not shared by major actors among the hemispheric states or in Western Europe. "Management" of U.S. foreign policy in these circumstances in the future will require a world view in which the hemisphere is less the dependent variable it has been historically, and more an integrated part of an emerging and new subsystem.

The often acrimonious debate surrounding the outcome of the March 1982 national election in El Salvador demonstrates the point. The Reagan administration argued that the election results confirmed the viability of democracy in El Salvador. Never mind that the apparent victor was the most conservative of the groups running for election to the Constituent Assembly. The inability of the guerrilla forces to disrupt the elections themselves, and the unwillingness of their political allies to return to El Salvador to campaign, demonstrated to the United States that they had been right—that the people of El Salvador, if given the opportunity, would employ democratic means to determine the future of their war-torn country.

Others argued that the March elections were admirable but a singular event, not a process that would lead to a settlement. Events following the elections indicated growing skepticism in the United States Congress about the strategy being pursued by the administration in El Salvador. The six-month certification debates have become more rancorous. By early 1983, Assistant Secretary of State Thomas O. Enders visited Madrid amidst a flurry of rumors that the socialist government of Felipe Gonzalez or the socialist movement in Europe would be utilized in seeking a negotiated political settlement in Central America. The very fact that the United States at least turned to Europe for advice and consultation is significant, and clearly demonstrates the viability of European initiatives in Latin America. It also raises the important question of whether the United States will finally comprehend the difficulty of attempting to transplant to Central America institutions and political processes that were the result of a very different historical period and a profoundly different political culture.

In another area, politics is no longer "party politics" in Latin America as it may have appeared in the 1950s and in the heyday of the Alliance for Progress in the 1960s. Party politics in Latin America are ideological politics, in that serious social and broadly societal questions need to be dealt with by the state to avoid polarization and breakdown. They cannot be left to the private sector. Social Democracy and Christian Democracy both suggest alternatives that are comfortable. They correspond to the sorts of collaborative arrangements in Latin America that have been normal in Western Europe in the postwar period. These parties provide a "bridging" function between

·the state and society that American political parties cannot and would not pretend to provide. European parties also accept and encourage, in contrast with Democrats and Republicans in the United States, international activity by the Roman Catholic Church and trade union movements. The parties bargain and negotiate across national boundaries. Monies are transferred for worthy—and perhaps unworthy—purposes. Social action projects and political involvement in Latin America, and elsewhere in the Third World, are widely viewed as both desirable and necessary. Such activities also provide important legitimizing functions for parties in the international and domestic arenas. The claim to global involvement strengthens transnational projection and institutional viability of the parties as well.

The debate in the United States between liberals and conservatives about the future of Latin America is viewed by both the Social Democrats and Christian Democrats as irrelevant in political terms. That debate is framed in terms of democratic values particular to U.S. democracy, not the social and political needs of Latin America today. Involvement of the more advanced Latin American states, through this set of transnational and state-private relationships in Central America, is symptomatic of the changing and more confident role of political institutions in the hemisphere.

Leaders of Latin America and Western Europe have spoken out with increasing frequency. Former President Lopez Portillo of Mexico captured the mood of the more progressive leaders in stating that "in our continent, social injustice is the true womb of unrest and revolutionary violence. The theory that foreign subversion is the origin of our ills is unacceptable to the democratic nations of the area" ("Mexico and Venezuela Plan" 1981). Responding to a reporter's query about Colombia's role in Central America and the Caribbean, recently-elected President Belisario Betancur stated in early 1983 that "Colombia must make its voice heard and its good offices available so that the conflicts encounter resolutions. . . . I offer the mediation of Colombia in pursuit of this noble and urgent objective. Colombia wants to be the mediator of peace" ("Bogota Begins Seeking" 1983). Such language was not impossible two decades ago, but it received little attention. Today, when combined with the interdependence of world politics and the growing concern in Latin America about its own future, it represents an important, perhaps profound, assertion of regional autonomy. The United States has no comparable offer to make to Latin America. The state-to-state relations between the

United States and the countries of the hemisphere are adequate for certain bilateral and multilateral purposes, but they do not provide the overarching and integrating functions of the European alternatives.

U.S.-Latin American relations today are basically private sector relations. Multinational corporations and private banks dominate the profile. Public transfers of development assistance are minimal. Security assistance means slightly more, but is involved increasingly in bitter domestic political battles. Cultural and educational ties diminish, while the West European ties increase. Reassertion of American hegemonic pretensions in the Caribbean Basin is viewed with alarm both in Latin America and in Western Europe. American economic might is no longer sufficiently impressive or leading to command absolute deference on the part of either the West Europeans or the Latin Americans. The European Option, for Latin American states, is at least as good as is the American, given the short-term difficulties being experienced domestically and globally by the United States.

One of the ironies of the current state of relations between the United States and Latin America is the complex and delicate foreign debt negotiations. While U.S. private banks are the principal source of capital for Latin America, the U.S. government has become involved in these negotiations reluctantly and belatedly. A protagonist of greater importance than the U.S. government has been the International Monetary Fund (IMF), which has collaborated closely with private banks in an effort to put together bridging loans, new money, imaginative repackaging schemes, and other forms of financial aid for the hard-pressed and deeply indebted states of Latin America.

As it became obvious in late 1982 that massive new financial resources would be required to prevent debtor states from declaring a moratorium or defaulting, the U.S. government was adamantly opposed to substantial increases in contributions to the IMF. While the debtor states called for an increase of 100 percent in 1982, the United States initially proposed 25 percent. In January 1983 negotiations, the United States suggested that an increase of 40 percent would be sufficient. In February 1983 negotiations, the United States reluctantly agreed to a 47.4 percent increase. Although a number of bilateral initiatives have been taken by the United States in the cases of Brazil and Mexico, the overall impression in Latin America—the most indebted of the regions of the Third World—is that once again, the U.S. government is either disinterested in or unaware of the dangerous and precarious financial situation of a majority of the region's economies.

Concomitantly, the central bankers of Western Europe and Japan were far more realistic in assessing the potential damage to the world economy if Latin American countries defaulted. Beginning at the Toronto meeting of the World Bank and the IMF in September 1982, they have been making strong efforts to convince the United States to support immediate and large increases in financial support.

THE FUTURE OF THE UNITED STATES IN LATIN AMERICA

To date, the United States has not identified an all-encompassing strategy for dealing with Latin America in the 1980s and 1990s. It is doubtful that the American government will assume the role of the West European state in urging private sector groups such as labor unions, churches, or political parties to become more involved in social and political interaction with their Latin American counterparts. The present, narrow focus by the Reagan administration on strategic and geopolitical issues in Central America, and the insistence on further isolating Cuba in the hemisphere, are viewed as both unwise and dangerous by Latin American states as well as by West European governments. The inability of the United States to accept ideological diversity and pluralism, and its insistent drumbeat on the strategic dangers of such diversity, are profoundly disturbing to Social Democratic and Christian Democratic forces in the region. A concomitant rush to reinitiate military ties and security assistance with Chile and Argentina, for example, is viewed as short-sighted and perilous.

West European involvement in Latin America and the Caribbean will grow. Private sector and state involvement promises to become more complex. Interlocking social and political issues will increasingly be mediated by and dependent on extraterritorial institutions. Elimination of social injustice, which Lopez Portillo appropriately identified as the cause of unrest and revolutionary violence in Central America, will remain a principal goal of Social Democratic and Christian Democratic forces. The interpenetration is too great and too profound for the United States to be able to afford the belief that we can either return to the *status quo ante* of the Cold War or build barriers against European and transnational involvement in the region's affairs. At a time when the United States policy on human rights has a low priority, social injustice concerns are increasing in importance to many Latin American groups. As the United States seeks to isolate Cuba, many Latin American states see the Castro regime as the result, not the cause, of unrest. And as social development and economic growth grow in priority, the United States is seen, on the one hand, as being unable to provide much support and help financially, and on the other hand, as most concerned about strategic issues which involve a warped view of the pattern of East–West relations that has recently emerged in global politics.

If the conservative or rightist U.S. position is unacceptable to many Latin Americans, the well-meaning but ultimately vacuous liberal position is less than appealing. The liberal option for the center, for the middle, for the tranquil salvation of moderate forces, may have been viable a decade ago, but it is too late in the 1980s. Liberal longing for change—slowly—requires the kinds of economic assistance that are no longer available. As Viron P. Vaky (1981) has commented, "there is, in short, a real question as to whether U.S. policymakers will have available either the level of resources or the degree of popular support required for regional (or world) leadership." In a time of economic desperation in the United States, and with a clear public choice for a conservative political and economic order, the possibility of the United States being able to provide the financing needed is highly doubtful. Moreover, the liberal option traditionally abhors Marxist or revolutionary political regimes—precisely the type of regime favored by the Mexicans, for example, in Nicaragua (not a classic totalitarian system, but one in which elements of Marxism and revolution coexist and survive). Is such an alternative possible? Increasingly, large numbers of Latin American and West European leaders think it is.

To have a future in Latin America, the United States needs to understand that the countries of the region are and will remain increasingly assertive in pursuing their external relations and in seeking answers to internal problems. West European institutions provide a known and flexible mechanism for finding short-term solutions and may offer longer-run options. Subregional and regional forms of cooperation will continue to emerge—some successful, some not—as a way not only of pursuing Latin American solutions to Latin American problems, but also of counterbalancing new hegemonic pretensions. Ideological pluralism will continue to characterize a growing number of states in the hemisphere. Growth of trade union movements and involvement of European political parties and social action groups will increase and receive widespread legitimacy among Latin American leaders—and increasingly their publics as well.

The future of the United States is inextricably tied to cooperation with these new forces, although it is historically ill-prepared to accept that fact. In the short term, the European presence in Latin America may trigger controversy and confusion in American relations with its allies. Ideally, it will be understood in the not too distant future that the European role in Latin America is both legitimate and useful. It expands economic options, offers reasonable political alternatives, and broadens the strategic and geopolitical debate to emphasize international interdependence. It is essential that it be understood neither as an effort to "tie" Latin America to Europe, nor to link action in the region to other Western Alliance foreign policy and strategic concerns. In and of itself, Latin America is assuming greater international importance. Conduct of the advanced developed countries in the hemisphere, therefore, requires comprehension in an overall context. "Going it alone" has created serious regional difficulties in relations of the United States and Latin America since independence. To pursue such a policy now would both threaten U.S. bilateral relations with states such as Mexico and Venezuela and isolate those forces, present and growing in many countries, that seek reasonable alternatives to the capitalist economic model and the linked democratic model, and to the possibilities of continued authoritarianism of the right or aggressive Marxist regimes of the left. To understand the realities of Latin America today, it is less than useful to employ an East–West prism. The learning of this first lesson may be long and painful for the United States.

The Falklands/Malvinas crisis must be seen in the context of a steadily diminishing presence of the United States in Latin America. It has been a process long under way (Roett 1982). The shockwaves that the crisis sent through the Inter-American System should be sufficient for the United States to reassess its future in the hemisphere, and to undertake a basic reassessment of its interests as well as those of its neighbors. Failure to do so will merely confirm the opinion of many that the United States is unable to define its national interests in the hemisphere in a way that will coincide with the realities of today's Latin America.

REFERENCES

Barrow, Simon. "Europe, Latin America, and the Arms Trade," in *The European Challenge: Europe's New Role in Latin America.* London: The Latin American Bureau, 1982.

"Bogotá Begins Seeking 'New Partners' Among Nonaligned." *New York Times,* 9 January 1983.

Leiken, Robert. "Eastern Winds in Latin America." *Foreign Policy,* 42 (Spring 1981), 94–113.

"Mexico and Venezuela Plan to Counter Outside Intervention in Caribbean." *New York Times*, 9 April 1981, 1, 14.

"The South Atlantic Crisis: Background, Consequences, Documentation." U.S. Department of State, Bureau of Public Affairs, Selected Document No. 21, August 1982.

Roett, Riordan. "Beyond the Falklands: Our Latin Clout Weakens." *The Washington Post*, Outlook Section, 9 May 1982.

Vaky, Viron P. "Hemispheric Relations: Everything Is Part of Everything Else." *Foreign Affairs*, 59:3 (1981), 640.

13

THE UNITED STATES AND WESTERN EUROPE: THEIR PLACE IN LATIN AMERICAN INTERNATIONAL POLITICS

Juan Carlos Puig

To understand the place held by the United States and Western Europe in Latin American politics, two things are necessary: a historical framework, to enable us to assess what is happening now and what is possible in the future; and a conceptual framework, to enable us to identify the causal relationships among the various components of the historical record.

My conceptual framework has four basic propositions. First, that the possibilities with respect to strategic games of expansion and containment are circumscribed by the extent of the permissivity obtaining in the international environment. This means essentially what the less powerful countries can get away with without retaliation. It does not, therefore, imply that the more powerful countries necessarily give permission for such action. Nor does it imply that the less powerful countries will necessarily take such action. It is simply a statement of the possibilities.[1] Second is that international politics is, construed to mean international actions and nonactions that contribute to the formulation of the international political situation—even reactive behaviors on the part of "dependent" states. Third, I suggest that it is inappropriate to speak of Latin American unity in this context, because the various Latin American countries do not constitute a unified block that acts as a unit in the international political arena. The fourth proposition is that the international community is a human group that functions politically as any other "micro" or "macro" human group. This means that, as in other groups, there are rulers (supreme and subsidiary) and subjects, and subregimes or subsystems of different types (Rosenau 1969). In this chapter I shall emphasize different zones of dominance (Singer 1969).

From the point of view of its relationship with the respective dominant power, a state affiliated to a given zone of dominance may follow one of four basic policies: (a) *paracolonial dependence*, characterized by a formal system of national decision-making, but one which actually works as an appendix to the government apparatus of the dominant power; (b) *national dependence*, characterized by acceptance of asymmetrical relations but, at the same time, an effort to make the most of the advantages that are inherent in the "accepted" dependence, even at the risk of creating important conflicts with the dominant power; (c) *heterodox autonomy*, characterized by increasing decision-making autonomy within the overall recognition of the leadership of the dominant power, which is backed up in those matters which that power considers vital from a strategic point of view; (d) *secessionist autonomy*, characterized by a cutting of the umbilical link with the dominant power and decision-making autonomy even against the vital strategic interests of the power.[2]

The historical framework I shall use for my discussion has three main periods of change in the "zones of dominance" of Latin America and the types of foreign policy followed by the client states. The first one is the nineteenth and first part of the twentieth centuries, up to World War I: the period of European hegemony. The second one embraces the period between the World Wars: the mirage of European hegemony. The third period of change is the period since the beginning of World War II: American–Soviet dominance. Each will be discussed in turn.

EUROPEAN HEGEMONY

From the early nineteenth century until World War I, the supreme international rulers were the governments of the Great Powers of Europe. Within this group, England stood out above the rest. From the formal standpoint, England was similar to her European partners in the maintenance of the balance of international power; but in practice she was able to exercise a sort of veto power over other countries' overseas ventures. Canning could rightly say that he had brought together the new world in order to reestablish the equilibrium of the old (Schuman 1953).[3]

The regime operating in that zone of influence was open in itself. The only requisite for entering the club of the Great Powers was to accept the rules of the game and have a potential comparable to that of its already accepted members. In principle, political and religious disparities did not prevent the states from becoming part of the "club"—a rule applied as early as the sixteenth century, when the French King Francis I wanted to incorporate the Ottoman Empire into the European equilibrium system. A good sign of the regime's open quality was the way the wars usually ended. Once the immediate objective (normally clearly localized) had been obtained, yesterday's loser continued to be an accepted partner.[4]

Although the regime was open, however, vertical mobility was extremely difficult. Because of the balance of power, the Great Powers (the real supreme rulers of the regime) had the means of access under their control. Virtually the only two additions came from extra-European regions: the United States and Japan (setting aside the promotions of Germany and Italy, which came from state unifications).

The case of the United States deserves special attention because certain of its characteristics set it apart from the other states in that region of the globe. In the first place, it had manufacturing and maritime experience, although still backward compared to European industrial countries. Even in the colonial period, American shipyards made ships more cheaply than did the British. Its international trade was also far more diversified in terms of markets as well as of products than the rest of the Americas: "Tobacco, rice, indigo, corn, flour, meat, fish, rum, furs, wood, found markets in England, the European continent, Africa, the West Indies" (Pratt 1965, 29). The U.S. population was also far more cultured and trained for basic agricultural and manufacturing tasks than the populations of Latin America. Finally, immigration and territorial expansion enabled them to develop more fully the advantages they enjoyed at the beginning of their independence (Droz 1966).

Their international politics from the beginning was that of heterodox autonomy; and their skillful use of their position in both internal and foreign policy was a powerful additional factor. Although internally they favored liberalism, political as well as economic, they embraced protectionism in foreign trade. Thus, they accepted the British criterion of preventing intervention by the European countries but rejected the suggestion of a joint British–American declaration, which would have condemned the intervention in general terms thus jeopardizing later American expansion in the continent. This is the deep sense of the Monroe Doctrine (Puig and Colombo Imaz 1974). With Jefferson and Washington, the United States proclaimed an isolationist policy, but reduced it in practice to not taking part in the political and military European affairs. Isolationism was not an obstacle, for example, to the coercive opening of Japanese ports by Commodore Perry in 1853; nor was it an impediment to American occupation of the Philippines after the Spanish war (Puig, Imaz, and Irureta 1968).

Latin American countries, in contrast, were straightforward clients of the European powers, especially England. They were purveyors of raw materials and buyers of European manufactures; they absorbed capital and facilitated foreign investments in the main extractive activities. Any possibility of autonomous development in Latin America was soon thwarted by the free trade and free exchange championed by Great Britain.[5]

Could it have been another way? One can never know for certain, but it must be admitted that the Latin American starting point was not comparable to that of the United States. It is also true that whenever the American alternative was considered explicitly, it was promptly discarded,[6] and that Latin Americans really believed that liberalism would bring development automatically (Bagu 1966). Nevertheless, it must be admitted that, within the dependent policy followed by Latin American countries generally, at least some of them, even at the risk of serious conflicts with the dominant power, reserved a few areas for independent decision. Typically, these had to do with the status of foreigners, the diplomatic protection of European investors and companies, and the possible occupation by force of the territory as a coactive measure for alleged illegal torts committed by the Latin American country. Argentina (Puig 1980a), Brazil (Lafer 1973), Chile, and Mexico may be included among these.

The U.S. heterodox autonomy (to use my earlier classification) provoked a permanent controversy with Great Britain, especially with regard to Latin America. Such controversy was, however, handled with skill by the Americans. They did not defy the dominant power explicitly; they simply broadened the scope of their autonomous decision-making (Rippy 1929). Thus, for instance, after James N. Polk's government established a *modus vivendi* between the United States and Great Britain, the latter tolerated the American territorial expansionism at Mexico's expense, in return for which the United States promised not to interfere in the rest of the continent (Merk 1963, 1966; Rippy 1929). The War of Secession, in which Great Britain made the mistake of siding openly with the South, gave the triumphant North new opportunities to follow an independent Latin American policy in front of Great Britain.

By the late nineteenth century, their leaders' skills had enabled the United States to graduate to a successful autonomous secessionist policy and become one of the first-ranking powers on the international scene. Important American confrontations with the British during this period include the First Pan American Conference (1889–1890) and the sending of a powerful naval force to Rio de Janeiro to ensure the unloading of American goods, in defiance of a blockade imposed by promonarchical revolutionaries (1893) who counted on British benevolence (LaFeber 1961). The negotiations that followed ended with the adoption of the Hay–Pauncefote Treaty. Great Britain accepted American sole responsibility for the construction of an interoceanic channel and, in so doing, recognized, at least implicitly, American hegemony in Central America and the Hispanic Caribbean. The United States, for its part, had assumed the obligation to honor British investments in that area and to respect global British interests in South America: a sort of nineteenth-century Yalta (Puig and Imaz 1970, 1972). The treaty was signed on 18 November 1901.[7]

THE MIRAGE OF EUROPEAN HEGEMONY

World War I set in motion a series of forces that changed the international system of power. First, the United States had accumulated a potential that surpassed that of the other Great Powers. Second, Great Britain had lost her economic and financial supremacy. Thus, the existing "balance of power" was no longer in balance. Nevertheless, as usually happens when deep, structural changes are taking place, the protagonists (or at least those that prevailed) failed to take note of the magnitude of the changes. The United States returned to its "isolationism" and the European states kept on behaving as if their hegemony had been maintained. The sad story of the League of Nations provides perhaps the best example of this. Without American collaboration, which was not forthcoming because the Republican party had prevailed in its opposition and won the battle in the Senate against it, the League could do nothing either to maintain the status quo dictated by the peace treaties or to promote realistic adaptations to new situations through successful peaceful change (Puig, Imaz, and Trureta 1970; Puig 1974). Further, in matters of strategy and of enlarging (or cutting down) spheres of influence, the United States imposed its will, especially in the areas near to it. This is exactly what happened in Latin America.

Two main trends characterized the period. First, once the war was ended, the decline of European influence—not only economically but also, and above all, politically and strategically—left a vacuum that was progressively filled by the United States. This process reached its climax with the Great Depression, which compelled Great Britain to reorder her relations with countries belonging to her various spheres of influence. British preference was for the members of the Commonwealth, and the Imperial Conference of Ottawa in 1932 left no doubt about it (Conil Paz and Ferrari 1971). Argentina was possibly the only exception to this new frame of reference, since the Roca–Runciman Pact of 1933 confirmed the traditional special relationship with Great Britain and maintained the old imperial linkage (Villanueva 1975)—a situation that was to have troublesome repercussions later on.

Second, the establishment of fascist regimes in Europe (Germany, Italy, and above all Spain) led to an ideological offensive all over the subcontinent. Publications, tourism, fellowships, organization of groups of citizens residing abroad (numerically important in some Latin American countries), schools—all were important instruments. And this was accompanied by a commercial offensive. In 1938, for example, the total trade of Latin America with the Axis nations amounted to U.S. $518 million, second only to the United States (Dozer 1972; Goldhamer 1972). In Brazil, Germany even displaced the United States, becoming the main exporter of goods to Brazil in both 1936 and 1937.[8]

The progressive U.S. takeover of the continent changed the center of political gravity for the countries of Latin America. All (except perhaps Argentina) reproduced the same basic patterns they had followed with the European rulers, adapting them as necessary to the new situation. Some followed a paracolonial policy; Chile, Brazil, Mexico, and Argentina, as before, preferred national dependence.[9]

Evolution of the Pan American system clearly showed the new trends. The failure of the First Pan American Conference in 1890 and the subsequent Anglo–American understanding with respect to their respective spheres of influence in the new continent paved the way for a formal diplomatic sequence which was ineffectual from both political and economic points of view (Puig and Colombo Imaz 1972). As Thomas and Thomas (1968, 17), among others, have said: "Not much success might be ascribed to the Pan American Movement or to Pan American cooperation, given the situation in which they found themselves after 30 years of existence, on the eve of World War I." Nevertheless, after the war, the Pan American Conferences began to pose at least an arena for confrontation between the United States and Latin American countries. The reason was fear of U.S. intrusion. As long as Great Britain (and, in second place, the other European countries) acted as centers of gravity, South American countries had their security guaranteed against the United States; when they began to feel European protection vanishing and American pressures become increasingly stronger, they tried to obtain at least diplomatic assurance that they should be free from coercive interference and from the political fluctuations of American expansion, which had left deep tracks in Central America. They recognized the new dependent relations, but at least the major states of South America pretended not to be subject to visible coercive measures nor, as a result of them, to the occupation of their territory. That explains why in the 1920s the main subject debated at the Pan American Conferences was "multilateralization of the Monroe Doctrine." The Latin American countries were pretending that the United States had assumed a pledge of nonintervention in the continent. That the Monroe Doctrine was strictly unilateral and, therefore, not interpretable or enforcible by any other government was completely unacknowledged. Only with the change of administrations in Washington was the situation relieved. In the 1930s Roosevelt and the Good Neighbor policy performed the miracle; nonintervention became a principle accepted formally, even enthusiastically, by the United States.[10] As a token of good will (and owing also to the success of Sandino's troops), the marines left Nicaragua. Open intervention was abandoned and subtle intrusion began to take its place.

But the new Good Neighbor policy had a string attached; the United States expected to set up institutional mechanisms to implement Latin American solidarity with the United States in case of "aggression." This aim was fulfilled in the Conference for the Consolidation of Peace in Buenos Aires, 1936, and in the Eighth Pan

American Conference in Lima, 1938. The consultation procedure was established and then put into effect from 1939 (the year in which the First Meeting of Consultation was convened) on. Argentina was the only country that maintained its aloofness. It continued to belong to the British orbit, thereby facilitating its ability to resist U.S. pressures. Even its neutrality during the war favored the British (Puig 1980a).

AMERICAN-SOVIET DOMINANCE

World War II and the meetings at Potsdam and Yalta defined the international scene that would clearly prevail. There was no doubt on anyone's part about the European decline or about the huge potential of the two superpowers: the United States and the Soviet Union. Their governments were clearly the new international rulers, and a new criterion for acceptability into the top level of international stratification was established: the power of massive destruction. At the same time, new substantive criteria for dominance appeared, one of which deserves special attention: block impermeability. Spheres of influence were now formally established through two important blocks—Western and Eastern—each under the supervision of one of the superpowers. Within the Western block, Western European powers assumed mediation roles—sometimes important—but by their own definition their roles were not comparable to the responsibility of making decisions on a world scale. It was also clear that these blocks would be "waterproof," meaning that each assumed the obligation of not intervening (especially in the sense of "military" intervention) in the opposite block, and that interference by one of the superpowers in the internal affairs or distribution of power within its own block would not be curbed by the global and regional security systems set up after the war. The veto power in the UN Security Council was the only exception.[11]

Latin America became an integral part of the U.S. block. It is not surprising, then, that the policies and strategies implemented with reference to the dominant power followed the same types we have already noted in previous paragraphs. The small countries maintained paracolonial dependence; the biggest ones, national dependence generally and heterodox autonomy on occasion. (Arévalo and Arbenz's Guatemala, Perón's Argentina, Cárdenas' Mexico, Vargas', Quadros', and Goulart's Brazil, Allende's Chile, and Alvarado's Peru are all good examples.) Sometimes, autonomist Latin American policies provoked U.S. (either open or concealed) intervention. Guatemala and the Dominican Republic are perhaps symptomatic, not only of the deepness of the U.S. engagement, but also of the uselessness of recourse to the United Nations and to the OAS. Thus, they proved beyond doubt that the real juridical principle of contemporary international relations is not nonintervention but block impermeability (Claude 1964).

Cuba is an example of a successful autonomous secessionist policy, but it also shows that the secession must take place without military help or massive foreign assistance. The discussion still continues as to the real reasons for Marxism–Leninism establishing itself in Cuba. Was it a desired course of action? Did American intransigence affirm the power of the more radical elements and push Fidel Castro, being an opportunist, to climb on top of the waves in order to remain in power? Though it is true that on the 2nd of December, 1961, he said that he was a Marxist–Leninist and would be so for the rest of his life, most people forget that on the 13th of January, 1959, he had said, "Neither I nor my movement are communist" (Thomas 1971, 1049 ff).

Relations between the Latin American countries and the United States are shaped by the margins of heterodoxia, the factors of power, the most influential pressure groups in each country that the U.S. government is willing to tolerate, the perceptions that Latin Americans have of these factors, and their will to take advantage of the margins they have.

Defining these margins, however, is a difficult exercise because indicators of the degree of permissiveness are neither tangible nor clear (Jaguaribe 1972). Interpreting clues, however, allows us to draw some tentative conclusions. Thus, for instance, nationalization of U.S. companies and purchase of Czechoslovakian armaments by Guatemala stimulated strong intervention by the United States; but the actions of the Peruvian government after 1968, though similar in quality and significance and even more intense in degree, did not provoke such a reaction.[12] The policy of statism introduced by Allende in Chile stimulated immediate U.S. hostility and sanctions, but the Andean Pact and its autonomist resolutions were more or less tolerated. Such apparently contradictory positions have led analysts to differing interpretations of U.S. policy toward the subcontinent. Thus, Ianni (1974, 48) has developed the thesis that such variations in American foreign policy are due to confusion: "the imperialist domination loses sometimes the perspective of its own interests or does not understand the real significance of the events." Bourricaud (1975), on the contrary, interprets the new structural approaches of the United States as marking the "end of a game" in Latin America.

In my judgment, the experience of the last decades indicates that the United States has taken a new look at their real national interest in Latin America. It seems that a firm stand against communism (above all from the external point of view) makes "progressive" policies in the socioeconomic field and stronger links with the Soviet block in economic matters "tolerable." Even arms trade with communist countries seems to be tolerated, provided it is not on a massive scale.

In fact, such developments and their rationale had been clearly anticipated 20 years ago by Adolf A. Berle (1962, 23–24). This is his comment on the possible basis for American–Latin American understanding.

> An implacable criterion of judgment has to be that of the safety of the United States. The fact that a new order is different or unfamiliar to us is wholly secondary in importance to the question whether it is, in the context of the prevailing world struggle, dangerous to our own survival. The United States can, and during most of its existence has, coexisted quite happily with all manner of social systems governed by all manner of political organizations. It is, for instance, quite possible to imagine systems not based on the institution of private property (though we might be dubious about their success), and for the United States to work happily with them—provided they do not assert as a necessary concomitance that they must join with others in conquering the United States, or insist (as Castro does) that they will, in some fashion, attack the American political–economic system.

If one bears in mind the relative loss of U.S. power in the continent and in the world (Lowenthal 1977; Lowenthal and Fishlow 1980; Pinto 1974), the increased influence of the transnational corporations (Sunkel and Fuenzalida 1979), and the increasingly accurate understanding on the part of Latin Americans of the real borderlines existing in their relationship with the United States,[13] it becomes clear that the "macrovision" generally prevails over the "private microvision" in the Latin American policy of the "colossus of the North" (Pinto 1974, 134). From the strategic point of view, it is presently the possibility of the secession of a client–state that primarily affects the national interest of a dominant power. Although one cannot yet speak of a net trend in such a direction, events that are taking place in both orbits seem to signal at least the feasibility of macrovision approaches to the solution of intrablock crises (for example, Nicaragua and Poland).[14]

The increasingly sophisticated understanding by Latin Americans of the real structure and functioning of the international regime and of the existence of given criteria and fundamental rules shared by the United States and the Soviet Union merits a further word or two. Within such a background, cold war, peaceful coexistence, and détente are nothing more than different stages of a political game, played to obtain minor gains without questioning the existing strategic understandings. It seems that the Latin Americans are tired of continuously adapting their policies and strategies to the hesitations and changes of the United States in their perception (usually tactical) of their relations with the Soviet Union. This is, above all, because "each change of political orientation in the United States has dangerous repercussions on all those regimes whose policy does not conform to the priorities of the American policy at each moment" (Grabendorff 1977, 437).

Let us now turn to Europe. As Europe's recovery after the war took place, its relations with Latin America increased considerably in the economic and cultural fields (Goldhamer 1972). Sometimes there has even been some interest in giving that relationship a certain sense of political solidarity; however, this has never lasted, except in rhetoric or to justify specific economic concessions or arms sales. A good example was the Gaullist policy. As has been rightly emphasized by Goldhamer (1972, 23), "French prestige and influence did gain perceptively from General de Gaulle's state visits, from his hostility toward and independence of the United States, and from the sale of Mirages, but this gain was not sustained." The same could be said of the Saragat and Fanfani attempt to implement a triangular policy in 1962–65 to include Latin America as one of the three points in a proposed triangular set of alignments (with Europe and the United States) which would bring Latin America into closer association with Europe and, by compensating for stresses in U.S.–Latin American relations, ensure a greater degree of Western unity and security. But, as Goldhamer also says (20), "This geometric image was not supported by a policy with sufficient specificity to alter anything in the political or military arrangements of the Western Powers."

This, in fact, is the crucial point. Are the Western European powers willing to uphold Latin American aspirations of a greater autonomy within the area *against* the will of the United States? There are positive answers to this question. Thus, Grabendorff (1977, 440) announces that "the relationship between Europe and Latin America will become closer in the future." To other European specialists, however, the conclusions are frankly negative. Boselli (1977, 428) says that, "although the geopolitical framework in which the relations between Latin America and Europe developed is characterized by the necessity of looking for an alternative to the U.S. presence as a hegemonic power in the Latin American complex reality, [those relations] must not ever be interpreted as rivalry between the Communities and the United States." And it was clearly pointed out by Delorme and Langer (1976) that, from the Suez question on, France and Great Britain will not be able to intervene, even in their own spheres of influence, against the will of the United States. It is possible that such a behavior does not correspond to the real power the United States could exert, but the governments act as if it were true, and that is what really matters in terms of political analysis (see Puig 1980a).

So, where are we? In the first place, it seems correct to say that generally, the Western European powers consider that Latin American security and strategy (political and military) are largely in U.S. hands for two main reasons: (1) from the point of view of European security, Latin America is a region of secondary importance; (2) the United States has primary responsibility for the region for reasons of geographic proximity, regional understandings, and cultural ties.

It should be emphasized that in recent years there has been a trend to intensify European entanglement in Latin American political and strategic subjects in, for example, relations with Cuba, human rights, nuclear assistance, and military equipment. One can also venture a guess that this trend will continue in the future, particularly when the first European reactions to the new American administration's Latin American policy have been carefully assessed. However, on the road to a more dynamic and fruitful Latin American–European understanding, there are huge obstacles. One of them—an important one—is the restrictive commercial policy of European communities vis-à-vis Latin America. This is a dramatic fact. Between 1955 and 1979, Latin American exports to Western Europe fell from 7.3 percent to 3.1 percent; and Latin American imports from Western European sources fell from 7 percent to 3.4 percent. The relative importance of Western Europe in Latin American foreign trade is also in sharp decline. In the same period, for example, Western European exports fell from 31 percent to 24 percent, and their imports from Latin America fell from 28 percent to 23 percent. Community restrictions on Latin American trade are all the more regrettable because they are not necessary to preserve European economic health, as the last World Bank research program on the penetration of the markets of industrial countries by exports of manufactures from developing countries made clear.[15] Unfortunately, final admission of Spain, Portugal, and Greece into the Communities will damage still more Latin America's economic relationships with Western Europe. Another important obstacle is the absence of a European policy with respect to Latin America.[16] This should not come as a surprise since, in fact, no integrated European international policy exists, particularly with respect to helping Latin American aspirations to autonomy.

A final point should be noted. If there is any real tightening of Western European relations with Latin America politically and strategically, it will inevitably transform at least some of the foundations of the international regime, enhancing Latin American mediation powers to the detriment, obviously, of the United States and Western Europe.

NOTES

1. See Jaguaribe (1972, 1979) and Puig (1980b) for a general discussion of this issue. See also Boulding (1959) and Jervis (1970).

2. The aim is to part with the block (which does not guarantee in all cases that the seceding country will not fall again, trapped in a diabolical dialectical process, under a different sphere of influence). For a more detailed explanation of these ideas, see Puig (1980a).

3. This assertion, in my opinion, has a meaning by no means akin to the one generally accepted. What Canning wanted to say was that England, having contributed to preventing Spain from recovering her colonies and the other European powers from acquiring them, had succeeded in keeping those colonies from adding to the potential of the latter. All this made easier the maintenance of the balance of power in the region (obviously under discreet British supervision). As the newly independent Latin American countries entered into the British sphere of influence, from the commercial and financial points of view, British maritime and economic power was increased which, in turn, facilitated the British role of "watchman of the European equilibrium" (Albrecht-Carrie 1958, 23 ff).

4. This explains the "forgetfulness" clauses so frequent in the peace treaties at that time.

5. This trend started, in fact, in the years before Independence, owing precisely to both the decline of Spanish power and British economic expansion. That is why, for instance, in 1806 in Buenos Aires, while the *vara* (Spanish unit of length, about 2.8 feet) of national cotton was worth 2 or 2.5 *reales*, the same amount of British cotton was worth 1 *real*. Even the "ponchos" were woven in England; they were sold for 3 pesos when the national ones amounted to 7 pesos. See Alvarez (1914, 23).

6. Alberdi (1963, 33) explained why the American alternative should have been put aside in Argentina: "On separating from a naval and manufacturing power, the United States had the capacity and the means to become one thing or the other, and it was better for them to march against foreign intervention, through exclusions and tariffs. But we have no factories, nor navy on behalf of which we should restrain, through prohibitions and regulations, the foreign shipping and industry which are willing to trade with us."

7. This fact explains why the American government was so "unreceptive" to the Drago Doctrine, announced by the Argentines on the occasion of the European (including the British) intervention in Venezuela in 1902. However, as the Monroe tradition implied, a punitive expedition could not be the beginning of a territorial occupation. It was the task of the next American government to find a way of repelling the European intrusion without affecting the spirit of the understanding previously reached. That explains, again, the Roosevelt Corollary to the Monroe Doctrine. Whitaker (1956, 115) is right when he says, "if Drago's ideas had been implemented, the whole history of inter-American relations of the following decades would have been different." Two recent pieces of research make clear this aspect of the question: Conil Paz (1976) and Herwig and Helguera (1977).

8. This was true even though Getulio Vargas himself considered that Brazil had engaged dangerously in this way, and tried to mend economic relationships with the United States; even by 1938, Brazilian purchases of German goods were still impressive (Green 1972).

9. Mexico and Argentina, in particular moments, even embarked on an autonomist heterodox policy—Lázaro Cárdenas' Mexico, for example, and Argentina, at least during World War II. Francis (1976) is very interesting on this subject. As he says in his conclusions (246): "By 1943 the Argentine political system had worked itself into a position in which the amount of coercion the United States could generate (which was limited by geography, the necessity of winning the war, the need to protect U.S. business interests, and England's precarious economic situation) could only accomplish the opposite of what the United States wanted."

10. On this subject and, in general, on a sociopolitical explanation of the Pan American system, Connell–Smith (1966) offers probably the best approach.

11. As to this question and the repercussions of new developments in the United Nations and regional organizations formally reducing the veto power, but in fact reinforcing it, see Puig (1974). This American–Soviet dominance meant a basic understanding on the part of the governments of the superpowers (international "rulers") about the supreme criteria on which the regime rests. As is true of every political regime, a basic understanding does not imply a permanent agreement on everything between the different groups contending for power, otherwise the political struggles would make no sense. Nor does it mean that, within the structure of the

regime, there is no margin for incremental gains—nor even that incremental gains could eventually lead to such a major change. So far, however, the American-Soviet struggle seems a normal political competition, both of them trying to obtain more important scopes of influence in international decisions within a structure whose basic criteria both respect. The functioning of the current international system is explained in detail in Puig (1980a). Let me simply say here that the criterion of impermeability between the blocks has worked unharmed since World War II, and that the increase (or diminution) of the influence of the superpowers in Afro-Asiatic countries not assigned to either block has followed the fluctuations of the relative conventional strength of the concerned powers and of the will to play the game of forcing or checking an expansion (Vincent 1976; Connell-Smith 1977; Puig 1979).

12. With reference to one of the most risky episodes of the Peruvian-American relations at that time—the confiscation of IPC assets—see Puig (1972).

13. This is a very important point, since the internal elite is beginning to learn that more autonomy in relations with the United States does pay in the long run, even having in sight its internal supremacy. The case of Argentina in recent years is particularly relevant.

14. This reappraisal of the dominant power national interest in the stated terms is connected to the whole "conception" of the empire. The point has been well made by Jaguaribe (1972, 1979). Reasoning from history, he has suggested three possible alternatives: (1) *ethnocentrism*, as a way of maximizing interests of the center in the historical short range; (2) *central culturalism* incorporating peoples and elites identified with the central culture; (3) *ecumenism*, which presupposes the gradual overcoming of centralism and the expanding on a universal level of all benefits of society to all peoples.

Ethnocentrism implies the permanent domination and exploitation of the periphery to the benefit of the center, supported by material forces of the center. On the other hand, central culturalism presupposes incorporation of the peoples and, above all, of the elites identified with the central culture and the main strategic considerations of the dominant power. This is not the place to go into the details of this approach and to sketch a criticism (for this, see Puig 1980b). However, leaving aside small differences, if one refers to recent U.S. history, one can maintain that the Carter administration identified itself with the pattern of central culturalism, within which obviously the macrovision can be freely followed and the autonomy of decision of client-states is enlarged. The Reagan administration, on the contrary, seems to follow the patterns of ethnocentrism. Although it is premature to make a final judgment, significant symptoms are the new rearmament program of the United States, the emphatic assertion made in all official documents that there is no foreign policy without an adequate military power, the reaffirmation of open hegemonic pretensions, the distinction made between "totalitarian" and "authoritarian" governments, etc. The real question is whether ethnocentrism can be sustained in a world where military potential is each time less conclusive, where the spiritual forces constitute a resource of power that is increasingly important, and where it is progressively more difficult for the dominant powers to subsidize governing elites of client-states.

15. See the World Bank Staff Working Papers on Market Penetration Research Project, Nos. 425 on.

16. See, for instance, *Integración Latinoamericana* (April–May 1980), 5:45–6.

REFERENCES

Alberdi, Juan Bautista. *Bases*. Santa Fe: Castellví, 1963.

Albrecht-Carrié, Albert. *A Diplomatic History of Europe Since the Congress of Vienna*. New York: Harper, 1958.

Alvarez, Juan. *Estudios sobre las guerras civiles argentinas*. Buenos Aires: 1914.

Bagú, Sergio. *El plan económico del grupo rivadaviano, 1811-1827*. Rosario: Universidad del Litoral, 1966.

Bailey, Norman. *Latin America in World Affairs*. New York: Walker & Co., 1967.

Berle, Adolf A. *Latin America, Diplomacy and Reality*. New York: Harper & Row, 1962.

Boselli, Luigi. "Die Beziehungen zwischen der Europaischen Gemeinschaft und Lateinamerika. Auf dem Wege zu neuen Zielen?" *Europa Archiv*, 32:14 (1977).

Bourricaud, François. "Fin de partida en América Latina." *Trimestre Politico*, 1:1 (July 1975): 86–92.

Chalmers, Douglas. "Developing in the Periphery: External Factors in Latin American Politics," In James N. Rosenau (ed.), *Linkage Politics*. New York: The Free Press, 1969.

Claude, Inis L. Jr. "The OAS, the UN and the United States." *International Conciliation*, 547 (March 1964).

Conil Paz, Alberto. "Historia de la Doctrina Drago." In *Homenaje al doctor Luis Maria Drago*. Caracas: Oficina Central de Información, 1976.

Conil Paz, Alberto and Gustavo Ferrari. *Política exterior argentina. 1930-1962*. Buenos Aires: Biblioteca del Oficial, 1971.

Connell-Smith, Gordon. *The Inter-American System*. London: Oxford University Press, 1966.

————. *Los Estados Unidos y la América Latina*. Mexico: Fondo de Cultura Económica, 1977.

DeLorme, Hélène and Frederique Langer. "L'Europe des Neuf et le nouvel ordre economique international." *Révue Française de Science Politique*, 26:4 (August 1976):3–42.

Dozer, Donald Marquand. *Are We Good Neighbors? Three Decades of Inter-American Relations, 1930-1960*. New York: Johnson Reprint Co., 1972.

Drekonja, Gerhard. "Aproximaciones a la política exterior latinoamericana." *Estudios Internacionales*, 14:53, (Enero–Marzo 1981):89–104.

Droz, Jacques, Lucien Genet, and Jean Vidalenc. *La época contemporanea*. Buenos Aires: Eudeba, 1966.

Fralon, José. *L'Europe, c'est fini*. Paris: Calmann-Lévy, 1975.

Francis, Michael J. *The Limits of Hegemony. United States Relations with Argentina and Chile During World War II*. Notre Dame: University of Notre Dame Press, 1976.

Gleich, Albrecht von. "Algunos comentarios a las relaciones actuales entre América Latina y la Comunidad Europea." *Mundo Nuevo*, 4:13/14 (July/December 1981):172-6.

Goldhamer, Herbert. *The Foreign Powers in Latin America*. Princeton: Princeton University Press, 1972.

Grabendorff, Wolf. "Lateinamerika und die Vereinigten Staaten." *Europa Archiv*, 32:14 (1977).

Green, David. *The Containment of Latin America. A History of the Myths and Realities of the Good Neighbor Policy*. Chicago: Quadrangle Books, 1972.

Greville, J. A. S. "Great Britain in the Isthmian Canal." *The American Historical Review*, 61 (1961).

Herwig, Holger H. and J. Leon Helguera. *Krupp Salvos at Fort Libertador: Germany and the International Blockade of Venezuela, 1902-3. A Study in Gunboat Diplomacy*. Caracas: Ministerio de Relaciones Exteriores, 1977.

Ianni, Octavio. "Diplomacia e imperialismo en las relaciones interamericanas." In J. C. Cotler and R. R. Fagen (eds.), *Relaciones políticas entre América Latina y Estados Unidos*. Buenos Aires: Amorrortu, 1974.

Jaguaribe, Helio. *Desarrollo político: sentido y condiciones*. Buenos Aires: Paidós, 1972.

———. "Hegemonía céntrica y autonomía periférica." In Eduardo Hill and Luciano Tomassini (eds.), *América Latina y el nuevo orden internacional*. Santiago de Chile: Corporación de Promoción Universitaria, 1979, 17–48.

Jervis, Robert. *The Logic of Images in International Relations*. Princeton, NJ: Princeton University Press, 1970.

LaFeber, Walter. "Background of Cleveland's Venezuelan Policy." *The American Historical Review*, 66 (1961).

Lafer, Celso. *Argentina y Brasil en el sistema de relaciones internacionales*. Buenos Aires: Nueva Visión, 1973.

Lowenthal, Abraham. "El fin de la presunción hegemonica." *Estudios Internacionales*, 10:37 (Enero–Marzo 1977):45-67.

Lowenthal, Abraham and Albert Fishlow. "Los nuevos intereses de los Estados Unidos en el hemisferio occidental." *Estudios Internacionales*, 13:49 (Enero–Marzo 1980):54-69.

Merk, Frederick. *La doctrina de Monroe y el expansionismo norteamericano*. Buenos Aires: Paidós, 1966.

———. *Manifest Destiny and Mission in American History. A Reinterpretation*. New York: Knopf, 1963.

"National Images and International Systems." *The Journal of Conflict Resolution*, 3 (1959).

Pinto, Aníbal. "Las relaciones económicas entre América Latina y Estados Unidos: algunas implicaciones y perspectivas." In J. C. Cotler and R. R. Fagen (eds.), *Relaciones políticas entre América Latina y Estados Unidos*. Buenos Aires: Amorrortu, 1974.

Pratt, Julius W. *A History of United States Foreign Policy*. 2nd ed. Englewood Cliffs, NJ: Prentice-Hall, 1965.

Puig, Juan Carlos. *Derecho de la comunidad Internacional*. Buenos Aires: Depalma, 1974.

———. *Doctrinas internacionales y autonomia latinoamericana*. Caracas: Ediciones del Instituto de Altos Estudios de America Latina (IAEAL), 1980a.

———. "El Caso de la International Petroleum Co." In *De la dependencia a la liberación. Política exterior de América Latina*. Buenos Aires: La Bastilla, 1972, 11–54.

————. "El principio de no intervención en el Derecho internacional público interamericano. Influencia de la nuevas relaciones internacionales." *Anuario Jurídico Interamericano* (1979).

————. "Hacia una nueva ciencia política para un mundo nuevo." *Mundo Nuevo. Revista de Estudios Latinoamericanos*, 3:9/10 (July/December 1980b).

Puig, Juan Carlos and Delia Colombo Imaz. "El movimiento por la unidad interamericana. Ensayo de sistematización en base al método estructural." *Revista de Derecho Internacional y Ciencias Diplomáticas*, 19:37/38 (1970).

————. "Panamericanismo por inercia." *Revista de Derecho Internacional y Ciencias Diplomáticas*, 21:41/42 (1972).

————. "El Fracaso de la iniciativa latinoamericana en el panamericanismo." In J. F. Petras, et al. (eds.), *Política de poder en América Latina*. Buenos Aires: Pleamar, 1974.

Puig, Juan Carlos, Delia Colombo Imaz, and Hugo Irureta. *Historia política contemporanea*. Buenos Aires: Pleamar, 1968.

Rippy, J. Fred. *Rivalry of the U.S. and Great Britain over Latin America (1808–1830)*. Baltimore: The Johns Hopkins Press, 1929.

Rosenau, James N. "Toward the Study of National-International Linkages," In James N. Rosenau (ed.), *Linkage Politics*. New York: The Free Press, 1969.

Schuman, Frederick L. *International Politics. The Western State System in Mid-Century*. New York: McGraw–Hill, 1953.

Singer, J. David. "The Global System and Its Subsystems." In James N. Rosenau (ed.), *Linkage Politics*. New York: The Free Press, 1969.

Sondermann, Fred A. "The Linkage between Foreign Policy and International Politics." In James N. Rosenau (ed.), *International Politics and Foreign Policy*. Glencoe, Ill: The Free Press of Glencoe, 1961.

Sunkel, Oswaldo and Edmundo Fuenzalida. "Capitalismo transnacional y desarrollo nacional." In Eduardo Hill and Luciano Tomassini (eds.), *América Latina y el nuevo orden económico internacional*. Santiago de Chile: Corporación de Promoción Universitaria, 1979, 49–68.

Thomas, Ann van Wynen and A. J. Thomas Jr. *The Organization of American States*. Dallas: Southern Methodist University Press, 1968.

Thomas, Hugh. *Cuba. The Pursuit of Freedom*. New York: Harper & Row, 1971.

Villanueva, Javier. "Economic Development." In Mark Falcoff and Ronald H. Dolkart (eds.), *Prologue to Perón*. Berkeley: University of California Press, 1975.

Vincent, J. R. *Nonintervention and International Order*. Princeton, NJ: Princeton University Press, 1974.

Whitaker, Arthur T. *La Argentina y los Estados Unidos*. Buenos Aires: Proceso, 1956.

Winkler, Max. *Investment of United States Capital in Latin America*. Boston: World Peace Foundation Pamphlets 11:6, 1929.

14

THE UNITED STATES AND WESTERN EUROPE: COMPETITION OR COOPERATION IN LATIN AMERICA?

Wolf Grabendorff

The international system of the 1980s is different from that of earlier decades.

- The United States can no longer be viewed as the principal link between Latin America and the rest of the world.
- State and nonstate actors from outside the Western hemisphere affect increasingly not only Latin America's economic but also its political life.[1]

In other words, the Monroe Doctrine has outlived its usefulness—the Falklands/Malvinas conflict being merely the most recent case in point. This fact, noted by Latin American policymakers earlier than by most of their U.S. counterparts (at least in part because of their interest in reducing the "shadow" of the former hegemonic power of the United States), requires a new definition of Latin America's role in the international system.

THE CONTRAST BETWEEN U.S. AND WESTERN EUROPEAN INFLUENCES ON LATIN AMERICA

Measuring their development in Western European or U.S. terms is an old tradition in Latin American societies, and there can be no doubt that the influence of both countries has been, and still is to some degree, an important determinant of Latin American development. This importation of Western political and economic models, as well as consumption and lifestyle patterns, has led to a cultural affinity with Western values and traditions which contrasts sharply with Latin America's structural affinity with the rest of the Third World—a contrast that has produced an ambiguous but at the same time very specific role for Latin America in the international system (Nitsch 1977; Atkins 1977), and a "stability of instability" with respect to the majority of their political institutions.

There are important contrasts between the influences of Western Europe and the United States, however, which are important to understand because they will increasingly influence their relationships with Latin America during the 1980s. First, Western Europe is more like Latin America than is the United States in the generally stronger ideological nature of their political actors and the more important role of the state in their societies. This gives Western European models a certain attractiveness for those Latin American elites looking for a way out of their economic and political bondage through military-dominated political systems. Second, the conceptualization of political and economic development is much more pluralistic in Western Europe than in the United States. Thus, looking to Western Europe for models to follow allows more room for choice than does looking to the United States. Third, the traditional North–South pattern of domination—United States–Latin America, Western Europe–the Middle East and Africa, Japan–Southeast Asia—tends to carry with it a heavier historical burden than do diagonal relationships like that of Western Europe with Latin America. A certain geographical distance tends to make power imbalances easier to accept and interventions of all types a little less likely. The absence of common borders or neighbors reduces the number of potential conflicts—even though the Falklands/Malvinas conflict has demonstrated how rapidly the existing ones can explode—and different perceived threats from outside, make security discussions less divisive. Conceptualization of diagonal relationships can, therefore, be tailored more flexibly to serve the interests of both parties.

Finally, and most decisively in the U.S.–Latin American case, Latin America's relationship is with a superpower. In the case of Western Europe, Latin America's relationship is with a group of relatively diverse states. These countries' experiences with two world wars and their aftermaths, furthermore, have made them, on the one hand, reluctant to try to exercise any great influence over other countries, and have contributed greatly, on the other hand, to their willingness to live side-by-side with ideologically radically different states and to seek compromise resolutions rather than confrontations with them.

Since internal developments in Latin American countries are of paramount importance in determining their foreign policy postures, these differences provide the only context within which the contrast between U.S. and Western European relationships with Latin America can be properly understood.

LEGACY OF THE MONROE DOCTRINE: U.S.-LATIN AMERICAN RELATIONS

The United States views its relationship with Latin America mainly within the framework of its steadily declining influence (Lowenthal 1976, 1978), to which different administrations have reacted differently. The Carter administration seemed—at times at least—resigned to letting Latin American states develop in their own way and choose their own alliances. The obvious preoccupation of the Reagan administration with the global balance vis-à-vis the Soviet Union, in contrast, has moved Latin America into the forefront of the East–West conflict. The reason is that the Reagan administration's concept of reasserting U.S. influence in the world is based on having a strong position in the Western hemisphere. Outside interference in Latin America in general, and the Caribbean Basin in particular, is viewed by the United States as threatening to its international position.[2] That makes highly undesirable not only Cuban and suspected Soviet interest in the region, but also, though to a much lesser degree, Western European influence. Stable, "moderately repressive authoritarian regimes"[3] are an acceptable choice for the Reagan administration, compared with the chances that their destabilization might bring about radical Marxist states hostile to U.S. interests in the future. The development of Nicaragua is seen as an example of undesirable internal political change aided by outside forces. As in other parts of the world, the fight against terrorism—a term that is also used to identify guerrilla movements—in Latin America has taken the place of a U.S. policy stressing human rights. To avoid political change by violent means has become more important than pressing for fewer violations of human rights in the region. What is overlooked is that, by attempting to control political change, the process is very often accelerated and, in consequence, the political outcome becomes a self-fulfilling prophecy. By trying to impose on these countries a particular domestic order and "acceptable" external behavior, the United States runs the risk of leaving revolutionary regimes no other option but to approach the socialist camp.[4]

On the assumption that the world position of the United States will suffer greatly without U.S. control of political developments in its immediate vicinity considered hostile to its national interest, re-establishing its influence in Latin America has become a priority issue in U.S. foreign policy.[5] As a consequence, geopolitical and security issues are much more on the minds of Washington policymakers to-day than are Latin America's political, social, and economic development needs.[6]

The reason why such a policy is unlikely to be successful is clear when the reasons for the decline in U.S. influence are identified. Are they really to be found in the inept policy-making of previous administrations? Are they to be found in the meddling of Cuban and Soviet interests in Latin American affairs? Both are unlikely. The reasons lie, rather, in the changing international context. It was the Vietnam war and its aftermath that gave Latin American states the opportunity to enter the international system without the consent of the United States. Detente was another important factor, because reduced U.S. preoccupation with the possible effects of regime changes in Latin America on the East–West power balance gave Latin American countries—Brazil, Cuba, Mexico, Venezuela, and Argentina, to name the most prominent—new room for a more independent internal course. Further, the preference of the Carter administration for an overall foreign policy as opposed to one that treated Latin America as a special region, accepted Latin America *de facto* as part of the Third World, and contributed externally to its identification with the positions of Asian and African states in the North–South conflict (Fagen 1979; Lowenthal and Fishlow 1979).

It should be noted that these trends in U.S. policy toward Latin America had very pragmatic origins. Limitations of U.S. power seemed to make indirect or direct interventions in Latin America—not least because of domestic political costs—less and less feasible. Preferential treatment for Latin Americans on economic issues, therefore, became less and less advantageous and, as a consequence, less and less available.

A similar effect has occurred in the field of moral superiority as the concept of human rights did not, as intended, strengthen the political influence of the United States in Latin America but, rather, contributed to its weakening. Given the relatively low strategic importance of Latin America as seen by the Carter administration, it seemed logical that human rights violations would be used as politically expedient tools there, more than in other parts of the world. The immediate effects of this policy, however, were to strengthen not only the internal opposition forces in any given Latin American country, but also a growing anti-Americanism in the ranks of the traditional elites, which grew rapidly into active distrust toward the United States (Grondona 1977). Some of the U.S.-trained officers went so far as to doubt not only the readiness but even the willingness of the Carter administration to defend their regimes against internal subversion. The resulting insecurity on the part of ruling Latin American elites led to the search for new foreign partners and contributed to the general weakening of the U.S.–Latin American relationship.

The Reagan administration has found it difficult to reverse this trend, even though it has shown great willingness to accommodate the interests of these elites. Any recently-restored trust in U.S. policies has, of course, been shattered by the posture of the Reagan administration during the Falklands/Malvinas conflict. It was not only in Argentina that the military felt "betrayed" by the lack of support. The traditional anti-Americanism of the Latin American left has now been joined by an anti-Americanism of the Latin American right. Canceling of military aid arrangements during the Carter administration and the continuous changing of military suppliers have also contributed to the decline of U.S. influence where it used to be strongest—in the Latin American military (Marcella 1980).

The increasing economic interdependence of the United States with its neighbors to the immediate south—the Caribbean and Central America, including Mexico, Venezuela, and Colombia—is another important factor weakening the U.S. position in Latin America. In the last decade there has been an obvious shifting of concentration of U.S. interest in that new direction. This reorientation is only partly due to increasing interests in securing energy. A much more important factor is the immigration pattern, which has led to the presence currently of some 20 million "latinos" in the United States.

The long-term effects of what is now the most striking border between the First and the Third World—the U.S. border with Mexico and the Caribbean—have barely begun to evolve. Internal consequences of a possibly politically active minority of such dimensions may well have a greater impact on United States–Latin American relations than anything since the Cuban Revolution. International and domestic aspects of the proximity of societies that are entirely different politically, socially, economically, and culturally, in the context of steadily increasing possibilities of communication and transport, will make necessary a new network of cooperative agreements among all the states involved. So far no such mechanism has been developed. The Caribbean Basin Initiative (CBI),[7] which was launched by the Reagan administration in cooperation with Mexico, Venezuela, Canada, and later Colombia, seems to contain some elements of a new approach to the region of the U.S. "third border." But so far it shows no signs of success because it lacks funds, and there is obvious disagreement among the participating countries about developmental objectives and priorities. What is clear is that, since certain U.S. neighbors show an increasing ability to export some of their problems to the United States (Cuba, Mexico, and Haiti), the political and social fabric of these countries will be getting more and more attention in Washington, as well as in the southern states of the United States that are immediately affected by these new issues in U.S.-Latin American relations.

For all these reasons, although it is as yet an open question whether the formulas of the Reagan administration will contribute to a strengthening of U.S. influence in the region, it must be considered unlikely. To the extent that they do appear to have the desired results, it will probably only be on a short-term basis and in the smaller, more dependent Latin American countries. By the end of the 1980s, their long-term effect may well be the opposite. Because of the rapidly crumbling community of interests between Latin America and the United States, and the U.S. unwillingness to transfer any substantial resources for development to its Latin American neighbors, U.S. influence in the region will further decline (although it might remain strong in selected countries). All efforts to revive the Monroe Doctrine are bound to fail, since its basis—the community of interests between the United States and Latin America and the ability of the United States to keep other powers out of the hemisphere—cannot be reestablished.

POLITICS OF ATTRACTION: WESTERN EUROPEAN-LATIN AMERICAN RELATIONS

Until well into the 1970s, Western European politicians did not feel they had to pay much attention to Latin America. Except for the missile crisis in 1962, nothing much happened there that was considered of international importance, and the continent seemed to have been spared from the superpower rivalries. There was a tacit understanding that the United States would take care of the "lesser" problems in Latin America, while cultural and economic relations between that region and Western Europe would continue to flourish.

Recently, however, the rise of regional powers like Brazil, Mexico, Venezuela, and Argentina has led to a much closer relationship with Western Europe. Given the strong economic performance of some Western European countries in the 1970s, their desire to diversify their foreign and trade relations to avoid pressure from the United States in situations of conflicting interests, and their increased willingness to translate their economic position into a bolder international role, Western Europe has become an attractive partner for Latin America. Offering almost the same possibilities with regard to capital, technology, and access to markets, Western Europe had neither the capacity to exert political pressure or the desire to exercise moral leadership. This made them preferred as business partners by many Latin American states. Especially in sensitive areas of special significance to Latin American perceptions of sovereignty, like weapons and nuclear technology transfer,[8] the "European connection" proved to be more reliable and politically less difficult to manage—until the Falklands/Malvinas conflict—than that of the United States. Fully aware of the tough competition between the Western European and U.S. business interests in a variety of fields, certain Latin American countries even became able to play off these interests against each other. The history of the Brazilian nuclear deal with West Germany is only the most spectacular case of many.[9]

The political bonus for the emancipation process of Latin American states resulting from the greater Western European role in Latin America has not yet been fully recognized. Latin America still views Europe as an option available to increase its bargaining power versus the United States, rather than an alternative to U.S. influence. And many Western European politicians still regard the attractiveness of Latin American markets and investment possibilities as overshadowed by the fact that the majority of Latin American political and social systems are not compatible with the democratic consensus of the respective Western European societies.[10] Visiting presidents—usually generals—from Latin American military regimes to Great Britain, France, or West Germany are often reminded of that fact.

This combination of factors has prevented state-to-state relations between specific European and specific Latin American countries from being the predominant type of link. Within the basic democratic consensus, however, as noted, there is a pluralism in Western

European societies: the more conservative sectors praise law and order in authoritarian governments as the means to achieve economic growth; the more progressive groups in Western Europe favor social change as the only basis for long-term development in the region. This very pluralism has led to the perception of Latin America in Western Europe increasingly as an area of experimentation for political, social, and economic development strategies. The result is a pattern of relations between Western Europe and Latin America that has changed over the years from the state-to-state level to a great variety of substate relations. Cooperation between the political parties is probably best known; but the trade unions, the churches, a number of pressure groups, and scientific institutions have also contributed importantly to what is now considered the "European connection" in Latin America. The willingness of European institutions to transfer human and material resources to support political and/or social interests through these channels has contributed definitively to strengthening the civil elites in many Latin American countries.

These transnational elements of Western European–Latin American relations are of increasing importance for both sides. From the Western European perspective, such cooperation allows for the support of counterelites in those Latin American societies in which the political system is seen as particularly unstable.[11] At the same time, the development of a democratic perspective is aided, because it is hoped that the pluralistic bias of Western European political philosophy will be accepted by the various groups who benefit from outside support. From the Latin American perspective, this type of cooperation is engaged in as part of the process of searching for a way out of the vicious circle between military and civilian governments. Since the "technocratization of the military" through the help of the United States has resulted in more military competence and more military governments in the region, some politicians in Western Europe hope the "technocratization of the politicians and labor leaders" through the help of Western European counterparts might lead to more civil competence and more civil governments. These Western European relationships with Latin America also have obvious attractions for both sides. Economically, Latin America's options are increased, and the possibilities for Western Europe are expanded. Politically, Western Europe can make good use of her cultural, linguistic, and religious affinity with Latin America in offering a variety of ideological concepts and participatory solutions to social problems, and Latin America is free to choose which—if any—fits her needs and aspirations.[12]

A number of institutions and their roles within their respective societies correspond in the two continents, and identification and communication seem much easier for many Latin Americans with Western Europe than with the United States.[13]

Two recent developments have, however, changed Western European perceptions of Latin America considerably. One is the relevance of Central American turmoil for the East–West conflict, the other is the conflict between Great Britain and Argentina over the Falklands/Malvinas. Inasmuch as Western Europe liked to see itself in a mediating position in the former—counseling restraint to the United States in her reaction to revolutionary change in Nicaragua and El Salvador—it had to accept a similar role for the United States in the latter—Great Britain being asked not only to consider her own national interest but also the effect of the conflict on overall U.S.-Latin American relations. For many Western European politicians, the time had come to make a choice for or against what was perceived as Latin American interests. In Central America what was at stake appeared to be a commitment to the possibility of revolutionary change once other options were exhausted, hoping that political pluralism and a mixed economy would characterize the newly evolving systems along with a foreign policy of nonalignment. In the case of the Falklands/Malvinas conflict, the stakes were much higher and the possible damage closer to home. Great Britain was given all-out solidarity to prove the European Community's readiness to stand by its members and to help to enforce a principle highly cherished in Western Europe—nonaggression. A deterioration of relations with a number of Latin American states had to be expected and was an accepted result of the economic sanctions imposed on Argentina. The apparent North-South character of that conflict and its possible long-term political and economic consequences, however, should not be underestimated. They may well make Western Europe a much less attractive partner for Latin American states in the years to come.

UNEASY PARTNERSHIP: COOPERATION AND COMPETITION BETWEEN THE UNITED STATES AND WESTERN EUROPE IN LATIN AMERICA

Different perceptions of the United States and Western Europe with regard to Latin America, and their different receptions by Latin Americans, have led to the development of an uneasy partnership between the two in recent years. The basis of such a partnership is a set of common goals for the region and its relationship to the Western industrialized nations.

- To avoid adherence of additional Latin American states to the socialist camp.
- To avoid regional or internal instability through interstate or intrastate violence.
- To guarantee economic cooperation with Latin American states through support of free market economies in the region.

The common ground for the United States–Western European partnership in Latin America is their interest—the United States a little more, Western Europeans a little less—in the preservation of stability. This common interest in regional stability tends to lose ground, however, when discussion turns to how such stability should be achieved, especially in areas of crisis or tension like Central America and the Caribbean. The best way to reach social change, which both sides claim to strive for, is heavily disputed within the uneasy partnership, in part reflecting the controversy within the Latin American societies themselves about that politically divisive subject. The U.S. position then tends to center on short-term solutions: Western Europeans are more likely to argue that short-term instability has to be taken for granted to reach long-term stability. U.S. strategic priorities seem to be more willing to tolerate social injustice as long as the regime in question seems to be able to guarantee stability. Western European strategists are more inclined to press for social change because of their association with some of the political groups who would benefit directly from such change. They are also convinced that democratic development in Latin America cannot take place in any real form until the majority of the population gets a chance to participate economically and politically.

The tolerance level with regard to the type of development model evolving in some Latin American states is also inclined to differ widely between the United States and Western Europe. Although Peru from 1968–75 and Nicaragua since 1979 have been seen as dangerous political models by the United States for example, both experiments have been praised and aided considerably in Western Europe. A development of autonomous socialist systems that would not serve the interests of the Soviet Union would be viewed with little alarm in Western Europe (a generalization that does not exclude great displeasure by some groups); such a trend would probably be seen in the United States, in contrast, as a serious threat to U.S. interests in Latin America. Although Western Europe seems resigned to accept a great deal of ideological pluralism in the Third World, the United States— and especially the Reagan administration—seems unwilling to tolerate such developments in the Western Hemisphere, citing Cuba as a prime example of the implicit dangers for U.S. security.[14] Only after a "winning situation" has been achieved—be it in El Salvador or Nicaragua—and a signal of U.S. power assertion has been sent, not only to the radical forces within Central America, but also to the Third World in general and even more so to the Soviet Union, will the Reagan administration consider lessening its preoccupation with security in its "front yard."

All security-related issues in Latin America are much more sensitive issues for the United States than for Western Europe. In spite of the geopolitical explanations that are generally offered, this fact seems hard to understand for Western Europeans and Latin Americans alike, against the background of a superpower position. The explanation lies in the tremendous shock that the Cuban missile crisis left in the minds of American policymakers, which alone can explain the continuous preoccupation of the United States with Cuba, Grenada, and Nicaragua.[15]

Arms transfers from outside the region have been another point of disagreement within the uneasy partnership in Latin America. During the 1960s most of the military hardware for Latin America was supplied by the United States, but this picture has changed entirely during the last decade. Now Western Europe, plus Israel, provide the vast majority of all arms shipments to Latin America, rendering various U.S. measures to extend political pressure through limitation of arms sales ineffectual in a number of Latin American countries. U.S. ability to exert pressure in cases of warfare by threatening to withhold spare parts has likewise diminished considerably, as was demonstrated in the Falklands/Malvinas conflict. The United States holds Western Europe responsible for most of these developments. In an effort to change the situation, the Reagan administration decided early-on to enter the arms market in Latin America again, and has started to compete with the now-established arms suppliers in Western Europe.

Similar disagreements developed over the nonproliferation issue. The Carter administration tried vainly to block all sales of sensitive material to Third World countries, to avoid the risk of nuclear disaster developing from a combination of internal political instability and nuclear capacity. Most Western European suppliers believe, in contrast, that a policy of denial would result in increasing political problems between the status-conscious countries of the Third World and the Western industrialized countries and postpone their nuclear development for a couple of years at best. They favor, instead, a concept of controlled cooperation, in which the new nuclear countries like Brazil and Argentina would be integrated into the control mechanisms of the International Atomic Energy Agency (IAEA). It was not coincidental that the disagreements between the United States and Western Europe were never drawn into the open quite as much as in the case of nonproliferation policy in Latin America. Aside from the multibillion-dollar business involved, the underlying question was to what extent the United States—former hegemonic power over Western Europe as well as over Latin America—could control the technological emancipation process of her allies.

By far the greatest agreement within the uneasy partnership can be found with regard to economic policies in and vis-à-vis Latin America. Preservation of the rules of the free enterprise system and the market economy within the economic systems of Latin American states, as well as in their relations with Western Europe and the United States, are top priorities for both partners. Any major changes of the rules of the game, as advocated or tried by some Latin American states, are to be resisted. Latin American tendencies to support radical Third World demands for a New International Economic Order (NIEO) are criticized by the United States, as well as by Western Europe as contrary to "their [the Latin American states'] own best interests." To avoid further Latin American leadership in the North–South conflict, a common strategy to co-opt some Latin American states into the Organization for Economic Cooperation and Development (OECD) may be evolving. It is in this area that the full cooperation between the United States and Western Europe in Latin America will be most likely to occur.

While competing for certain markets and for access to raw materials in all of Latin America, there exists a certain degree of informal division of economic influence within the uneasy partnership. The United States concentrates not only political and security attention on the Caribbean Basin, it concentrates economic interest also. The large energy reserves in that area of easy access and convenient location make it a prime target. European participation is only in demand with regard to development aid in the Caribbean, in the context of the Caribbean Basin Initiative.

Western European interest, in contrast, has historically tended toward the Southern Cone, including Brazil. In the postwar period, U.S. economic engagement there was overwhelming as well, but since the 1960s Western European influence has been rising steadily. Even though Western Europe is much more dependent on export earnings and access to raw materials and markets than is the United States, its economic profile in Latin America will probably increase little in the near future, if at all. The specific conditions of the European Community and its preferential relations with other parts of the Third World are probably the single most important reason for this. Certain countervailing measures in the aftermath of the Falklands/Malvinas conflict will probably contribute to it as well. Western Europe as well as the United States will find Latin America in general a much less attractive region for their economic activities—for a variety of reasons—than in the recent past.

THE PROCESS OF EMANCIPATION: LATIN AMERICA'S NEW ROLE IN THE INTERNATIONAL SYSTEM

The United States and Western Europe each have their difficulties in dealing with Latin American states as they become increasingly assertive within the international system. They have not yet accepted that foreign policy in Latin America has always been a strategy for survival—survival in the sense that modernization has historically been impossible without foreign capital and foreign technology, and the dependence that came with it. A direct result of the asymmetry that was an inevitable part of that dependence has been the constant desire of Latin American countries to demonstrate some independence and distance from the very countries on which they depended.

To realize such independence, it has been necessary to search for new international partners, to both diversify the dependence and also to open new options and alternatives in the case of political or economic pressures. Latin America's belated integration into the international political system—which came many generations later than integration into the world market—has been accompanied by a series of efforts to diversify foreign relations through the creation of new alliances that offer alternatives to the classic North–South spheres of influence. More than other countries in the Third World, Latin American states have demonstrated the capacity to form such alliances. The distinguished role of Latin American leadership in the creation and development of the major organizations of the Third World is well known. Its ability to globalize regional problems has enhanced its bargaining power considerably vis-à-vis the United States. The European connection is probably only one card—albeit a strong one—in that game. Another is the strengthening of the South–South relationship, in which Latin America as the most developed part of the Third World would command an advantageous position. If Latin American international relations remain a strategy for survival, the attention of the region may indeed soon shift to the Arab countries. Brazil has already taken the lead, for example, in reorienting itself to the centers of oil and wealth.[16]

Latin America's new role in the international system will give neither Western Europe nor the United States special preference because of any historical ties or hegemonic presumptions. It will deal with each of them according to the national interest of the Latin American countries in question—an interest that will most probably differ considerably from Western European and U.S. interests. In the context of future disputes about the division of power, influence, and welfare between the industrial countries and the Third World, Latin America will be on the side of the status seekers; Western Europe and the United States will find themselves on the side of the status defenders. This is because the future problems of Latin America's position in the international system will not be dominated by her relations with the United States or Western Europe, but by her ability to continue to form new alliances to gain or preserve political maneuverability. Given the increasing international importance of Latin America as a region and of certain Latin American states in particular, it does not seem far-fetched to expect that the United States and Western Europe may have to compete for Latin America's cooperation in the near future. In that context, Western Europe, with her own experiences in dependency and vulnerability, may turn out to be a more tolerant partner than the United States.

NOTES

1. For the new position of regional actors, see Grabendorff (1980).
2. See especially The Committee of Santa Fe (1980), and Theberge (1980).
3. This was advocated by Kirkpatrick (1979).

4. For a convincing analysis of how to avoid such developments, see the article by the French Minister for Cooperation and Development, Jean-Pierre Cot (1982).

5. The clearest expression of this policy can be found in the writings of the current U.S. Ambassador at the United Nations (see Kirkpatrick 1981).

6. For a discussion of U.S. security interests in the region, see Hayes (1980), and Domínguez (1980).

7. See President Reagan's address before the Organization of American States (OAS) on February 24, 1982 (U.S. Department of State 1982a, 1982b). For a critical discussion of the Caribbean Basin Initiative, see the articles by Lowenthal, Johnson, Hernández–Colón, Corrada, Weintraub, Feinberg, and Newfarmer, in *Foreign Policy* (Summer 1982).

8. For an overview of Western European arms transfer to Latin America, see Barrow (1982). For a comparison of Western European and U.S. positions in the field of arms and nuclear technology transfers, see Kolodziej (1980).

9. For the discussion of the controversial German–Brazilian Nuclear Agreement and its aftermath, see Haftendorn (1978); Wonder (1977); Gall (1976); Lowrance (1976).

10. For a typical example of the ambivalence of the relationship, see Grabendorff (1981).

11. I have discussed this elsewhere for the case of Central America (Grabendorff 1982a).

12. The roles of the Christian and Social Democratic parties in that process in Latin America are discussed by Solorzano (1980), Huebener (1982), and Evers (1982).

13. For the different levels of cooperation, see Grabendorff (1982b), and Roett (1981).

14. For a detailed analysis by the U.S. government, see U.S. Department of State (1981).

15. Only while detente lasted could the tolerance level be stretched a little with regard to accepting ideological pluralism once more in the case of Nicaragua.

16. For an overview of Latin America's relations with the Arab countries, see MEED–LAN (1981).

REFERENCES

Atkins, G. Pope. *Latin America in the International Political System*. New York: The Free Press, 1977.

Barrow, Simon. "Europe, Latin America and the Arms Trade." In Jenny Pearce (ed.), *The European Challenge: Europe's New Role in Latin America*. London: Latin American Bureau, 1982, 176–216.

The Committee of Santa Fe. *A New Inter-American Policy for the Eighties*. Washington, DC: Council for Inter-American Security, 1980.

Cot, Jean-Pierre. "Winning East–West in North–South." *Foreign Policy*, 46 (Spring 1982): 3–18.

Domínguez, Jorge I. "The United States and Its Regional Security Interests: The Caribbean, Central, and South America." *Daedalus*, 109:4 (Fall 1980): 115–33.

Evers, Tilman. "European Social Democracy in Latin America: The Case of West Germany." In Jenny Pearce (ed.), *The European Challenge: Europe's New Role in Latin America*. London: Latin American Bureau, 1982, 80–129.

Fagen, Richard R. "The Carter Administration and Latin America: Business As Usual?" *Foreign Affairs*, 57:3 (1979): 652–69.

Foreign Policy 47 (Summer 1982): 114–38.

Gall, Norman. "Atoms for Brazil, Dangers for All." *Foreign Policy*, 23 (Summer 1976): 155–201.

Grabendorff, Wolf. "Brazil and West Germany: A Model for First World–Third World Relations?" In Wayne A. Selcher (ed.), *Brazil in the International System: The Rise of a Middle Power*. Boulder: Westview Press, 1981, 181–200.

———. "The Central American Crisis and Western Europe: Perceptions and Reactions." *International Politics*, Research Institute Friedrich–Ebert–Stiftung, Bonn (1982a).

———. "Latin America and Western Europe: Towards a New International Subsystem?" In Jenny Pearce (ed.), *The European Challenge: Europe's New Role in Latin America*. London: Latin American Bureau, 1982b, 41–58.

———. "Perspectivas y Polos de Desarrollo en America Latina." *Estudios Internacionales*, 13:50 (April/June 1980): 252–78.

Grondona, Mariano. "South America Looks at Detente (Skeptically)." *Foreign Policy*, 26 (Spring 1977): 184–203.

Haftendorn, Helga. *The Nuclear Triangle: Washington, Bonn and Brasília*. Washington, DC: Georgetown University, 1978.

Hayes, Margaret Daly. "Security to the South: U.S. Interests in Latin America." *International Security*, 5:1 (Summer 1980): 130–51.

Huebener, Karl Ludolf. "The Socialist International and Latin America: Problems and Possibilities." *Caribbean Review*, 11:2 (Spring 1982): 38–41.

Kirkpatrick, Jeane J. "Dictatorships and Double Standards." *Commentary*, 68:5 (November 1979): 34–45.

———. "U.S. Security and Latin America." *Commentary*, 71:1 (January 1981): 29–40.

Kolodziej, Edward A. "European Perspectives on Europe's Roles in the World: The Partial Partner." *Working Paper No. 17, International Security Studies Program*. Washington, DC: The Wilson Center, 1980, 45–54.

Lowenthal, Abraham F. "Latin America: A Not-So-Special Relationship." *Foreign Policy*, 32 (Fall 1978): 107–26.

———. "The United States and Latin America: Ending the Hegemonic Presumption." *Foreign Affairs*, 55:1 (October 1976): 199–213.

Lowenthal, Abraham F. and Albert Fishlow. "Latin America's Emergence: Toward a U.S. Response." *Headline Series*, 243 (February 1979): 1–80.

Lowrance, William W. "Nuclear Futures for Sale: To Brazil from West Germany, 1975." *International Security*, 1:2 (1976): 147–66.

Marcella, Gabriel. "Las relaciones militares entre los Estados Unidos y América Latina: Crisis e interrogantes futuras." *Estudios Internacionales*, 13:51 (June–September 1980): 382–400.

MEED-LAN. "Latin America and the Middle East." A MEED-LAN Special Report. *Middle East Economic Digest* (September 1981).

Nitsch, Manfred. "Latin America in the Third World." In Wolf Grabendorff (ed.), *Latin America and the Third World*. Special Issue, *Vierteljahresberichte*, 68 (June 1977): 91–105.

Roett, Riordan. "Tienen los Estados Unidos algun futuro en América Latina?" *Estudios Internacionales*, 14:56 (October–December 1981): 517–29.

Solorzano, Mario. "El papel de la Democracia Christiana en la actual coyuntura Centro Americana." *Nueva Sociedad*, 48 (May–June 1980): 22–33.

Theberge, James D. "Rediscovering the Caribbean: Toward a U.S. Policy for the 1980s." *Commonsense*, 3:2 (Spring 1980): 1–20.

U.S. Department of State. "Cuba's Renewed Support for Violence in Latin America." *Special Report*, 90 (14 December 1981).

———. "Caribbean Basin Initiative." *Current Policy*, 370 (February 1982a).

———. "Democracy and Security in the Caribbean Basin." *Current Policy*, 364 (February 1982b).

Wonder, Edward F. "Nuclear Commerce and Nuclear Proliferation: Germany and Brazil 1975." *Orbis*, 21:2 (1977): 377–406.

CONCLUSION

Riordan Roett

Our study of the changing relations among the states of Latin America, Western Europe, and the United States, and the issue of whether a New Atlantic Triangle is feasible, clarified a number of recent trends in international relations. Three are of most significance for the possible emergence of a pattern of new and dynamic relations between Latin America and the United States and Western Europe. First, the slow but perceptive growth of Latin America toward "middle income" status in the international system is clear. Second, as a parallel to that development, important changes in the influence of the United States in world affairs have emerged. Third, Western Europe appears to offer to Latin America an increasingly useful alternative to the United States as it seeks to identify its authentic role and to maximize its opportunities in a rapidly changing global power structure.

THE EMERGENCE OF LATIN AMERICA

Almost imperceptibly during the 1960s and 1970s, Latin America moved fitfully into middle-class status in the international system. Economic changes initiated in the region in the postwar years resulted in the formation of a significant industrial base and an increasing role in world trade. During the halcyon days of the last two decades, prior to the oil price shocks, Latin America diversified both its export profile and its export partners. Trade liberalization benefited both exporter and importer. The United States became less important, although still of great influence. Intra-Latin American trade improved. Japan became a new and growing commercial factor in some countries.

At the same time that trade flows increased in volume and diversified in terms of markets, financial relations between Latin America and the United States were modified. Official bilateral aid flows dropped and were replaced by private bank lending. Latin American growth and expansion were directly linked to the lending policies of the private banking system in the OECD countries, with the United States playing a leading role.

New patterns of economic interdependence were accompanied by new thrusts in foreign policy. The contentious debate surrounding the New International Economic Order (NIEO) and the special sessions of the United Nations General Assembly in the early and mid-1970s, gave way to a more coherent Latin American position on issues of trade, protectionism, capital flow, and the North–South dialogue. The Group of 77, the United Nations Conference on Trade and Development (UNCTAD), the Non-Aligned Movement, and the North–South Conference in Cancun (Mexico) in 1981 all addressed the need for sustained support for development in the South. There was near unanimity of opinion that the North had refused to acknowledge the legitimate development goals of the Third World. The consensus among the major states in Latin America, as to both their vulnerability and their right to be heard, led to important statements at the United Nations General Assembly in September 1982 by the Presidents of Brazil and Mexico and, less than a year later, in the April 1983 Declaration of Cancun. That declaration, for the first time, carefully identified a common perception on the part of these two leading industrial states in the hemisphere. The two states were also the most buffeted by the recent downturn in world trade and heavily dependent on international capital markets in the North to finance their burgeoning foreign debt.

By 1983, the debt question had indeed become a key policy issue among the partners of the Triangle. Of Brazil's foreign debt of approximately U.S. $90 billion, 34 percent was held by U.S. banks and 28 percent by West European financial institutions. In Argentina, the foreign debt held by U.S. private banks equaled 60 percent, with the Europeans representing 23 percent of the approximately U.S. $37 billion total. Similar figures characterized the other major Latin American debtors. In the absence of a strong economic recovery in the United States and Western Europe, and with the persistence of high interest rates and loans needed by Latin America to service the debt, the issue was increasingly contentious. The possibility of an increase in nonperforming loans mounted and the banks and the International Monetary Fund became involved in what appeared to be continual meetings to seek "packages" of aid for hard-pressed Latin American states. It is clear that the debt issue will remain a common agenda item, for Latin America, the United States, and Western Europe for years to come.

The global thrust of the Latin American states was matched by a new feeling of optimism in intra-Latin American relations. The rapprochement between Brazil and Argentina survived the war in the South Atlantic and a series of government changes in Buenos Aires. Brazil and Mexico were working more closely together than at any time in recent memory. Governments of Colombia, Mexico, Panama, and Venezuela seized the initiative in 1983 and organized the "Contadora group" of states to seek a political solution to the continuing turmoil in Central America. The Amazon Pact of 1979, which brings together all those states bordering on the Amazon Basin to discuss its development, demonstrated a growing awareness of the need for joint planning and development of natural resources. The Economic System of Latin America (SELA), established in 1975, confounded skeptical observers of Latin American multinational efforts by surviving and slowly solidifying a presence in the economic and trade relations of the region. Dissatisfied with the progress of LAFTA (Latin American Free Trade Association), the Latin American states in 1980 created ALADI (the Latin American Integration Association), in hopes of spurring regional economic development.

The process by which Latin America began to insert itself into the international system was uncertain, but perceptible. Greater economic and commercial potential, a larger industrial base, a growing role in South–South trade and financial ties, and the beginnings of a search for a coherent Latin American position on world issues have characterized the last 15 years. Those changes were due to some degree to the perceived and real decline of the United States.

THE DECLINE OF THE UNITED STATES

One must not exaggerate claims as to the decline of the United States, specifically in Latin America and, more generally, in the world. However, it is true that the 1960s and 1970s saw a slowing down of the capacity and the will of the United States to impose its world view on the international system. In part, the aftermath of the Vietnam War set the stage for a painful review within the United States of that country's global role. It also sharply raised the question of the limits of power, even for a superpower. Further, it opened a debate in the United States, which has not ended, about the relationship between domestic politics and the formulation of foreign policy. Not only Vietnam but Central America, in the early 1980s, began to define the limits of American power in the world—and in the Western Hemisphere specifically.

America's diplomatic, cultural, and educational presence in Latin America also declined in the 1970s. Trade ties loosened. Between 1950 and 1970, the proportion of U.S. exports to Latin America dropped from 28 percent to 15 percent of total exports. This level remained steady during the 1970s, increasing slightly in 1980 (to about 18 percent). U.S. imports from Latin America followed a similar path. Imports dropped from 35 percent of all U.S. imports in 1950 to 25 percent in 1960 and to 14 percent in 1970. Again, there was a slight increase in 1980 (bringing imports to 16 percent). By the 1980s, the strongest ties between the United States and Latin America were between the private banks. Even these transnational actors appeared to follow U.S. policy less than their own economic and profit imperatives in structuring their relations with the states of Latin America. Latin America's foreign policy increasingly diverged from stated U.S. interests. The war in the South Atlantic between Argentina and Great Britain dramatically illustrated the drift in U.S.–Latin American relations. The willingness of Latin American states to challenge American assumptions about relations between the North and the South, about economic growth, protectionism, and related matters escalated. Increasing divergence over the U.S. role in Central America and the Caribbean motivated a new assertiveness on the part of Latin American states to seek regional solutions with less regard for United States' opinion. Indeed, the United States appeared to many Latin American actors as part of the problem of their underdevelopment, not as a factor in solving it.

THE RETURN OF WESTERN EUROPE

The silent partner in Latin America's international relations during the last decade has been Western Europe. While the trade and financial ties between Europe and Latin America are not as strong as those between the United States and Latin America, there are a host of areas in which Europe has taken new and important initiatives. The role of Western Europe in the Triangle is still evolving. It is imprecise, but clearly of increasing interest to the states of the hemisphere. It is as much a cultural and historical role as it is a "dollars and cents" role at this time. But its evolution will deeply affect both the ties between the United States and Latin America and the latter's role in international affairs in the coming decades.

The decline of the United States in the region during the last two decades went unnoticed in Western Europe at first. However, as Latin America began to assert its autonomy in the 1970s, and the conflicts between the United States and other states of the hemisphere multiplied, Western Europe became aware of the possibility of mediating United States hegemony in the area. The more Latin America assumed a world view, the more important became the finding of sympathetic diplomatic and political allies. The affinity between the two world areas was strengthened by similar views on the role of the state in development, for example. Socialism or statism held little fear for either West Europeans or Latin America, whereas it continued to be a cause for concern in North American society. The interventionist state and mixed economy that resulted were familiar in both Europe and Latin America.

Ideological political parties were another component of the relationship. Growth in Latin America of Social Democratic and Christian Democratic parties in Chile, Venezuela, Peru, Ecuador, and other countries provided an important bridge between Latin America and Europe. Not only was there a commonality of structure and purpose, but important financial and political support was available—and deemed appropriate—from the Europeans for their Latin colleagues. West German party foundation, the Socialist International, party-linked labor union organization, and community action groups all became relevant to the struggle to reduce the role of the military in Latin American societies, to spur the search for new forms of social and political organization, and to consolidate support for civilian rule and social justice. The Roman Catholic Church entered the scene as a significant actor in Latin America, providing the support of priests and nuns, as well as much needed financing.

By the late 1970s and early 1980s, a new and more sinister reason emerged for a higher profile in Latin America. Efforts of the Reagan administration to define all conflict, real and potential, in terms of an East–West confrontation between the United States and the Soviet

Union began to alarm many European governments. To argue that the Soviet Union and its surrogates in Cuba and Nicaragua were responsible for all the ills confronting American policy in the Caribbean Basin appeared far-fetched. The Mexican-French declaration of August 1981 illustrated the new concern and the new willingness to state unequivocally the common interests of both regions. It was followed by the February 1982 initiative of President Lopez Portillo of Mexico to open a dialogue and begin negotiations to resolve regional conflict.

These initiatives were paralleled by a growing concern that the Reagan administration was pursuing a futile policy in Central America. The West Europeans grew increasingly worried that the East–West bias of Reagan's policy would lead to serious tension between the two superpowers and a resulting hardening of Moscow's attitudes in Europe on a wide variety of subjects of great importance in West European capitals. As the Socialist government in Spain consolidated its grasp on power, Prime Minister Felipe Gonzalez emerged as a straightforward and effective spokesman for European democratic forces. In a widely heralded visit to Latin America in June 1983, Gonzalez strongly endorsed the efforts of the Contadora countries—Colombia, Venezuela, Panama, and Mexico—to seek a peaceful solution to Central American conflict. He called for a major shift in American strategy. Gonzalez said that the root causes of conflict in the region were social injustice and misery, rather than Communist penetration; the path to stability is through democracy and social and economic development, he argued.

But to argue that the Latin Americans seek broader ties with Western Europe and other world areas is to denigrate neither the legitimate interests nor the real linkages between the United States and Latin America. Indeed, it can be argued that the political, institutional, and cultural ties between Europe and Latin America will remain vague and ultimately without value if they are not consolidated in strategic and/or economic terms. That is the conventional wisdom and it is certainly accepted by many current observers of American foreign policy. In effect, the Latin American states have nowhere to turn "when the going gets tough." That they are, and will remain, in the United States' "backyard" is a given of that approach to America's ties in the hemisphere. It is simply to take a more pragmatic and realistic view of the evolution of those ties over the last 20 years and to argue that there are important new factors at work that may be recognized.

The essays in this book have attempted to indicate how the long-standing historical, cultural, and social ties between Latin America and Western Europe were submerged by North American economic and security interests earlier in this century. The occurrence of the Cold War, the creation of the Inter-American Security System after World War II, and the almost total dependence of Latin America on the United States for a market for its exports and as a provider of essential imports, obscured the previous relations. With the diminishing of American power and will in the 1970s, and with the concomitant development of Latin America, politically and economically, new—and old—options were sought by the Latin states. Common concern about the thrust of American foreign policy, as well as affinities of an institutional sort, were found to be comfortable and viable.

That Latin America will not seek to substitute Western Europe for the United States should be evident from the 1982 war in the South Atlantic between Argentina and Great Britain for possession of the Malvinas Islands. To the dismay of the Latin states, the United States joined its European allies in taking harsh economic and political steps to censure Argentina and to support the English war effort. The Inter-American System as well as the political and diplomatic relations between Latin America and Western Europe suffered a serious setback. The Latin states understood that the Western Alliance will stand firm on Third World or Southern issues that are viewed as threats to sovereignty or to vital security interests. While many Latin American governments privately condemned Argentina's use of force, all publicly endorsed Argentina's sovereign rights in the islands and rejected the right of Great Britain to use force to assert its claim.

The Malvinas War and the situation in Surinam illustrate the new and complex ways in which Latin America will interact with the states of Western Europe and with the United States. The era of automatic alignments is over. Independent foreign policy has become a hallmark of Latin American sovereignty. Transnational relations will characterize Latin America's new insertion into the global system, both economically and politically. New coalitions in the South and between sectors of the South and the North will emerge. As Latin America continues to see itself as both Western and as an active part of the Third World, there will be inconsistencies in policy and periods of confusion about appropriate means and ends in Latin America. But the "moments of opportunity" to buy space in the international system will increase for the states of Latin America in the coming decades. Latin America, while part of the West, will not willingly again become a prisoner of the West.

The Atlantic Triangle Conference has attempted to illustrate the dynamic change under way in Latin America and in its relations with the states of Western Europe and with the United States. The process has begun; it is impossible to predict its eventual outcome in terms of the vital interests of any of the partners in the Triangle. What is certain is that, in an interdependent and multipolar international system, a vital and engaged Latin America is optimally part of a needed process of system consolidation and value confirmation. Latin America needs to multiply its global linkages, ironically, to be able to more effectively defend and enhance the system of values and the societal concerns that ultimately identify the permanent interests of all three partners in the Atlantic Triangle.

Index

advanced technology transfer 101
African policy, of Brazil 121
agricultural export sector in Latin America 41
agricultural modernization, Argentina 43
air communications 13–14
Alliance for Progress 66, 137, 232
Alvess, Joaquim 23
American-Soviet dominance 246–51
anarchism 5
Andean Group 61, 62, 86, 210
anti-Americanism in Brazil 111
Aranha, Oswaldo 23
Argentina: British influence on economy 43; EEC restriction on agricultural imports 62; European immigrants 3; German military influence 3; relations with Soviet Union 172; war with Great Britain 224; during World War II 18
Argentinian railways, British control 43
armaments, international transfer 105
armed forces, political role 113
arms technology, transfer 70
arms transfers 267
Atlantic Triangle 166, 167; revival of 169–73
atomic energy, agreements for peaceful use 61
Auswärtiges Amt 7, 10; Auslandsorganisation (AO) and 16

bankruptcy 158
Barbosa, Ruy 4
Barboza, Gibson 127
Baruch, Bernard 27
Blaine, James G. 7
Bolivia, democracy 173
Branco, Castelo 104–5, 124–26

Brazil: agreement with Argentina 108; air traffic foundation 13; anti-American feelings 96, 111; anti-Communism 104; anti-Communism foreign policy 105; application for IMF help 136; armed forces 106; armed forces political readjustment 112; arms industry 187; arms sale to industrialized countries 187; arms sale to Iraq 188; British influence on economy 43; British intelligence agencies 19; British political influence 4; changes in military institution 125; civil war 115; commercial rapprochement policy toward Socialist countries 127; concept of Western world 108; debt 98; decline in trade with U.S. 97; democracy restoration 132; democratic regime 110; domestic policy 112–15; economic cooperation with Africa 108; economic cooperation with Eastern Europe 108; economic cooperation with Europe 86; economic nationalism 126; economic policy changes 115; economic relations with Europe 23; economic tension 115; European perception of 124; export capacity 100; foreign debt 118; foreign debt service payment freezing 118; foreign interests in 29; foreign policy strategy 25; future foreign policy 118; future internal policy 117; as German military espionage center 19; independent foreign policy 106; inflation 118; internal policy 96, 117; intrazonal trade 108; joint Iranian-German ventures 186; middle classes 113; middle class improvement 118; military agreement with U.S., breaking of 107; military assistance from Europe 24;

ABOUT THE EDITORS AND CONTRIBUTORS

Wolf Grabendorff is Senior Staff Member of the Stiftung Wissenschaft und Politik, Research Institute for International Affairs, in Ebenhausen, Federal Republic of Germany. Among his professional experiences in Germany and abroad, he has been Visiting Scholar at the Institute of Latin American Studies, Columbia University; Visiting Fellow at the Center of Brazilian Studies, School of Advanced International Studies, The Johns Hopkins University; and, for three years, Latin American correspondent for the German Television System (ARD) in Buenos Aires. Among his extensive writings on many facets of Latin American politics and international relations are *Lateinamerika—Kontinent in der Krise* (Hamburg 1973, edited), *Brasilien: Entwicklungsmodell und Aussenpolitik* (Munich 1977, coauthored), and *A donde Latinoamérica?* (Madrid 1979).

Riordan Roett is Professor of Political Science and Director of the Latin American Studies Program and the Center of Brazilian Studies at The Johns Hopkins School of Advanced International Studies in Washington, DC. He is a member of the Executive Board, International Economic Assessments, and of the Working Group on Western Interests in the Caribbean Basin, The Atlantic Council. Roett has written widely in the area of Latin American politics, with particular emphasis on Brazil. Among his most important works are *The Politics of Foreign Aid in the Brazilian Northeast* (Nashville 1972), *Brazil in the Seventies* (Washington 1976, edited), and *Brazil: Politics in a Patrimonial Society* (New York 1984).

Ulrich Albrecht is Professor of Peace and Conflict Studies in the Department of Political Science, Free University of Berlin. He is chairman and founding member of the German Association for Peace Research, and has served as an expert consultant to numerous organizations, including NATO, the United Nations, and the World Council of Churches. His special expertise is in international politics, technology, and arms control. Albrecht has published widely. Among his more recent major works are *Kuendigt den Nachwestungs-beschluss* (Frankfurt 1982), *A Research Guide to Arms and Armed Forces* (London 1978, coauthored), and *Reustungskonversionsforschung* (Baden-Baden 1978).

Werner Baer is Professor of Economics, University of Illinois (Urbana–Champaign). He has been Visiting Professor at the University of São Paulo, Program Advisor to the Ford Foundation, and Rhodes Visiting Fellow at St. Anthony's College, Oxford. He is a member of the Editorial Board of *World Development* and Advisory Editor of the Cambridge University Press Latin American Series. Among Baer's many contributions to the economic literature on Latin America are *Dimensões de desenvolvimento Brasileiro* (Rio de Janeiro 1978, coedited) and *Export Diversification and the New Protectionism: The Experiences of Latin America* (Champaign 1981, coedited).

Gerhard Drekonja Kornat is a member of the Austrian Institute of Latin American Studies in Vienna. A political scientist with wide-ranging international experience, he has been Latin American correspondent for *Die Presse* (Vienna), head of the Latin American Department in the Seminar Center of the German Foundation for International Development in West Berlin, Research Associate at the Center for Latin American Studies at the University of Pittsburgh, and Visiting Professor of Political Science at the Universidad de los Andes, Bogota. His numerous publications on Latin America include *Ecuador, hoy* (Bogota 1978, edited) and *Colombia: Política Exterior* (Bogota 1982).

Roberto Fendt Jr. is Research Director at the Foreign Trade Studies Center (CECEX)—a private nonprofit foundation devoted to research in the areas of foreign trade and foreign policy—and Professor of Economics at the Graduate School of Economics, Getúlio Vargas

Foundation, in Rio de Janeiro, Brazil. Before joining CECEX in 1976, Fendt served as Professor of Economics at the University of São Paulo and as senior economic advisor to the Brazilian Minister of Finance. He is an international editor of *Studies of Comparative International Development*, published at the Georgia Institute of Technology. His many articles and studies have appeared in leading economic journals and in book form, including a book on monetary policy (*Política Monetária e Mercado Aberto*, 1977) and studies on international trade and foreign exchange policies, the most recent of which appears in John Williamson's *Exchange Rate Rules: The Theory, Performance and Prospects of the Crawling Peg* (New York 1981).

Walder de Góes is Professor of Political Science at the University of Brasília, Brazil. A journalist of distinction, he has been a correspondent for the *Jornal do Brasil*, *Veja*, and Associated Press International. In his capacity as political commentator for the newspaper *O Estado de São Paulo*, De Góes has traveled to Peru, the United States, Switzerland, France, Germany, Yugoslavia, Italy, and Great Britain. In addition to innumerable articles on many facets of Brazil (including Brazil's military regime, international relations, and nuclear program), he has published *O Brasil do General Geisel* (Rio de Janeiro 1978).

Maria del Rosario Green is Professor of International Studies at the Colegio de México, and also holds a professional appointment at the Universidad Nacional Autónoma de México. She has served on several editorial boards and is currently a member of the editorial council of the *Journal of Inter-American and World Affairs*. Her many publications in the area of Latin American and international affairs include *El Endeudamiento Público Externo de México, 1940–1973* (Mexico City 1976) and "Development, Foreign Debt and Dependency: The Case of Mexico," in *Mexico–United States Relations* (New York 1981).

Stanley E. Hilton is Professor of History at Louisiana State University. He has been Director of the Centro de História Contemporânea, Arquivo Nacional, in Rio de Janeiro, an outside consultant to the U.S. Department of State, and a Distinguished Visiting Professor at the U.S. Air Force Academy. Among his many major works in political history are *Brazil and the Great Powers, 1930–1939: The Politics of Trade Rivalry* (Austin 1975), and *Hitler's Secret War in South America, 1935–1945: German Military Espionage and Allied Counter-Espionage in Brazil* (Baton Rouge 1981).

Carlos E. Pérez Llana is Professor of International Relations and Director of the Postgraduate Program of International Relations at the University of Belgrano, Buenos Aires. He is a founding member of *Foro Latinoamericano* and a member of the Editorial Board of *Revista Estudios Internacionales*. Among his numerous contributions to literature on Latin America in the world arena are "Las Opciones de América Latina en el diálogo Norte–Sur," in *Nuevo Orden Economico Internacional* (Santiago 1979) and "La Argentina y el Mundo en la Década del '80," in *La República Posible* (Buenos Aires 1981).

Carlos Juan Moneta is a political scientist with the Sistema Economica Latinoamericano (SELA) in Caracas, who has held professorships at the Universidad del Salvador, Buenos Aires, and other universities in Argentina; visiting academic appointments at the University of California at Los Angeles and the Universidad Nacional Autónoma de México; and most recently, a special fellowship at the United Nations Institute for Training and Research. He has published widely in Argentina, Uruguay, Chile, Mexico, Venezuela, Germany, Rumania, and the United States. Examples of his work include "The Impact of World Order Studies in Policy-Making," in *Political and Institutional Issues of the New International Economic Order* (New York 1981) and "Political Obstacles to Regional Economic Cooperation," in *Regionalism and the NIEO: A Strategy for Progress* (New York 1981).

Juan Carlos Puig, a lawyer with special expertise in the field of international relations, is Professor in the Instituto de Altos Estudios de América Latina of the Universidad Simón Bolívar in Caracas. He has been Foreign Minister of Argentina, President of the Argentine Association of International Law, and has held visiting professorships at the University of Paris, the Free University of Brussels, and the University of Brasília, Brazil. His body of distinguished research includes *De la Dependencia a la Liberación. Política Exterior de América Latina* (Buenos Aires 1973) and *Doctrinas Internacionales y Autonomía Latinoamericana* (Caracas 1980).

Roberto Russell is Secretary of the International Orientation Program and Professor of Latin American Foreign Policy and Latin American History at Belgrano University, Buenos Aires, Argentina. Among his professional experiences outside Argentina he has been a Fulbright Scholar at the School of Advanced International Studies of The Johns Hopkins University and a Visiting Scholar at the Latin American Studies Institute, London University, England. He has published widely on Latin America generally, and North–South relations in particular, and recently coauthored a book on the Arab–Israeli Conflict.

Alexandre de Souza Costa Barros is Associate Professor of Political Science and Senior Researcher at the Instituto Universitário de Pesquisas do Rio de Janeiro. He has had Visiting Professorships at Georgetown University and the University of Florida, and is on the editorial advisory board of *Armed Forces and Society*. His publications include "The Diplomacy of National Security: South American International Relations in a Defrosting World," in *Latin America: The Search for a New International Role* (Beverly Hills 1975) and "Military Intervention and Withdrawal in South America," *International Political Science Review* (1981, coauthored).